The American History Series

SERIES EDITORS

John Hope Franklin, *Duke University*
A. S. Eisenstadt, *Brooklyn College*

Justus D. Doenecke
NEW COLLEGE OF FLORIDA

John E. Wilz

From Isolation to War

1931–1941

THIRD EDITION

HARLAN DAVIDSON, INC.
WHEELING, ILLINOIS 60090-6000

Library of Congress Cataloging-in-Publication Data

Doenecke, Justus D.
    From isolation to war : 1931–1941 / Justus D. Doenecke, John Wilz.—3rd ed.
            p. cm.— (The American history series)
Includes bibliographical references and index.
    ISBN 0-88295-992-1 (alk. paper)
    1. United States—Foreign relations—1933–1945. 2. United States—Foreign
relations—1929–1933. I. Wilz, John Edward. II. Title. III. American history
series (Wheeling, Ill.)
    E806.D63 2003
        940.53'2273—dc21

                                        2002006078

Cover: A small boat rescuing a seaman from the burning USS *West Virginia* in
Pearl Harbor, Dec. 7, 1941. *Courtesy of the FDR Library.*

Manufactured in the United States of America
04 03 02 01 1 2 3 4 5 VP

For Carol and Susan

FOREWORD

Every generation writes its own history for the reason that it sees the past in the foreshortened perspective of its own experience. This has surely been true of the writing of American history. The practical aim of our historiography is to give us a more informed sense of where we are going by helping us understand the road we took in getting where we are. As the nature and dimensions of American life are changing, so too are the themes of our historical writing. Today's scholars are hard at work reconsidering every major aspect of the nation's past: its politics, diplomacy, economy, society, recreation, mores and values, as well as status, ethnic, race, sexual, and family relations. The lists of series titles that appear on the inside covers of this book will show at once that our historians are ever broadening the range of their studies.

The aim of this series is to offer our readers a survey of what today's historians are saying about the central themes and aspects of the American past. To do this, we have invited to write for the series only scholars who have made notable contributions to the respective fields in which they are working. Drawing on primary and secondary materials, each volume presents a factual and narrative account of its particular subject, one that affords readers a basis for perceiving its larger dimensions and importance. Conscious that readers respond to the closeness and immediacy of a subject, each of our authors seeks to restore the past as an actual present, to revive it as a living reality.

The individuals and groups who figure in the pages of our books appear as real people who once were looking for survival and fulfillment. Aware that historical subjects are often matters of controversy, our authors present their own findings and conclusions. Each volume closes with an extensive critical essay on the writings of the major authorities on its particular theme.

The books in this series are primarily designed for use in both basic and advanced courses in American history, on the undergraduate and graduate levels. Such a series has a particular value these days, when the format of American history courses is being altered to accommodate a greater diversity of reading materials. The series offers a number of distinct advantages. It extends the dimensions of regular course work. It makes clear that the study of our past is, more than the student might otherwise understand, at once complex, profound, and absorbing. It presents that past as a subject of continuing interest and fresh investigation.

For these reasons the series strongly invites an interest that far exceeds the walls of academe. The work of experts in their respective fields, it puts at the disposal of all readers the rich findings of historical inquiry, an invitation to join, in major fields of research, those who are pondering anew the central themes and aspects of our past.

And, going beyond the confines of the classroom, it reminds the general reader no less than the university student that in each successive generation of the ever-changing American adventure, from its very start until our own day, men and women and children were facing their daily problems and attempting, as we are now, to live their lives and to make their way.

John Hope Franklin
A. S. Eisenstadt

CONTENTS

PREFACE

Over the past decade, many new books and articles have been written on American foreign policy during the years 1931–1941. Such circumstance is hardly surprising, for it was during this time period that the United States changed from a nation crippled by depression to become a world power about to enter the greatest conflict in world history. This new edition of *From Isolation to War* involves an effort to share much of this fresh research with the general reader.

As with the second edition, published in 1991, this version involves extensive change. Every sentence has been checked for accuracy and clarity, and many have been altered. At times language has been changed to be made more exact. The word "pacifist," for example, is now used in a much stricter sense, with the term "peace group" often substituted. Similarly, the term "isolationist" has often given way to the more accurate "anti interventionist." Chinese spellings are now in Pinyin (e.g., Beijing) not in Wade-Giles (e.g., Peking), though when first introduced the traditional Western spelling is also offered.

Certain material has been reorganized. Coverage of the Nye Committee and the Ludlow amendment are placed in a narrative chapter rather than in the introductory one.

In other cases material has been expanded. Here one must mention such topics as the perspective and background of anti-interventionism (including disillusionment with World War I), major peace groups, the London Economic Conference of 1933, the Ethiopian conflict, the Spanish Civil War, the Nye Committee, the Munich conference, exclusion of Jewish immigration, the Soviet-Finnish war, American public opinion, the Hull-Nomura talks, possible options to FDR's Japan diplomacy, Roosevelt's last-minute assurances to Lord Halifax, and the latest Pearl Harbor revisionism. The meaning of such Far Eastern agreements as the Taft-Katsura and Root-Takahira accords is sharpened as is the Atlantic Charter and FDR's freezing order of July 1941. The bibliography, of course, is totally updated.

Most important of all, some material is entirely new. One notes the introduction of material on the leadership style of Franklin Roosevelt, the recognition of the Soviet Union, U.S. policy towards Cuba and Mexico, Pan-American conferences, U.S. naval policy, the 1940 mission of Sumner Welles, the Four Freedoms, and the U.S. Army victory plan of autumn 1941.

I am thankful to Wayne S. Cole for his thorough reading of much of this text and to Jonathan G. Utley for clarifying certain Far Eastern controversies. The influence of J. Garry Clifford always remains with me.

Justus D. Doenecke

ACKNOWLEDGMENTS, SECOND EDITION

This revision of *From Isolation to War* has involved considerable rewriting, including matters of content, style, and organization. Yet it is to be hoped that the verve and clarity that gave John Edward Wilz's original text such distinction have been preserved. It is a privilege to serve as coauthor with him. Some material is completely fresh, and here one must note such topics as the recognition of the Soviet Union, rejection of the World Court, United States–Japan relations in the late 1930s, the blocking of Jewish immigration, debates over conscription in 1940 and 1941, Hitler's invasion of Russia, and isolationist reaction to certain specific Roosevelt policies, including U.S. intervention in Asia. Other parts of the text have been greatly expanded in light of twenty years of fresh research. Here one points to material on the Manchurian and Shanghai incidents of 1931–1933, general perceptions held by Roosevelt and his opponents, the Atlantic Charter conference, a possible Roosevelt-Konoye meeting, American ships sunk in 1941, and responsibility for the Pearl Harbor attack. An entire new generation of scholars is introduced to the reader, while of necessity much older historiography has been dropped. This revision could never have been written without the help of others. Frederick W. Marks III kindly suggested my name to Harlan Davidson, Inc. Among my colleagues at New College of the University of South Florida, past and present, I note with gratitude Laszlo Deme, William Hamilton, Charlene Levy, and Eugene Lewis; among my students,

Chelsea Jones and Gina Lanier; and among my fellow teachers of Manatee County, Florida, Linda Boyer and Elaine Cox. Raymond G. O'Connor and Gerald E. Wheeler shared their matchless knowledge of U.S.-Asian relations. Suggestions both numerous and wise came from the editors of this series, John Hope Franklin and Abraham S, Eisenstadt. Robert A. Divine and Waldo Heinrichs each provided an analysis of the first draft that was both detailed and helpful. Maureen Hewitt and Andrew J. Davidson of Harlan Davidson, Inc., have been all that editors should be: sensitive, supportive, and rigorous. Four scholars deserve special mention for the extraordinary time they gave to a critique: J. Garry Clifford, for his awesome mastery of bibliography and his ability to probe long-range issues deeply; Richard A. Harrison, for deep learning in regards to American diplomacy, particularly in the 1930s; and Ralph B. Levering and Thomas C, Reeves, for their meticulousness in matters of organization and style. The librarians at the Sarasota campus of the University of South Florida, especially Holly Barone, deserve special thanks. As in all my efforts, my wife Carol has been with me at every step.

Justus D. Doenecke

ACKNOWLEDGMENTS, FIRST EDITION

I wish to express my gratitude to John Hope Franklin and Abraham S. Eisenstadt for the invitation to contribute to this series. To Douglas G. H. Hall and my colleagues at the university of the West Indies in the academic year 1965–66 I am grateful for providing such pleasant surroundings for composition of this book. The palms and poincianas swaying in the Caribbean breeze made me feel that I lived in a world removed from diplomacy and war. I want to thank Shinobu Iwamura, chairman of the Center for Southeast Asian studies, Kyoto University, Japan, for his recollection of events and people in Japan in the 1930s. At that time Professor Iwamura was a ranking official in the Japanese government news agency. I am grateful to Justus D. Doenecke for making available unpublished materials on America's response to the Manchurian incident. My thanks also to my colleague James T. Patterson of Indiana University who criticized two chapters before going on leave to Germany. Above all, I want to thank Robert H. Ferrell who spent many hours going over this manuscript word by word, catching errors here, striking superfluous sentences and paragraphs there. Indiana colleagues and students who have submitted their prose for the "Ferrell treatment" can appreciate the value of this criticism.

John E. Wilz

CHAPTER ONE

In Search of Peace

As the first gray light of dawn was breaking over Washington, D.C., windows of government buildings were ablaze with light. Automobiles jammed the streets. At the Capitol workmen, their breath visible in the frosty morning air, were driving wooden stakes into the ground around the House of Representatives' wing. Others followed, stringing wire cable to hold back the crowds expected later in the day. By midmorning policemen and marines, with fixed bayonets, were swarming around Capitol Hill.

Slightly over a mile away, at 1600 Pennsylvania Avenue, anxious crowds pressed against the iron fence of the mansion, while dozens of police patrolled the grounds. At 11:30 A.M., two open automobiles filled with Secret Service men moved into the driveway of the White House and rolled to a stop under the portico. Riot guns hung menacingly from the automobiles' sides.

At 12:00 P.M. sharp, the big glass doors of the building swung open, and into the chilly midday air walked President Franklin D. Roosevelt, supported by his son James, who was wearing the uniform of a marine officer. Grim-faced and silent, the president slowly descended the steps and entered a limousine bearing the White House insignia. Other automobiles quickly filled with aides, officials, and members of the chief executive's family. A moment later the cars were moving down the driveway, through the East Gate, turning right on Pennsylvania Avenue. Quiet crowds lined the streets. Skies were leaden, the temperature in the upper forties. A few brown leaves still clung to the city's larger trees.

Minutes later the presidential caravan entered the Capitol plaza and rolled to a special entrance. Onlookers broke into a cheer. His mouth tightly drawn, the president ignored the cheering, slowly lifted himself from the limousine, and went into the office of House speaker Sam Rayburn (Dem.-Tex.).

Members were taking seats in the House chamber. Meanwhile Senators were entering two-by-two down a long corridor and through the rotunda to the House side. A moment later the black-robed justices of the Supreme Court, led by Harlan Fiske Stone, entered the chamber and marched down the center aisle. At 12:24 the vice-president rapped his gavel, and everyone stood up. Down the aisle filed the president's cabinet, led by the white-haired secretary of state, Cordell Hull. Then, at 12:29, Rayburn rapped for silence and announced: "The President of the United States." Automatically the members of Congress, guests at the rear of the chamber, officials, diplomats, and a handful of servicemen and ordinary citizens rose to their feet. For an instant, there was silence, then applause. The clapping increased, but ended abruptly when Rayburn pounded the gavel. Still supported by James Roosevelt, the president appeared, slowly making his way up a ramp to the rostrum. More applause, then cheering, and for the next two or three minutes Roosevelt received the most tumultuous ovation of his presidency. Powerful lights enveloped the president in a blazing glow, movie cameras whirred, a dozen microphones made a jagged pattern across the rostrum.

After the House chaplain offered a brief prayer, the president, dressed in formal morning attire, stood alone. The large clock at his back showed 12:34, and at that moment a hush fell over the Republic. Millions of Americans turned toward radios to receive their president's words. Roosevelt opened a black loose-leaf notebook, and in restrained, staccato tones began: "Yesterday, December 7, 1941—a date which will live in infamy—the United States was suddenly and deliberately attacked by naval and air forces of the empire of Japan."

Several of those in the House chamber could remember a similar day just twenty-four years before, when President Woodrow Wilson had made an identical trip to the Capitol. He asked Congress to recognize that a state of war existed between the United States and Germany. The parallel between April 1917 and December 1941 made the drama of FDR's message curiously poignant.

I

When, in November 1918, quiet had finally settled over the Western Front in France, President Wilson made his plans to attend the peace conference in Paris. Over the past year and a half, he had led what he saw as a crusade for democracy; now he would direct the world to a settlement resting on justice and supported by a League of Nations. And that December, as the steamer *George Washington* slipped out of New York Harbor, the president jauntily paced the deck, smiling, full of confidence. He had the support of war-weary people the world over, and when he landed in France a week later, he was met with unparalleled enthusiasm. A Paris newspaper reported that "never has a king, never has an emperor received such a welcome."

Then something went wrong. The U.S. Senate rejected the peace drafted at Paris. It refused to join the League of Nations, and by 1923 Wilson's successor in the White House, Warren Gamaliel Harding, could announce that the League issue was "as dead as slavery." Americans were determined to keep their distance—to insulate themselves from Europe's troubles. Over the next decade and a half, this sentiment increased, and by the mid-1930s Congress was writing isolation into law.

This is not to say, however, that Americans closed their eyes entirely to the rest of the world. They took considerable interest in events elsewhere, underwriting Europe's postwar recovery while continually expanding their own foreign trade.

When historians use the term "isolationism," they are really referring to opposition to intervention in wars overseas, particularly in Europe, and to such "entangling alliances" as collective security agreements or such international organizations as the League of Nations. Because the term "isolationism" connotes a host of vices—indifference, dangerous naiveté, appeasement of dictators—one finds "anti-interventionism" a far more accurate term. People harboring this sentiment often referred to themselves as "nationalists" or "neutralists."

Anti-interventionism was an old habit and one that had several roots. One source was geography. From its birth the United States had enjoyed security to a degree unparalleled in the history of modern nations. The Atlantic and Pacific oceans served as giant barriers against overseas aggression, and neighbors in the Western Hemisphere were too weak to threaten an attack.

Another source lay in continental expansion. The North American continent, awaiting axe and plow, offered such splendid rewards that Americans inevitably turned their energy to developing their own empire. Once new markets were secured, the nation's prosperity would be guaranteed.

Then there were precedent and patriotism. Americans remembered the counsel of their first president. In his famous Farewell Address of September 1796, George Washington had warned of "the insidious wiles of foreign influence," urged "as little political connection as possible" with foreign countries, and noted the advantages of "our detached and distant situation." Thomas Jefferson, who used the very term "entangling alliances," shared these sentiments. More important, so did most Americans, who saw the Old World as corrupt, quarrelsome, autocratic—the antithesis of a truly democratic nation. Conversely, the New World was perceived as an Edenic utopia, or in the words of Thomas Paine, "an asylum for mankind." To use the metaphor of Abraham Lincoln, the United States was "the world's last best hope," the final outpost against feudal despotism or revolutionary anarchy. Down to the closing years of the nineteenth century, no responsible politician dared challenge Washington's position, and isolation became identified with Americanism.

By the 1920s the Old World held two particular dangers to those fearful of foreign involvement: British imperialism and Russian Bolshevism. The United States, anti-interventionists maintained, could not afford to be the unwitting agent of either colonial despotism or revolutionary terror.

From 1776 on, many Americans had regarded Britain with the greatest of suspicion. Not all were as vocal as the nineteenth-century diplomat Townsend Harris, whose parents had supposedly raised him up to offer prayers, fear God, and hate the British. In their eyes, however, England was ever seeking to rescue its domestic plutocracy and archaic empire. So long as it maintained dominion over much of the globe, it would be oppressing billions of subjects and attempting to hoard much of the world's wealth. All too often, so it was claimed, the U.S. was serving as the unwitting instrument of "Perfidious Albion." Just before World War II broke out in Europe, pundit H. L. Mencken accused the United States of serving as "the client and goon" of its traditional enemy, in fact acting "precisely like an English colony." Even the urbane news analyst Quincy Howe wrote a book in 1938: *England Expects Every American to Do IIis Duty.*

The Union of Soviet Socialist Republics embodied a newer threat, but one no less pernicious. To more conservative Americans, the Soviet Union stood for the persecution of religion, failure to pay the debts incurred by the Tsarist regime, and the liquidation of the entire Kulak class. True, for many liberals, not until the middle of the 1930s did Russia become "the God that failed." Even reformers, however, became deeply disillusioned by the famines in the Ukraine, the extermination of the top army command, the obviously trumped-up accusations of Stalin's purge trials, and the establishment of labor camps later known as the *gulags.*

It is hardly surprising that anti-interventionism was particularly strong among certain ethnic groups, among them Americans of German, Irish, and Italian origin. In the 1920s, German Americans were embittered over the harshness of the Versailles *Diktat,* Irish Americans furious that their beloved *Eire* had not been granted independence, and Italian Americans disappointed by the meager gains secured by Italy at Paris. Urged on by the Republicans, these ethnic groups reacted against the Democrats—the party of Woodrow Wilson, who was committed to a League of Nations and an "internationalist" approach to world affairs. When war again threatened in the 1930s, many among these groups, though seldom sympathizing with the Axis, feared that involvement would make the United States a full-scale partner of Great Britain. As there was no chance of an American alliance with Germany and Italy, the only alternative was aloofness.

Yet even by the end of the nineteenth century, the anti-interventionist tradition seemed to weaken. As a result of the Spanish-American War, the United States began to acquire an overseas empire, one that included the Philippines and Puerto Rico. President Wilson sent American youths to France in 1917–18, and when the war ended sought to take the United States into the League of Nations. The departure from old lines of thought, however, had been more apparent than real. It was easy for the anti-interventionist habit to reassert itself in the next two decades, and in 1935 Representative Maury Maverick (Dem.-Tex.) was undoubtedly expressing a popular sentiment when he announced: "In our Revolution against the British, Lafayette came over here, and Baron von Steuben, also a foreigner, came to train our Revolutionary troops, and we were glad to have them; but we do not like foreigners any more."

II

Americans, disillusioned by the results of the conflict of 1914–18, turned inward. In the 1920s, as historian William E. Leuchtenburg notes, the Great War (as people continued to call it) became "a dirty, unheroic war which few men remembered with any emotion save distaste."

Why had this happened?

America's leaders, historians agree, had oversold the World War. Instead of presenting U.S. participation as a matter of national interest, distasteful but necessary, they had turned it into a crusade for democracy. At the Paris peace conference and after, however, the public saw as much selfish nationalism in the world as before, and if anything less democracy. Many felt disgusted for having been so foolish as to become party to what they saw fundamentally as a European affair, that is, a war fought over European problems for European ends. No American interest, it was concluded, had ever been at stake. Millions of people agreed with Senator Homer T. Bone (Dem.-Wash.) when he said in 1935 that "the Great War . . . was utter social insanity, and was a crazy war, and we had no business in it at all." As late as January 1937, 70 percent of those polled responded that entry in the conflict had been a mistake.

Particularly disillusioning was the vindictive settlement the victors had imposed at Paris in 1919. Many Americans had thrilled to President Wilson's idea of a "peace without victory." They had hailed his Fourteen Points, the last item of which endorsed "a general association of nations" that would afford "mutual guarantees of political independence and territorial integrity to great and small states alike." Upon hearing that in Paris's superheated atmosphere Wilson had compromised principle and acquiesced in a conqueror's peace, they rejected the League. The United States, they believed, must live in isolation. As the *New Republic,* a liberal weekly, editorialized, Americans had hoped that "they would participate in a Europe so chastened by the war that the interests of a lasting peace would take precedence over every other national advantage. The European governments have chosen differently. Well and good. That must be their affair. It certainly should not be America's affair in the sense that American lives and American interests are entangled in it."

What was soon to be called "revisionism" strengthened such suspicions. Revisionism itself, as historians use the term, means a challenge to a conventional or generally accepted version of the past. In other words, revisionism has always been critical of what happened, how it happened, and why it happened. Contemporary opposition to public policy, new evidence, unexpected turns of history, plain political ambition—all have been, and will continue to be, reasons for "revising" interpretations of past events.

From the summer of 1914, when hostilities broke out, most Americans had accepted the view that it was the Germans in particular who were the aggressors. It was they who had fired the first shots on the Western Front, raped neutral Belgium, and plunged into France. When, in 1917, the U.S. entered the war, its leaders stressed that the conflict was the product of German militarism and sheer will to power.

Once, however, the combat was over, some writers concluded that Germany had been far from exclusively responsible. In a series of articles in the *American Historical Review* appearing in 1920–21, Sidney Bradshaw Fay denied that Germany was uniquely, or even primarily, culpable. Fay's great work, *The Origins of the World War* (1928), contained the claim that "Germany did not plot a European War, did not want one, and made genuine, though too belated efforts to avert one." Another writer, Albert Jay Nock, brought out a pamphlet entitled "The Myth of a Guilty Nation" (1922); it absolves Germany and deplored American support of the Allies. Sociologist-historian Harry Elmer Barnes, the author of a book titled *The Genesis of the World War* (1926), assigned responsibility for the war "in about this order: Austria, Russia, Serbia, France, Germany, and England."

Why then, many such people asked, had Americans failed to grasp the "truth" about the war and permit their nation to enter the conflict? Journalist C. Hartley Grattan (*Why We Fought,* 1929) was one who saw Allied propaganda playing a leading role, a view reinforced when some British officials admitted that the Allies had deliberately lied to the American public.

Others stressed the role of unscrupulous Wall Street bankers. It was common knowledge that American financiers had arranged huge loans to the Allied governments. When it appeared that the Allies might not win, the bankers—so the argument went—feared for their money and hence pressed Washington to enter the war. Although proponents of this "devil theory" offered no proof, the notion of Wall Street responsibility made sense to millions. It certainly strengthened the view that entry in Europe's bloodbath had been a mistake, and it heightened the nation's determination to avoid any new European conflict.

Still other explanations were more sophisticated, proponents claiming that the entire American economy, not just the banking community, had become increasingly dependent upon Allied war orders. Walter Millis, staff writer for the *New York Herald Tribune,* asserted in *Road to War—America: 1914–1917* (1935) that "if we now permitted the Central Powers to destroy our trade with the Allies, we should be risking a real and final economic collapse. No political administration could face that prospect." Charles A. Beard, who could well have been the most prominent historian in the entire United States, felt similarly. In his book *The Devil Theory of War* (1936), he wrote, "As the days and weeks passed[,] the fate of American bankers, manufacturers, farmers, merchants, workers, and white-collar servants became more deeply entangled in the fate of the Allies on the battlefield—in the war."

The controversy over war debts simply added to postwar disillusion. Late in 1914, when opposing armies struggled less than sixty miles from Paris, the Allies looked across the Atlantic for financial support. They worked through such banking houses as J. P. Morgan & Company, borrowing enormous sums. When the United States entered the war in 1917, the government opened its checkbook to the Allies. After victory the Allies managed to pay interest to the private financiers and bondholders, but they appealed for cancellation of debts owed the U.S. government—i.e., the American people. Such talk irked the public, who by then had determined that the war had been fundamentally a European venture that had only benefited that continent. Indeed Europeans, it was felt, should be grateful for American intervention and pay their debts to the last penny. Most Americans agreed with President Calvin Coolidge, who allegedly said: "They hired the money, didn't they?"

Europeans, of course, saw matters differently. So much was Germany's defeat in the American interest, they argued, that until April 1917 they were fighting the United States's battles for it. They also noted that the war had crushed their own economies while bringing prosperity to the New World. Little wonder the initials "U.S." now stood for "Uncle Shylock," who was demanding his pound of flesh from people who had shed blood in the common cause. European anger had scant effect upon the Americans; they continued to insist that the Allies honor all obligations. When the Allies defaulted in 1934, doing so under the impact of the Depression, their going into arrears was simply ascribed as additional evidence of Europe's ineradicable corruption.

Disillusion over the war reached its climax during the Great Depression of the 1930s, an event triggered in autumn 1929 by the New York stock market collapse. To many, including some economists, the war had planted the seeds of depression. Deflation, they reasoned, must follow inflation, and bust inevitably follows boom. During the war, a good number of Americans had enjoyed unprecedented prosperity, and in 1929 the reckoning was at hand. The future held a warning: to avoid another debacle, avoid war.

In 1940 a major Protestant weekly, the *Christian Century,* summarized the entire saga in six sentences:

First, a tremendous factory expansion to produce for a foreign war. Second, a rush of workers for the high pay which such emergency work will offer. Third, big profits for the shareholders in the "lucky" corporations. Fourth, the necessity to keep the expanded plant going if there is not to be an industrial crash. Fifth, peace—and no more use for the expanded plant. Sixth, the crash.

There was also the legacy of the recent war, including the continued demand for veterans' bonuses. Privates risking their lives in France had received $1.25 a day, while civilians in the factories and shipyards at home had earned ten times as much. There was logic in the argument that the country owed veterans some "adjusted compensation," although relatively few Americans favored being taxed to supply such bonuses. And where would the bonus business end? Historians could remind the country that the amount of money paid to Civil War veterans over the years since Appomattox had exceeded the cost of the conflict in 1861–65. There were, of course, the permanent victims of the 1917–18 war. Men who had suffered from shrapnel and gas needed sustained care. That took money, and these sad men were living reminders of the reality of war.

The politics of domestic reform provided still another incentive for isolation between the wars, particularly in the late 1930s. During the years 1901–17, the so-called Progressive Era, reform in America had moved from triumph to triumph, reaching a climax in President Wilson's domestic program of 1916. As the United States drew closer to war in 1915–17, most liberals urged that the nation keep out of Europe's conflict lest involvement stifle progressive legislation. When the country entered the war in 1917, their fears came true: the reform program nearly ended, and leaders of business were now more entrenched in power than ever.

The worst was yet to come, for war brought a highly conservative reaction to American politics. In the postwar decade, progressives labored in a political wilderness. Not surprisingly, they felt even greater hostility toward war, seeing it spawn the "do-nothing" era of Warren G. Harding and George F. Babbitt. Even when the New Deal was launched, some reformers feared that a war might nullify liberalism's newly secured gains. In 1940 Oswald Garrison Villard, an editor often to the left of the New Deal, warned that if the U.S. entered another war, it would witness "the destruction of everything we hold dear in American life and the loss of all our great gains under Roosevelt."

Paradoxically, many political conservatives too were anti-interventionist, for they feared that involvement in war imperiled the capitalist system. Full-scale mobilization, they warned, must lead to inflation, price and wage controls, and compulsory unionization. Senator Robert A. Taft (Rep.-Ohio) claimed in 1939, "The additional powers sought by the President in case of war, the nationalization of all industry and all capital and all labor, already proposed in bills before Congress, would create a socialist dictatorship," one "impossible to dissolve when the war ended." Aviator Charles A. Lindbergh was even more apprehensive, confiding to his diary in 1941, "Who knows what will happen here before we finish it [World War II]—race riots, revolution, destruction."

One thing was certain. Americans of all political persuasions could agree with Kansas editor William Allen White who found war "the Devil's answer to human progress."

III

Certainly war itself had lost its glamour. Reflecting on war, people were no longer inclined to envision cavalry charges with banners flying and sabers flashing. They saw mud, barbed wire, fear, desolation, death. Reinforcing the new image of war were such books as Erich Maria Remarque's *All Quiet on the Western Front* (1929), a bitter novel adapted into a movie (1930) that showed the disillusionment and death of Paul Bäumer, a German front-line soldier. Bäumer's American counterpart was Lieutenant Frederic Henry, the protagonist of Ernest Hemingway's *A Farewell to Arms* (1926). After the death of his fiancée, Henry commented on war in general:

You died. You did not know what it was about. You never had time to learn. They threw you in and told you the rules and the first time they caught you off base they killed you.

In the two decades after the armistice, some Americans concluded that most wars in history had been morally wrong. Others wrestled with the morality of killing enemies, even in a "just" war. In 1934 a young man wrote North Dakota's Senator Gerald P. Nye (Rep.-N.D.): "As a potential soldier, I object to the prospect of becoming cannon fodder in the 'next war'; as a future taxpayer, I object to enriching arms manufacturers by impoverishing fellow Americans; and, most important, as a Christian, I object to preparing to run a bayonet through my brother from another country."

Hence any discussion of the interwar quest for peace must include the peace movement. A variety of organizations strove mightily to sustain the nation's resolve to avoid war. Some were religious groups that saw war as violating scriptural injunction: most had the sole purpose of crusading against what they saw as organized slaughter.

The American peace movement had originated in the early years of the nineteenth century, after the Napoleonic wars in Europe. First was the Massachusetts Peace Society, organized in 1815. Then the American Peace Society, most influential of the early groups, appeared in 1828. Throughout its youth the peace movement amounted to little, for no enemies threatened the country and humanitarians found the problems of slavery, care of the insane, and inhuman prison conditions far more pressing. In the wake of the Civil War, when Americans turned to industrialization and westward expansion, the movement nearly expired. Even Andrew Carnegie's gift of $10 million, donated in 1910 to establish the Carnegie Endowment for International Peace, made little impact. After the First World War, however, the cause became a veritable crusade, and in the two decades that followed, it reached its pinnacle of influence.

Between the wars the peace movement had two wings, which one might label conservative and radical. Believing that peace required international cooperation, the conservative wing—the Carnegie Endowment, World Peace Foundation, Woodrow Wilson

Foundation, League of Nations Association—adhered to collective security. More prominent were such radical groups as the Women's International League for Peace and Freedom (WIL) and the National Council for Prevention of War (NCPW). One small group, the War Resisters League, was an outright pacifist body, pledging itself to "not to support any kind of war."

Like the conservatives, such militant groups at first favored international cooperation. In the 1930s, however, some found the League of Nations incapable of organizing united efforts against aggression. Others saw the League as a new alliance to enforce the status quo. Still others were fearful of anything smacking of an international police force. Harboring a rampant antimilitarism, they were dedicated to ridding the world of the "war habit." Time, they believed, was short, for at any moment the "militarists" might seize the initiative and plunge the world into conflict. This sense of urgency gave the radicals a zeal unmatched in conservative circles.

These radical groups, one should add, were in no sense mass organizations; membership was small, funds severely limited. At their peak they had fewer than a hundred full-time workers, usually located in Washington and New York. Yet, because of skillful organization, national disillusion over the Great War, and their own frenetic energy, they profoundly influenced American opinion.

Occasionally a comic note crept into the peace movement. In 1936, eight Princeton undergraduates organized the Veterans of Future Wars, which soon spread to fifty institutions. Demanding an immediate bonus of $1,000 for every man between the ages of eighteen and thirty-six, they claimed that many in that age group would not survive the next war and therefore deserved their bonuses immediately. The Veterans paraded with overseas caps worn at right angles to the usual position. Members greeted each other with a fascist-like salute, right arm extended but with palm upturned as though seeking a handout. For college women, the Veterans set up a Future Gold Star Mothers auxiliary; it demanded that the government award loved-ones pensions for trips to Europe, so that they could visit the grave sites of their future sons and husbands. In a parade near Columbia University, a drum major twirled a crutch, leading 150 girls dressed as nurses or war widows who carried "war orphan" dolls. They were followed by 200 young men displaying such signs as "You too can learn to play a machine gun." What began as a spoof on veterans' demands ended up as biting satire.

Apart from denouncing war and teaching "peace habits," what were the objects of the peace movement between the wars?

Disarmament was a cause dear to peace groups, conservative and radical, and both wings supported the disarmament conferences of the 1920s and early 1930s. In their view, bulging arsenals were, like tinderboxes, ignited by the slightest spark—such as the assassination of a European archduke. Recalling Europe's armament stocks in the years before 1914, peace groups agreed with Sir Edward Grey, Britain's wartime foreign minister, who had claimed that "the enormous growth of armaments in Europe . . . made war inevitable."

Peace groups also fostered a movement entering on nothing less than the "outlawry of war." Put forth early in the 1920s, the idea of outlawing war did not catch on until 1927, when Charles A. Lindbergh's solo flight over the Atlantic from New York to Paris brought an outpouring of Franco-American friendship. To capitalize on these sentiments, French Foreign Minister Aristide Briand proposed a pact between the United States and France that would bind the two countries never to fight each other. One of Europe's most clever diplomats, Briand enlisted the help of the American peace movement, which began to press President Coolidge to sign the accord.

The State Department suspected that Briand had hidden motives, in fact that he sought a virtual alliance with the United States, one that would protect France from a possible resurgence of German power. Not surprisingly, American Secretary of State Frank B. Kellogg was furious at his nation's professional peace workers ("a set of God-damned fools"), but he came forth with a shrewd counterproposal. If a bilateral treaty was such a good idea, why not a multilateral treaty pledging all nations to renounce war? Known as a man of peace—he was a former winner of the Nobel Peace Prize—Briand hardly could refuse the American suggestion. As for the peace movement, it mobilized American opinion behind a multilateral agreement.

In 1928 fifteen nations, including the United States, entered into the Kellogg-Briand Pact, also called the Pact of Paris, renouncing war "as an instrument of national policy." Other nations soon clamored to affix their signature. Peace groups hailed the treaty as the greatest step toward peace in human history. More cynical people called it "solemn ballyhoo" and "an international kiss."

By the mid-1930s, the peace movement had reached its peak of influence. Its solution for keeping America out of war: total isolation. Ignoring the troubles of the rest of the world was not enough. The United States should complete its insulation by cutting economic ties with warring nations as well. This idea attracted wide support and, as Chapter Three will show, resulted in a major congressional inquiry of what would later be called the military-industrial complex and in a series of congressional "neutrality" acts.

By 1938 any pacifist sentiment was beginning to wane, and in September 1939, after the outbreak of war in Europe, dilemmas became more acute. Moreover, peace groups were facing some gnawing questions. Could the United States remain faithful to its heritage as a beacon of democracy and at the same time stand by while this very system perished in Europe? Was it really true that a general war in Europe or Asia need not touch the interests of the United States? The more radical bodies, such as the WIL and the NCPW, still pushed for American isolation, while more conservative peace groups endorsed military aid to the British. Debate became increasingly sharp, then ended abruptly—on December 7, 1941.

So it was, in the decades between the two world wars, that Americans determined to isolate themselves from "foreign" embroilment. The word "peace" took on a theological quality, striking a chord whenever it found its way into a sermon, speech, or prayer. And when President Harding voiced moving sentiments about concord, he was not indulging in "bloviation," as he was wont to call some of his lesser oratory; Harding and others meant what they said. Through the decade of the 1920s, the anti-interventionist impulse manifested itself in hostility to the League of Nations in particular and collective security in general. Otherwise Americans were willing to participate in disarmament conferences, discuss ways of strengthening international law, and sign a treaty to outlaw war.

Then came the 1930s and collapse of the Paris settlement of 1919. Fearing another general war, Americans added a new dimension to their anti-interventionism: if war enveloped other parts of the world, the flames must not scorch America. Let the rest of the world destroy itself; America must live. In 1935, historian Beard captured this sentiment: "We tried once to right European wrongs, to make the world safe for democracy. Even in the rosiest view the experiment was not a great success . . . [Isolation] may be no better, for aught anyone actually knows. But we nearly burnt our house down with one experiment; so it seems not wholly irrational to try another line." In view of the international uncertainties of the 1930s, the claim appeared difficult to refute.

CHAPTER TWO

Manchuria

When, on September 19, 1931, readers scanned the front pages of the *New York Times,* their eyes moved to the lead story. It described a compromise between Governor Franklin D. Roosevelt and the Republican majority in the Albany legislature over unemployment relief. But in turning to the opposite side of the page, they saw a two-column headline declaring that Japanese troops had seized the Manchurian city of Mukden. The accompanying story reported that on the night of September 18, at about 10:20 Tokyo time, three companies of Chinese soldiers had begun destroying tracks of the Japanese-owned South Manchuria Railway at a village three miles from Mukden. According to dispatches datelined Tokyo, Japanese troops had driven off the Chinese, but the Chinese counterattacked with machine guns and cannon. Special trains reportedly were speeding fresh Japanese battalions to the scene of hostilities, and Japanese air squadrons based in Korea were preparing to strike. Japan's foreign office pledged that their country would soon withdraw its troops, but it quickly became apparent that the promise would not be honored.

In a subsequent "clarification," Japanese officials claimed that a small explosive charge planted by Chinese soldiers had ripped away

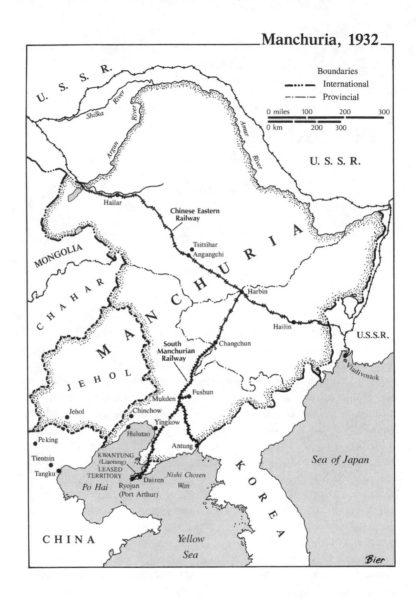

Manchuria, 1932

twenty-one inches of South Manchuria track. Nobody saw the gap, and there was no proof in the collection of bent spikes and splintered crossties that the Japanese exhibited a few days later to foreign newsmen. The Japanese, moreover, found it difficult to explain how the Mukden Express had passed over the line a few minutes after the alleged explosion. They simply said that the train had jumped the gap.

Today, of course, Japan's explanation appears outrageous. But within days after the railroad incident, the Japanese moved troops across the Korean frontier. They not only occupied Mukden, but seized towns a hundred miles away as well. Within a few months, claiming they were pursuing Chinese bandits, they had occupied most of Manchuria.

The American public did not comprehend what had happened, nor would it for several years. The peace created in the aftermath of World War I, however, had suffered its first serious fracture. In one sense, World War II had already begun.

I

If the Manchurian incident of 1931 was a beginning, it was also part of a stream of events that had begun in the 1850s, when Commodore Matthew C. Perry, under orders of president Millard Fillmore, entered Tokyo Bay with four steam-powered warships and persuaded the Japanese to accept a commercial treaty with the United States. Thus ended more than two centuries of Japanese isolation from the rest of the world. Through the door cracked open by Perry flowed the ideas and goods of Europe and America.

The result: a veritable revolution of Japanese society. Factories went up, a modern army and navy appeared, the people began to move outward. In 1894–95, renewal of an old rivalry with China over Korea led to a war that Japan won easily, and at the peace table the Japanese took Taiwan (Formosa), the Pescadores Islands, and the Liaodong Peninsula, Manchuria's outlet to the sea. Then the Island Kingdom became frustrated: Russia, France, and Germany compelled the Japanese to surrender the Liaodong Peninsula in return for an additional cash indemnity.

In the next few years, the Russians cynically elbowed their way into the Manchurian territory that they had insisted Japan relinquish.

They also began casting glances toward Korea, "the dagger pointed at the heart of Japan." In 1902 the Japanese responded by making an alliance with Great Britain, and two years later, they launched a successful attack against Russian forces in the Far East. By the Treaty of Portsmouth, engineered in 1905 by American President Theodore Roosevelt, Japan received important Russian holdings in Manchuria, including the naval base of Port Arthur and the beginnings of a line that became the South Manchuria Railway. Subsequent agreements with China confirmed Japan's new position in Manchuria. To protect their interests in the "leasehold," the Japanese were empowered to station troops in a narrow "railway" zone.

At first, many Americans welcomed Japan's victory over China, and a decade later they similarly applauded its triumph over Russia. President Roosevelt, who had feared Russian domination in Manchuria, admired Japan's technological prowess and hoped for a new balance of power in Asia.

Still, the United States had long engaged in commercial and missionary activity in China and, with the acquisition of the Philippines in 1898, it had become a full-fledged Far Eastern power. Soon official Washington was viewing Japan's new strength with misgiving. Fears for America's China trade grew as the great powers were carving up China into spheres of influence. Secretary of State John Hay sent circular notes to the great powers seeking endorsement of an "Open Door" there. The 1899 note stressed commercial equality within existing spheres of influence. The 1900 note, however, sought to preserve "Chinese territorial and administrative entity," that is its independence and territorial integrity. At best the replies the president received were evasive. Hay, however, expressed satisfaction with them, in the process leaving Americans to believe that their nation had preserved China's independence, actually preventing its dismemberment.

Two matters only served to cloud American policy further. One was a memorandum drafted on July 27, 1905, by Roosevelt's secretary of war, William Howard Taft, and Japanese prime minister Katsura Taro. Under this agreement, Taft conveyed the president's support for Japan's suzerainty over Korea, meaning that the U.S. president favored an arrangement by which Japan controlled Korean foreign policy. As noted by historian Raymond A. Esthus, the conversation was simply an honest exchange of views. Contrary to myth, it did not involve any pledge by Japan to keep its hands off the Philippines, something that Roosevelt would have considered unnecessary in any case, for such action would have triggered war with the U.S.

Another such agreement was reached on November 30, 1908, involving an exchange of notes between Elihu Root, American secretary of state, and Takahira Kogoro, Japanese ambassador to the U.S. The agreement declared their intention to support peaceful trade, defend "the principle of equal opportunity for commerce and industry in China," and to consult whenever Chinese independence and territorial integrity might be jeopardized. Again contrary to legend, the exchange did not give Japan any "free hand" in Manchuria, much less recognize Japan's disputed claims in South Manchuria, in return for any guarantee of the Philippines. Esthus writes that "historical accounts which have pictured the Root-Takahira episode as a moment of great decision in America's Far Eastern policy have greatly overdramatized the affair."

In 1910 Japan annexed Korea outright. Then, while Europe was convulsed in the Great War, Tokyo moved quickly. Seeking to enlarge Japanese holdings in Manchuria and Shandong (Shantung) and to cripple the Chinese government, in January 1915 it placed its "twenty-one demands" before China. Had all these demands been accepted, Japan would have totally controlled the Chinese government. Four months later, over American protests, Japan signed a treaty with China that granted Japan all but the most severe exaction. Japanese predominance in South Manchuria was explicitly recognized. So too was Japan's dominant position in Shandong and East Inner Mongolia. Moreover, it was acknowledged to have a special interest in an industrial base in Central China.

The United States, fearing that Japan might ally itself with Germany, moderated its position when, in the spring of 1917, it entered the European war. The shift was reflected in an exchange of notes between the U.S. Secretary of State Robert Lansing and Viscount Ishii Kujujiro, a special Japanese envoy. Called the Lansing-Ishii agreement and signed that November, it recognized Japan's undefined "special interests" in China. The phrase "particularly in the part to which its possessions are contiguous" could easily be interpreted as meaning such areas as southern Manchuria.

The end of the First World War brought no weakening of Japanese ambition. At the Paris Peace Conference, the Japanese overcame the opposition of President Wilson and secured Germany's economic holdings in China's Shandong Peninsula. By means of a League of Nations mandate, they also gained Germany's islands in the Pacific north of the equator.

There was also the matter of Siberia. In 1918, the Allied powers had sent troops there, doing so in the hopes of getting Russia back into the war against Germany. Two years later, the Japanese declined to withdraw, even when the other Allied forces, including the Americans, left. That same year, the United States and Japan began quarreling over the island of Yap, a cable station in the Carolines between Guam and the Philippines.

If Americans found amusement in the jingle "Yap for the Yappers," the government in Washington took a more serious view of Japanese activity in the western Pacific and East Asia. Adding to the concern of America's leaders was the Anglo-Japanese alliance of 1902. Since the War of 1812, American security had depended heavily upon the British navy. The United States now had to ponder the consequences of drifting into war with Japan and finding the British fleet on the side of the enemy.

Was war with Japan likely? It certainly seemed a possibility just after World War I, especially if one took seriously the fulmination of Japan's military leaders. From the time of the Russo-Japanese War of 1904–1905, the high-water mark of Japanese-American friendship, relations between the two nations had deteriorated. Mutual suspicion had begun with the Treaty of Portsmouth, for it denied Japan the high indemnity it sought. Although the military situation at the time allowed Japan no leverage, its people blamed Theodore Roosevelt, and a wave of anti-Americanism swept throughout the Japanese islands. Then in 1906 came the insolent order of the San Francisco Board of Education directing Japanese-American schoolchildren to attend segregated schools.

At Versailles, the United States had proved the main obstacle to Japanese pride and expansion. The U.S. failed to support Japan's demand that the new League of Nations Covenant explicitly recognize the principle of the equality of all races. At the same time, it pressed Japan, who had ousted the Germans from Shandong during the Great War, to return that area to China. Furthermore, American fear of economic competition and general racism produced calls for the exclusion of Japanese immigrants.

By 1919, many Japanese, especially military men, talked wildly about war with the United States. In a book entitled *If Japan and America Fight* (1920), General Sato Kojiro accused the United States of hypocritically demanding that others observe the "open door" in China while harboring imperialist ambitions of its own. As for war, Sato recognized America's industrial power but felt confident that the "indomitable will" of the Japanese people would ultimately triumph. Using the analogy "a tree must have its roots," he pointed to British "roots" stretching to Africa, India, Australia, and Canada and to U.S. "roots" reaching Central and South America. Japan too must have "roots"—lest it shrivel and die.

Similarly, American naval strategists dreamed of converting Guam into the Gibraltar of the Pacific and envisioned the possibility of an "Orange Plan" by which the U.S. would conduct an offensive war, primarily naval in character, in the western Pacific. Moreover, the U.S. Army had been drafting contingency plans to land troops on the Japanese mainland. For its part, the American press frequently alluded to the dangers of war, and books entitled *The Rising Tide of Color, The Germany of Asia,* and *Must We Fight Japan?* sold widely.

It is hard to assess how much credence each side gave to the other. When, however, the Washington Conference of 1921–22 convened, the United States sought to stabilize the entire Pacific expansion. Several treaties emerged. A Four-Power Treaty of 1921 replaced the Anglo-Japanese alliance. By its terms the United States, Japan, Britain, and France pledged themselves to consult should their island possessions and dominions be threatened. The United States undertook no obligation: pressure by anti-interventionists in Congress assured that no commitment to armed force was involved.

The Nine-Power Treaty (the same four, plus Belgium, China, Italy, Portugal, and the Netherlands) of 1922 committed signatories to the open door of commercial equality and administrative integrity in China. No power, the agreement declared, should seek special privileges abridging the rights of others or threatening the security of friendly states. Here again, the signers undertook no obligation to enforce such provisions; Article VII merely allowed for "full and frank communication" if any signatory believed that conditions were becoming dangerous.

In the Five-Power Treaty (the United States, Britain, Japan, France, and Italy) of 1922, which was the most publicized agreement of all, the United States and Britain paid for abrogating the 1902 alliance and Japan's pledge of good behavior. A tonnage ratio of 5:5:3 was established for "capital" ships, that is warships of over 10,000 tons or carrying guns of over eight inches caliber. Though this ratio was five for Britain, five for the United States, and three for Japan, the agreement facilitated Japan's naval supremacy in the western Pacific. Tokyo's failure, however, to gain absolute equality aroused the ire of some nationalists. One Japanese diplomat later referred to the arrangement as "Rolls Royce: Rolls Royce: Ford." The British, Americans, and Japanese also agreed that certain Pacific islands should not be fortified further. Included under this ban were the Kuriles, Bonins, and Pescadores (all Chinese), Hong Kong (British), and the Philippines and Aleutians (U.S.).

Here was laid out what later would be called "the Washington Conference system," or simply "the Washington system," in some ways an Asian counterpart to the European order first established at Versailles (1919) and then modified at Locarno (1925). Rather than perpetuating an old diplomacy rooted in exclusive alliances, the major Pacific powers committed themselves to a new diplomacy based upon multilateral cooperation. Freezing the status quo was no more sanctioned than was fostering violent revolution. Instead Asian stability was to be ensured by the allowing of gradual and peaceful change. Because the participants possessed advanced capitalist economies sustained by the gold standard, historian Akira Iriye notes that one can label the Washington system "a capitalist internationalism, or even a new form of imperialism."

Although the powers had pledged themselves to foster China's evolution into a modern and independent state and not to expand at its expense, one thing must be noted. Despite such agreements, the international system established at Washington was most precarious. Indeed, it implied more of a moral commitment than a legal one; its only means of enforcement was the goodwill of the individual signers.

The Washington treaties brought about some improvement in Japanese-American relations. True, 1924 marked a temporary setback, for Congress passed a new immigration law that insulted the Japanese by excluding their nationals. Still, moderates had taken power in Tokyo, the influence of the army was in decline, and the Japanese seemed to have put aside those dreams of expansion that had so recently produced friction.

All this time, China was in ferment. In 1912 the tottering Manchu dynasty, which had ruled China since 1644, finally collapsed. There followed a long period of social and political turmoil. When in 1925, Dr. Sun Zhongshan (Sun Yat-sen), the father of Chinese nationalism, died, a new leader soon appeared-General Jiang Jieshi (Chiang Kai-shek), Sun's brother-in-law and a man whose position was augmented by marriage into the incredibly powerful Soong family. The generalissimo, as he was called, was motivated by a combination of personal ambition, patriotism, and the dream of a better life for his country's millions.

Throughout much of the 1920s, Jiang sought to eliminate foreign privileges. The Nationalist or Goumindang (Kuomintang) party espoused a passionate antiforeign ideology, one that often involved attacks upon U.S. and British interests in China. In 1927, Chinese crowds overran British concessions at Kiukiang and Hankou (Hankow) and Nationalist troops captured the Chinese section of Shanghai. When the Nationalists seized Nanjing (Nanking), British and American gunboats opened fire. In that same year, Chinese troops attacked American vessels, stationed to protect U.S. lives and property, some thirty-seven times. By the beginning of 1928, about 5,000 American troops were ensconced in Shanghai and in the Beijing-Tiangin (Peking-Tientsin) region.

Just as the Chinese Nationalists wanted to limit Western power in China proper, so they sought to curb Japanese influence in Manchuria. Although Japan had long treated Manchuria as if it were its colony, culturally and demographically it remained predominantly

Chinese. In 1931, 28 of its 30 million people were Chinese; all Japanese privileges were acknowledged in formal treaties with the Chinese government.

The rising Chinese nationalism could not help but affect the perceptions of Manchuria's leaders. Warlord Chang Tso-lin, whom the Japanese assassinated in 1928, had originally been Japan's client, but his son-in-law and heir, Chang Hsueh-liang, allied himself with Jiang Jieshi. To counter the Japanese, Jiang's government persuaded several million Chinese to emigrate to Manchuria to spur economic development. In addition, their presence would emphasize China's ownership of the province, something always tenuous. China also demanded the surrender of all extraterritorial rights in Manchuria and confronted Japan in other ways as well, urging a full-scale boycott of Japanese goods and developing ports at Hulutao and Yingkow to rival the Japanese port of Dairen.

Most important of all, China's leaders correctly saw the South Manchurian Railroad as the linchpin of Japan's power. To use the metaphor of historian Robert H. Ferrell, "The South Manchurian was a thread on which Japan had strung huge economic holdings." No mere railroad concern, it administered schools, libraries, police forces, agricultural stations, and public utilities. It owned ironworks and coal mines and had developed the port of Dairen. Late in the 1920s, Jiang's government violated a protocol made in 1905 by encouraging the local warlord to link one Chinese line with another, putting down a spur here and a section of a local track there.

Such aspirations were bound to meet with Japan's opposition, for no area played such a crucial role in the program of its expansionists. In 1927, the cabinet of Prime Minister Tanaka Giichi designated Manchuria as a special region, one that the government must defend at all costs. In creating this policy, the cabinet spoke for more than itself, for virtually every articulate segment of Japanese society—ranging from the prominent industrialists (known as *zaibatsu*) to farm and labor organizations—considered Japan's rights there to be completely legitimate.

Japanese entrepreneurs were permitted to operate in Manchuria almost as freely as on their own soil. By 1931, Manchuria held over half of Japan's foreign investment, some 1.2 billion yen, and Japan operated 690 miles of railroad there. Given this strong economic presence, it was hardly surprising that the Japanese economy had become increasingly dependent upon such Manchurian resources as lumber. Fifty percent of Japan's food and pig iron came from Manchuria, and a third of Manchuria's coal crossed the Yellow Sea to Japan. In addition, a quarter of a million Japanese subjects, mostly Koreans, lived in Manchuria, and about 40 percent of Japan's China trade centered there.

Manchuria's economic advantages became even more important in 1930, for the Great Depression reached Japan. Even during the 1920s, when Japan was relatively prosperous, its economy had been unstable. The people suffered first from inflation, then from chronic hard times. With each financial crisis, less silk was exported, more firms dissolved, more workers went on strike, and more families broke apart. Now, in one year, the export of raw silk had plunged by half, which reduced Japan's exports by more than 40 percent between 1929 and 1930. By the summer of 1931, Japan's economic situation was desperate. Compounding the problem was continued population growth: 65 million Japanese were squeezed into an area smaller than the state of Texas. Manchuria, a land mass the size of France and Germany combined, therefore, suddenly appeared most promising.

The United States contributed to Japan's hardships. The Smoot-Hawley tariff, enacted in June 1930, raised import duties on Japanese goods by an average of 23 percent, seriously affecting Japan's export of chinaware and canned goods. Then, by 1931, the U.S. had replaced Japan as the leading supplier of goods to China.

Protecting the Manchurian leasehold was one thing, but in the 1920s some Japanese had begun to have even wider dreams. Why should Japan merely hang on in Manchuria? The Chinese had never developed the territory. Despite the recent Chinese migration, it was essentially a frontier area of untapped mineral wealth. By expanding from the railway zone, the Japanese could broaden their industrial base, alleviate food shortage, and establish settlements to absorb surplus population.

The Russian factor was also important. In 1904–1905 the blood of Japanese soldiers had been shed on Manchuria's soil, making the leasehold a sort of hallowed ground. The battle for Mukden alone had taken seventeen days. Now Russia, Japan's ancient rival, had been stirring recently in northern Manchuria and was threatening to spread its new ideology of communism throughout East Asia. Soviet moves aroused Japanese patriots, stiffening their resolve to brook no nonsense from China.

The more Japan's patriots pondered, especially after the onset of the 1929 economic crisis, the more alluring the possibilities became. Manchuria would guard the home islands and Korea against the despicable Russians and their communist ideas. Furthermore, in Iriye's words, it "would be a self-sufficient haven of stability and prosperity, free from national egoisms and from radicalism." It would also link Japan and China, bringing those countries into a giant economic bloc that would end Occidental exploitation and thwart Soviet communism. In turn, this bloc would become a magnet, attracting all peoples of East Asia. Who would lead this "new order"? Obviously it would be the country having a "superior" culture, advanced technology, and a unified population.

Japan's civilian government was sufficiently liberal to give the appearance of evolving into a Western-style democracy. Although it was distressed by the country's economic problems and incensed by Chinese inroads in Manchuria, it nonetheless sought peaceful solutions and entertained no grand design for a new adventure in imperialism. Still, civilian authorities labored under serious difficulties. Factionalism and corruption ravaged Japan's political parties. Members of the parliament, called the Diet, were often in the pay of the zaibatsu. The entrenched feudal tradition subverted democratic ideas, and boiling just beneath the surface of life was a fanatical nationalism.

Many voices within Japan, and not just the army alone, saw the Washington system leading to nothing but disaster. Why were the Washington powers continually making concessions to China? Why was there collective recognition of the Nationalist regime located in Nanjing? Why should Japan sign new treaties to revise the Chinese tariff? Why were negotiations underway for abrogating extraterritoriality, the means by which foreigners retained significant autonomy on China's soil?

The Japanese raised other questions as well. Why should Japan's welfare depend upon fluctuations in international trade balances and rates of exchange? How could the nation cope with the new economic protectionism of the Western powers? Must Japan's very destiny be based upon the beneficence of the other Washington treaty powers and perhaps of China as well? Surely, the ultranationalists reasoned, if Japan were to avoid being at the mercy of outside forces, it must defy the Washington treaties.

This discontent centered in the army. Japan's unusual constitutional structure gave the Diet little control over the unruly armed forces, and the army and navy chiefs of staff were responsible to the emperor alone. Then there was the special status of the Guandong (Kwantung) Army, which received its name from the fact that it was garrisoned on the Guandong, or Liaodong, Peninsula in southern Manchuria. Long an elite corps, it acted as the Young Turks of Japan's military establishment. Its ideology included authoritarian rule, the curbing of zaibatsu power, and expansion on the Chinese mainland. It saw itself leading a *Showa* Restoration, that is, a government by patriots that in turn could introduce *Kodo*, or the Imperial Way: the supremacy of Shinto (the original religion of Japan), absolute fealty to the emperor, and obedience to all superiors. The conquered areas could serve as laboratories of social reform, combining state aid for economic development with limits on income.

In the meantime, the army's prestige was at a low ebb. The officers were piqued by shabby equipment, short rations, and cuts in military appropriations. Holding their government in contempt, they accused it of corruption and incompetence. Moreover, they saw Japan's civilian rulers as being "soft on China," resorting to endless negotiations over privileges long taken for granted.

One minor incident followed another. In 1931, a dispute between Korean tenants and Chinese farmers resulted in 91 killed and 102 wounded, and the Chinese quarter of Seoul, Korea, was razed to the ground. Then Chinese soldiers executed Nakamura Shintaro, a Japanese army captain engaged in unauthorized reconnaissance in a remote Manchurian area.

Late that summer, the young officers determined to act. A world disarmament conference was in the offing, scheduled to convene at Geneva the following spring. Remembering how Japan's civilian leaders had acquiesced in reducing its naval power at the London naval conference held the previous year, military leaders feared emasculation of the army. Anxiety over military budget-cutting in Tokyo, as well as rumors that important staff leaders would soon be transferred from Manchuria, made the Guandong Army ready to gamble.

A dramatic stroke would restore the army's prestige vis-à-vis the civilian government, prove the need of a strong military establishment, and undermine domestic advocates of disarmament. Inevitably thoughts turned to Manchuria, where a bold action also would open the way for a new and glorious imperialism, check Russia, and resolve Japan's economic difficulties. The upshot was the incident at Mukden.

II

When news of the Mukden affair spread through Japan, there was no rejoicing in the streets, only a feeling of satisfaction that Japanese soldiers were chastising the "upstart" Chinese. Few saw the incident leading to increased commitments. The government in Tokyo, however, was frightened. Though not surprised, having long suspected army intrigue in Manchuria, civilian leaders dreaded the risks of further imperialism. Their position, however, was difficult. The army's action in Manchuria was popular. The cabinet felt it could not afford to appear less patriotic than the army; nor could it be seen as less interested in defending Japan's Manchurian interests.

How have Japan's actions been evaluated?

The Japanese long claimed that their economic bind and China's attempt to undermine their Manchurian interests justified both the Mukden incident and subsequent occupation. They pointed to several factors: Japan's economic dependence upon Manchuria; the need for a place to emigrate; the example of United States preponderance in Latin America; the belief that John Hay and Theodore Roosevelt had recognized Manchuria as a Japanese sphere of interest that lay beyond the domain of the Chinese empire; and the economic prosperity Japan brought to the region.

Most American historians remain unconvinced. In the words of historian Robert J. C. Butow, "Manchuria was Chinese, and while that did not give the Nationalists any right to ignore China's treaty obligations toward other powers, neither did geographical propinquity or even special rights and interests confer upon Japan any kind of patent to sever the area from China the moment there was the slightest trouble."

When news of the imbroglio near Mukden began to filter abroad, Washington exhibited little concern. On September 19, President Herbert Hoover and Secretary of State Henry L. Stimson had left for a weekend outing at Hoover's camp on the Rapidan River in Virginia. Appearing far more ominous was Britain's departure from the gold standard two days earlier, an event that threatened the shaky foundation of international finance. Indeed, the Great Depression had pushed diplomacy to the background of American life. During the previous month, August 1931, 158 banks had closed, and in September the rate of bank failures doubled. Unemployment reached at least 8 million.

Like Washington, the capitals of Europe betrayed no sense of crisis. In London and Paris, as a matter of fact, there was much sympathy for Japan. The British and French had come to admire Japanese industry and efficiency while despising Chinese weakness and disorganization. The British remembered Japan as a faithful ally in the years 1902–22 and saw a parallel between Japan's problem in Manchuria and their own in India. Fearful of increasing Soviet influence in East Asia, British leaders envisioned Japan as an Oriental bulwark against communism. The French drew a parallel between their own determination to force Germany to abide by the Versailles Treaty and Japan's determination to compel China to honor treaty commitments. They also found similarity between their occupation of Germany's Ruhr in 1923 and Japan's recent action in Manchuria.

At Geneva the League of Nations reflected the thinking of its leading European members, who betrayed little alarm upon seeing that Japanese were operating outside the railway zone. No one realized that the affair around Mukden signaled the beginning of the League's decline. After all, the advance of a few Japanese infantry battalions hardly bore the markings of a grand military operation. Still, it seemed wise to investigate, and soon the League was inquiring whether the United States would appoint a representative to a Far Eastern investigating commission.

The League's nagging, as well as reminders from China that the United States had sponsored the Kellogg antiwar pact, forced Stimson to examine the Manchurian problem. An active policymaker,

Stimson had been secretary of war under William Howard Taft and a field artillery colonel during World War I. In 1927 he had negotiated a peace between insurgents and government forces in Nicaragua. In regards to Manchuria, he first responded cautiously, stressing that Japan had legitimate complaints against China. "The peace treaties of modern Europe," he confided to his diary, "made out by the Western nations of the world no more fit the three great races of Russia, Japan, and China, who are meeting in Manchuria, than, as I put it to the Cabinet, a stovepipe hat would fit an African savage."

Stimson also had faith in Japan's civilian leaders, particularly its conciliatory foreign minister, Baron Shidehara Kijuro. Having dealt with them at the London Naval Conference the year before, he respected them, in fact would give them every chance to get their army and navy under control. Hence he opposed China's proposal of a League inquiry and European requests that an American sit with the League Council. Fearing that public condemnation could only jeopardize chances for peace, he even denied that Japan had violated either the Kellogg or Nine-Power pacts.

Furthermore Stimson had the situation in America to consider. The United States had few interests in Manchuria. Its armed forces were weak, its mood isolationist. And, of course, the Depression remained the country's number one problem. As for assisting in a League inquiry, Stimson perceived a strong anti-League sentiment in the U.S. Close involvement with the world organization, he feared, would have adverse political repercussions at home.

All such sentiments were shared by the president. Herbert Hoover had entered the White House with the broadest of international experience, having been in turn mining engineer in Australia and China, director of Belgian relief during World War I, and economic director of the Supreme Economic Council at the Paris Peace Conference. Yet he could give the crisis little attention, for the worsening depression absorbed his energies. Bad relations with the press, a Democratic House, and powerful insurgents within Republican ranks all made his task more difficult, and it was hardly surprising that he willingly handed over Far Eastern policy to Stimson.

In the days before mass polling, opinion-leaders—editors and journalists—were seen as important indicators of public opinion. In

1931, such people shared the caution of their leaders, seeing watchful waiting as the correct policy. To them, the passage of time would ease this volatile situation, for both parties would eventually reach an agreement. Despite all the indictments made later against America's "sentimentality" toward China, few opinion-makers engaged in any emotional outburst of sympathy for the Chinese people per se. True, the year of the assault on Mukden was also the year of Pearl S. Buck's *The Good Earth,* a best-selling novel that presented a most positive picture of the Chinese people. Yet neither the welfare of the Chinese people nor the territorial integrity of China as a nation-state was deemed crucial. Rather, what always remained at stake was the Washington system, the informal structure that, so Americans believed, had preserved peace throughout the entire Pacific.

During the fall of 1931, Stimson kept hoping for signs that Japanese troops were retreating to the railway zone, or as he put it, "crawling back into their dens." Despite continual pressures, however, the Japanese showed no intent of returning, and they continued to "pursue" the "Chinese bandits" deeper into Manchuria. Then, on the morning of October 8, came reports that Japanese planes had bombed Chinchow, a city close to the Chinese border and some 200 miles away from the South Manchuria Railroad. Shocked, Stimson confided to his diary, "I am afraid we have got to take a firm ground and aggressive stand toward Japan."

But firmness presented as many problems in October as it had in September. The Hoover administration was so immersed in fighting unemployment that the goal of the entire Hoover cabinet could be summarized in one phrase: not to allow, in Stimson's paraphrase, "under any circumstances anybody to deposit that baby in our lap." Stimson concluded that some sort of joint action with the League might offer the best hope, and he persuaded Hoover to authorize an American representative to discuss the situation with the League Council. Even at this point, he told the press that Japan was "our buffer against the unknown powers behind her on the mainland of China and Russia." During the first three weeks of the crisis, he had remained impartial.

On October 16, Prentiss Gilbert, American consul general at Geneva, sat with the League Council, ostensibly to discuss possible violations of the Kellogg-Briand antiwar pact. Yet Stimson found himself disturbed by Japan's objections as well as by anti-interventionist opposition in Congress, so he ordered Gilbert to leave the Council table whenever discussions over the Kellogg Pact came to an end. On the following day, the League Council invoked the Kellogg Pact; both belligerents were formally requested to settle their dispute by peaceful means. Immediately Stimson demanded Gilbert withdraw from future sessions, whether the Kellogg Pact was discussed or not, for he felt little more could be done at present. Though a few vocal anti-interventionists protested the Gilbert mission, his seating had drawn a surprising amount of public support. Hence Hoover and Stimson might well have been exaggerating isolationist sentiment in order to justify their own reluctance to align the United States with the League. Furthermore, Stimson continued to hope that Japan's civil leaders would assert their authority over the military. America's position as possible mediator, he feared, might be jeopardized by giving the impression that the United States was joining forces against Japan.

The president harbored particularly strong misgivings about any collective action. In the latter half of 1931, for example, Hoover wrote in a memorandum, "Neither our obligations to China, nor our interest, nor our dignity require us to go to war over these questions. These acts do not imperil the freedom of the American people, the economic or moral fibre of our people. I do not propose to sacrifice American life for anything short of this." At any rate, the Japanese, so the president predicted, would never be able to "Japanify China and if they stay long enough they will be absorbed or expelled by the Chinese." At one point, he told an aide, "Well, just between ourselves, it would not be a bad thing if Mr. Jap should go into Manchuria, for with two thorns in his side—China and the Bolsheviks—he would have enough to keep him busy for awhile."

The League labored on, and on October 24 the Council resolved that Japan must return to the railway zone within twenty-three days. Japan's condemnation had begun. The international body then turned its attention across the Atlantic, hoping that the United States would endorse its resolution. But it looked in vain. Stimson, detecting the folly of such unenforceable deadlines, told Gilbert to remain silent and publicly asserted that America was retaining "complete independence of judgment as to each step."

Yet the secretary still refused to abandon hope. Early in November, he reminded Japan of the League's demand for evacuation, while shrewdly failing to mention the date the League had set. In addition, he said that Japan's departure should not depend upon the settlement of broader issues.

On November 16, the date of the League deadline, the League Council reassembled in Paris. Stimson again revealed his fear of Senate anti-interventionists, for he would not send an official representative to Council sessions. Instead, General Charles G. Dawes, ambassador to Great Britain and Calvin Coolidge's vice-president, consulted informally with League leaders while conspicuously avoiding official meetings. Dawes tacitly supported League efforts, secretly persuading the Chinese to endorse a resolution calling for an international investigation.

Seeking to wash its hands of the entire matter, the embarrassed Council readily agreed. On December 10, it approved the proposal, and the world sighed in relief. A lull had settled over the frozen Manchurian battlefront, and there was hope that Japan would halt its troop movements. An inquiry would give the appearance of activity and might by some miracle open the way for serious negotiation.

Pondering the bad press it was beginning to receive, Japan gave its blessing. Though appearing impartial, a League investigation could work to Japan's benefit. If the proposal were implemented, Japan could strengthen its position vis-à-vis the Council and, while the commission was conducting its hearings, press China to settle the entire affair on its own terms.

In reality Japan's agreement was evidence of the League's failure. Japan had not acceded to the League deadline, China had shown no inclination to negotiate directly with Japan, and the Guandong Army had destroyed all forms of Chinese civil authority in Manchuria. Stimson suspected that Japan would continue advancing. Although he endorsed the inquiry, he doubted if it would succeed. As British historian Christopher Thorne notes, "no one had the slightest desire to bell the cat."

The new investigative commission, headed by the second Earl of Lytton, was not only empowered to probe thoroughly; it could make broad recommendations concerning Northeast Asia. The Hoover administration was highly enthusiastic, apparently undisturbed by the fact that the League had not yet deprived Japan of a single gain. Even Stimson shared this general optimism. At one time he predicted that a Chinese boycott of Japanese goods, then in progress, was "likely to bring her to her knees." At another, he forecast that Tokyo would make a settlement on its own.

The League resolution of December 10 and Stimson's endorsement of the Lytton investigation met with apathy from Japan, who was busily bringing up infantry, cavalry, artillery, and aircraft against the Chinese. Throughout November 1931, one Manchurian town after another fell to Japanese forces, including the city of Tsitsihar, 370 miles north of Mukden. It was clear that Japan had designs on all of Manchuria. As for the civil government, it was powerless to curb the military; indeed its leaders were living under threat of assassination. By December, a more belligerent ministry came into power, one in which Inukai Tsuyoshi was premier. The nucleus of a puppet regime was already being formed.

Historian Iriye, in examining the first months of the crisis, notes how seriously the Japanese had miscalculated. They had insisted that the Manchurian issue be settled bilaterally, as befitting a minor affair involving treaty rights. They were thereby turning their backs upon their own professions of internationalism. Conversely, as Iriye notes, China seized the rare opportunity offered it. No longer conveying the image of a divided, unstable, and revolutionary country, it presented itself as a responsible member of the international community, indeed the very bastion of peace and order.

The focus of Japanese ambition now became the city of Chinchow, 175 miles southwest of Mukden. On December 23, 1931, when the Chinese refused Japan's ultimatum to halt "bandit operations" around Chinchow, the Guandong Army began to move. Weather was severe, the mercury frequently dropping to twenty degrees below zero, but the greatly outnumbered Japanese soldiers—clad in goatskin jackets, overcoats, and hoods—plodded on. As for the Chinese, their threadbare uniforms mirrored the poverty and weakness of their homeland. Cold, demoralized, and ill-equipped, they fell back, and on January 2, 1932, the Guandong Army entered Chinchow, the last outpost of Chinese resistance.

In Washington, Stimson was furious, and his anger intensified even more when the chief of the State Department's Far Eastern Division, Stanley K. Hornbeck, compared Chinchow with the last dish in a set; Stimson had been watching Japan break dish after dish, and now the last one had been smashed. After calming down, the secretary decided that his cautious policy had proved futile. Toughness would be the new line.

Pondering alternatives, Stimson saw immediately that anti-interventionist sentiment and military weakness ruled out the use of American forces. Japan could plunder Western possessions all the way to Southeast Asia before being challenged. Any war would undoubtedly take several years. The U.S. Navy could not even rescue the Philippines, as it lacked the needed fortifications and air power.

But what about putting an economic blockade or sanctions on Japan? Japanese industry depended on American oil and cotton, and Japan sold a third of its exports to the United States. Sanctions, so the reasoning went, would ruin Japan's depression-laden economy. On December 6, Hornbeck had drafted a lengthy memorandum, in which he argued that a joint boycott by the League and the United States was bound to be effective: it would cripple Japan's cotton factories, dry up its silk market, and wreck its shipping. These developments in turn would create unemployment and financial panic, and within six months Japan would be brought to terms. Surely Tokyo would give up aggression before experiencing sanctions.

Sanctions, of course, were risky, and there was no issue connected with the conflict that Americans debated more passionately. According to the most anti-interventionist citizens, the Japanese might retaliate, entangling the United States in war. Then too, Japan was one of America's best customers, no small consideration in a depression.

Another obstacle to the use of sanctions was the president, for Chinchow brought no change in Hoover's view. He still refused to indulge in "sticking pins in tigers." The Great Depression continued to overshadow even the most jolting events overseas. Parts of the United

States saw police fighting unemployed workers, and public debate centered far less on Manchuria than on such domestic issues as relief and even prohibition enforcement. In February 1932, the future of the economy appeared blacker than ever; Stimson privately commented that the country was "in an emergency like war."

Even Stimson found sanctions too drastic a move. Such action, he believed, would create "ill-will," and thereby "set back the cause of peace upon which we have been working." In a letter to a retired diplomat, he claimed to recognize the danger; there was, however, "no point in telling your enemy you have less ammunition than he thinks." Similarly he privately warned that a League embargo could risk war with Japan.

In retrospect, opponents of sanctions had the better case. Such pressure needed widespread international cooperation, a doubtful possibility. Had the United States levied sanctions, something most unlikely during the Depression, Japan could well have suffered greatly, both in its exportation and importation of strategic goods. Yet it still remains doubtful whether coercion could have been applied so quickly and so powerfully that the Guandong Army would have knuckled under. And, given the likelihood that it would not, Japan might well have blockaded China and struck at Western possessions in the Pacific. Any government that attempted to convince its public to run far greater risks, including a war that might last two years, would indeed be engaged in a perilous undertaking.

III

In January 1932, Stimson, blocked in the matter of sanctions and himself possessing serious misgivings, turned to a new solution: non-recognition of Japan's conquest. Despite Hornbeck's reminder that similar efforts by Secretary of State William Jennings Bryan, exerted over fifteen years earlier, did not restrain Japan, Stimson too believed that a public announcement, if backed by the other Western powers, "ought to have a very potent effect."

The result: a note handed to the Japanese ambassador on January 7, 1932, proclaiming a policy that would go down in history as the Stimson Doctrine. (It was, however, Hoover who first mentioned nonrecognition, telling his cabinet on November 9, 1931, that it was his "main weapon." Not realizing that it would be strongly criticized later, the president always sought to take credit for the policy, having his supporters refer to it as the "Hoover Doctrine.") The United States, said the secretary of state, would not recognize the legality of any treaty or agreement between China and Japan that impaired the treaty rights of the United States or its citizens in China. Nor would it acknowledge any new agreements "which relate to the sovereignty, the independence, or the territorial and administrative integrity of the Republic of China, or to the international policy relative to China, commonly known as the open-door policy." Furthermore, it would not recognize "any situation, treaty or agreement in violation of the Kellogg-Briand Pact." (An identical note went to China, a perfunctory step inasmuch as the Chinese were not threatening American treaty rights.)

Obviously assistance to China for China's sake was not the issue. Rather, to Stimson, Japan had broken the confidence that the world had placed in it, and in the process had endangered what Iriye calls "the fabric of world peace and security" woven so carefully after Versailles. One should observe that the note neither referred to Chinchow nor specifically protested against Japan's Manchurian activities. In fact, when Stimson spoke to reporters, he first emphasized the increasing American trade with the Orient, then tied this trade to the integrity of China and preservation of equal rights there. Unlike most opinion-leaders, Stimson himself was publicly stressing the Open Door, although his diary reveals that, like them, he saw the entire post-Versailles order at stake.

Of course, few opinion-leaders had clamored for nonrecognition, for the idea had never occurred to them. Yet, in looking at the entire interwar period, one seldom finds such enthusiastic support for an American policy. The manifesto helped ease consciences discontented over the United States's failure to condemn Japan. More important, it gave the impression of painless but effective action, holding the promise of Japan's inevitable downfall. The declaration hardly affected Japan's behavior, but if press response is any indication, the secretary had rallied much of his nation. The cynical pundit Will Rogers was in a decided minority when he warned that every time the Japanese receive a note, "they take another town they hadn't thought of till our note gave 'em the idea. . . . We had better quit writing notes to Japan or she will have all China."

Stimson's strategy included support by other powers, notably Britain and France. Though he had not consulted with their leaders before issuing the nonrecognition note, the secretary of state expected full support. His confidence was ill-founded. As far as Manchuria was concerned, Britain was primarily concerned with commercial equality, something that Japan had repeatedly promised after the Mukden incident. Britain had no interest in futile moral pronouncements that might impair trade and investment in Central China. It also feared that a belligerent Japan would threaten such Far Eastern holdings as Hong Kong, Malaya, and Burma. Furthermore, Britain's conservative circles saw Japan as a needed counterweight to possible Soviet expansion in East Asia.

The French held similar views: so long as the Japanese remained occupied in Manchuria, they would not covet their own colony of Indochina. In a few days, therefore, it became apparent that Britain and France would not support nonrecognition. Even the Chinese press was unappreciative, claiming that America's protest was not restraining Japan.

The moral tone of Stimson's nonrecognition note may have been pleasing to Americans, but its only consequence was to rouse Japanese hostility. From Tokyo came a reply to the note that reeked of cynicism. Regarding the Kellogg-Briand Pact, the Japanese said: "It might be the subject of an academic doubt whether in a given case the impropriety of means necessarily and always voids the ends concerned; but as Japan has no intention of adopting improper means, the question does not practically arise." Referring to the Nine-Power Treaty of 1922, in which Japan had pledged to respect the integrity of China, the Japanese declared that "the present unsettled and distracted state of China is not what was in the contemplation of the high contracting parties at the time of the Treaty of Washington." The note concluded with an insolent reminder that the United States itself had played the imperialist just a generation before, when it took Hawaii and the Philippines.

Hardly had Stimson absorbed Tokyo's rebuff when the Japanese landed troops at China's largest port, Shanghai. Chinese citizens of the city had been boycotting Japanese goods, refusing to sell to Japanese customers, and burning Japanese merchandise. These activities dated back to the Korean riots of the previous summer, but the Mukden incident strongly intensified passions. As Japan's prosperity depended upon the Chinese market, particularly in such crucial industries as textiles, its economy suffered greatly, and it was hardly surprising that many incidents arose. For example, on January 18, workers from a Chinese towel factory assaulted five Japanese. One of the five, a Buddhist monk, died from the attack.

The Shanghai foray commenced at midnight January 28, 1932, with the bombing of Chapei, one of the three Chinese boroughs of the city. The *New York Times* vividly communicated the roar of Japanese planes, the echoes of machine-gun fire. The press featured maps of the Shanghai area, with battle lines graphically presented. Woochow River, Soochow Creek, and the Woosung forts suddenly became familiar names. An Associated Press report told of Shanghai inhabitants who faced a "dilemma of terror": they could either burn to death by remaining in their huts or flee into the open, there to meet Japanese bullets or be torn to pieces by bursting bombs.

To anxious diplomats across the world, this affair looked like the second phase in a grand design to subjugate China. Such speculation was wrong, however, for the Shanghai incident was the work of an obscure rear admiral in charge of Japan's naval contingent there. The government in Tokyo was embarrassed. Only when it concluded that Japan's national prestige was at stake did it permit the operation to be enlarged.

Brutality and suffering were now reaching an area of Asia far more visible than Manchuria. It was one thing for Japan to invade a region in which the Western powers had little material interest; it was something quite different for Japan to fight in an area where Western holdings were extensive. Over 3,500 Americans resided in the city, with some 1,600 living in the International Settlement. As of January 1, 1932, 1,300 U.S. Marines were stationed in the city, to which 400 were added when the crisis broke. The city held such prominent missionary institutions as the University of Shanghai and the American Bible Society. American traders conducted an annual business of slightly over $150 million, and American investors controlled such enterprises as the Shanghai Telephone Company and the Shanghai

Power Company. In fact, Shanghai housed over 65 percent of all American capital invested in China. The United States participated in the city's government, supplying one of the fourteen governors of the Shanghai International Settlement. American naval and military units joined their British, French, and Japanese counterparts to form the Shanghai defense force. Little wonder Americans reacted to Shanghai with far more concern than they did to Manchuria.

Secretary Stimson put the attack on a par with Germany's invasion of Belgium in 1914, and recalled "how outraged we were when President Wilson did nothing to show the shame that we felt." He wanted to make a display of force by moving the Asiatic fleet from Manila to Shanghai. Hoover, in no mood for bluffs, refused consent, though he did permit one cruiser and six destroyers to protect U.S. property there. Articulate American sentiment reflected both outrage over the attack and fear that military measures would lead to war. The *Baltimore Sun* reflected much public opinion when it said, "War that is dollars instead of men . . . too easily could become war with men." Stimson next proposed an international conference under the aegis of the Nine-Power Treaty. Such a conference would require British support, and when their government turned down the idea, he concluded that the British were "soft" and "pudgy," "very cold-footed."

Again the secretary decided to make a moral pronouncement, although he did not want to express his thoughts in a speech. "I do not dare to send a note on the Nine-Power Treaty," he confided to his diary, "for fear of the yellow-bellied responses that I will get from some of the countries."

Stimson felt forced to settle for another unilateral declaration, similar, but more dramatic, to the nonrecognition note of January 7. Acting on a suggestion made by an aide, Stimson decided to write a public letter to William E. Borah (Rep.-Id.), chairman of the Senate Foreign Relations Committee. Dated February 23, 1932, the "Borah letter" reaffirmed commercial equality and, as a corollary, preservation of China's territorial and administrative integrity. It also contained a veiled threat: further Japanese aggression might cause the United States to reconsider the Washington agreements of 1922. Although his warning was not specific, Stimson suggested that additional violation of the Nine-Power Treaty might well cause the U.S.

to enlarge fortifications in Guam and the Philippines and increase naval tonnage beyond treaty limits. The implication was clear: a belligerent Japan might face an armed America. As historian Ferrell has remarked, the note was designed "to encourage China, enlighten the American public, exhort the League, stir up the British, and warn Japan."

As with the January 7 note, Stimson had given the appearance of acting in a forceful but painless manner, and hence had rallied domestic opinion to his side. International relations expert Quincy Wright reflected the views of many opinion leaders in saying the Stimson Doctrine could revolutionize international law: a nation seeking "to utilize the fruits of its violence . . . would be fair game for all states or insurgents who sought to embarrass its enjoyment of those fruits."

At first, the Borah letter seemed to be achieving results. Although the British again failed to fall in line, on February 29 the Japanese indicated their willingness to negotiate the Shanghai problem. The great port at the mouth of the Yangtze was not yet an object of Japanese imperial policy. The affair, moreover, was depleting much national energy, delaying consolidation of the Manchurian conquest, and bringing bad publicity. Suddenly Japan's leaders became sensitive to world opinion and took care to consult with the United States, Britain, and France.

Early in May, truce talks were successfully concluded, and by July 17, the Japanese had withdrawn to the International Settlement. All these actions, however, were prompted far more by the desire of both Japan's military and civilian leadership to terminate the affair, and by the efforts of the British ambassador to China, than by any clout exerted in Stimson's communication to Borah.

Meanwhile the Japanese had tightened their grip on Manchuria, deciding to establish there a puppet regime bound to Japan. To make the new state appear Chinese, they determined to revive the Manchu dynasty, which had been evicted from Beijing (Peking) in 1911. Fortunately for them, the Manchu "boy emperor" had survived the 1911–12 revolution and was living in Tianjin (Tientsin) under the name of Henry Pu Yi. After a fast journey by automobile, train, and boat to Mukden, the "unheroic hero" (as portrayed in the 1987 film

The Last Emperor) agreed to act as regent in the new kingdom. On March 9, 1932, the new country made its appearance under the name of "Manchukuo." Its national emblem consisted of the five bars of the old flag of Imperial China, emblazoned with Japan's rising sun.

By the end of April, the Japanese had sent over 600 "advisers" to the new Manchukuo government, completely dominating its home, finance, and foreign offices. On May 15, military extremists assassinated Japan's aged premier, Inukai Tsuyoshi, and a more belligerent cabinet took control. The Tokyo government hoped that such powers as Britain and France would recognize the new regime first, so it delayed its own formal recognition until August 12.

Japan's recognition came in the wake of continued frustration. The League Assembly was dominated by less powerful countries, who were more sensitive than the great powers to the danger of aggression going unpunished. It began to discuss the possibility of sanctions against Japan by invoking Article XVI of the League Covenant. Lest the Assembly embroil the League itself in a Far Eastern war, Britain and France jumped into the debate. In March 1932, they persuaded the Assembly, as a compromise, to endorse the American policy of nonrecognition.

While the Japanese fumed, the League's investigators quietly went about gathering information. From February to the middle of July, the five-man Lytton Commission, which included an American major general, held countless interviews in such cities as Shanghai, Nanjing, Beijing, Mukden, and Tokyo. Its research was impressive, its conclusions balanced. Its report took note of China's efforts to destroy Japan's sphere of interest, which was protected by treaty, but insisted that Japan's response to the events of September 1931 had far exceeded any provocation. As for Manchukuo, the report called the new country a Japanese creation, and it declared that recognition of its government would violate international obligations set forth in the Nine-Power and Kellogg-Briand treaties. The commission recommended demilitarization, an autonomous Manchurian regime within the Chinese Republic, and a guarantee of Japanese treaty rights in the area. Having already recognized Manchukuo in August, Japan ignored the recommendations.

As the League wrung its hands, Stimson insisted that Japan should not go uncensured. Obviously Hoover's defeat in the election of November 1932 had weakened the secretary's hand. Early in 1933, however, President-elect Roosevelt endorsed Stimson's Far Eastern policies. On February 24, an overwhelming majority of the League Assembly, over the opposition of conservatives in Britain and France, adopted the Lytton report. On March 27, Japan gave official notice it would leave the League in two years. Its chief delegate, Matsuoka Yosuke, told reporters that as Christ was crucified on the cross, so had Japan been crucified by the international body. To Japan, a puppet Manchuria was worth the price of League membership. Passing through the United States on his way home, Matsuoka explained that the powers of Europe had taught Japan the game of poker, but after acquiring most of the chips, they had pronounced the game immoral and taken up contract bridge.

On leaving the League, the Japanese enlarged their acquisitions, seizing Jehol province in North China early in 1933. With that conquest, their appetite for territory was temporarily satisfied. Both military and civil officials accepted what the army had seized, but agreed to advance no further . On May 31, 1933, hostilities between Japan and China, never formally declared, came to a temporary end. Officials of the two governments met at the town of Tangku near the Great Wall. After humiliating the Chinese delegates by forcing them to leave their special train and walk across a dusty roadway to the Japanese barracks, Tokyo's negotiators accepted a truce. It was purely a military agreement, not a diplomatic treaty recognizing Manchuria's new status.

The Manchurian crisis, as Christopher Thorne notes, has long been shrouded in myth. It did not, he notes, destroy an established international order in the Far East. Rather it demonstrated that no such viable system had been created. At best the Washington system had been a rickety one. Nor, claims Thorne, did the crisis cause the downfall of the League. Instead, it exposed the limitations inherent in that organization for all to see. Moreover, writes the British scholar, it did not make a future American war with Japan inevitable: Japanese policy still lacked any long-range blueprint.

In addition, as Thorne points out, neither the United States nor Britain could have coerced Japan without high risk. True, Japan had levied "the greatest blow yet struck against the post-1918 settlement and the accompanying hopes for the peaceful resolving of international disputes." The U.S., however, had too little at stake within Japan's reach, and Britain too much, to justify major risks. Even had the American people endorsed sanctions, it would have been most difficult to impose them with sufficient speed and power to bring Japan to terms. At any rate, by 1933 the West thought that Japan would face such a severe financial crisis that it would voluntarily withdraw from the area.

In the United States, however, optimism remained widespread as did the general sense of innocence. The belief in China's eventual triumph, the reliance upon such unenforceable pledges as the Stimson Doctrine, the continual association of moral sentiment with physical power—all, to say the least, show naiveté at its most extreme. Undoubtedly this general hopefulness had worked all during the crisis against advocates of sanctions. If Japan's withdrawal was inevitable, there was no need to risk economic pressure, with its accompanying danger of war. A few opinion-makers did fear that the crisis would result in a major conflict, but far more foresaw moral force, and moral force alone, eventually causing Japan's downfall. Columnist Heywood Broun spoke for many in writing that public opinion bore "a mightier ring than that of men and machine guns." Even early in 1933, when Japan announced it would leave the League, one need only compare the handful of war predictions with the host of bright forecasts.

With such optimism extending well beyond 1933, one can no longer claim that the Manchurian affair helped cause Americans to doubt whether the peace machinery was effective. In particular, it did not lead them to become disillusioned with the Kellogg Pact "outlawing" war. The faith in the peace system that so earmarked the late twenties did not end abruptly. It lingered a bit longer, at least until 1936. Much would depend on what Japan and other "revisionist" powers would do. In one sense, the story of Manchuria is not the story of lost illusions, but of ones sustained.

CHAPTER THREE

Dictators and Neutrality

While the Japanese were conquering Manchuria, trouble was appearing in another corner of the world. In central Europe Germany's republican government, torn by dissension and weighted down by economic depression, had begun its death throes. If few Germans mourned the passing of republicanism, many were uneasy. At the center of the nation's anarchy, and urging it on, were the political extremists, communists on the left and National Socialists on the right, and throughout 1932 the two parties struggled violently over Germany's political wreckage. As the country edged toward chaos, many Germans looked to that relic of the 1914–18 war, president of the Republic Paul von Hindenburg, who found no easy solution to bread lines and street battles. But when he pondered the situation, the aging president decided that he liked communists less than Nazis and, after much sordid jockeying, appointed the National Socialist leader, Adolf Hitler, as chancellor.

It was January 1933.

Hindenburg's act boded ill for the world, but neither he nor outsiders dreamed what the next dozen years would bring. Such ignorance had little excuse, for Hitler had been spelling out his aims for at least ten years. In foreign affairs, he wrote, he would reassert German power, recover "lost" territories, and expand his nation's borders to provide *Lebensraum*, that is additional territory deemed necessary for economic well-being. When he gained power, he sought to fulfill his vision down to the last detail.

In Italy, another strong man, Benito Mussolini, had appeared, and by the 1930s he too had thoughts of expansion. To *Il Duce*, as he was called, an adventure in imperialism would supply an outlet for Italy's surplus population and prove its greatness as a nation.

I

Early in 1933, while Hitler was consolidating power in Germany, Americans anticipated a new presidential administration. They waited in an atmosphere of frustration and despair, for the Great Depression had reached its nadir. The change in national leadership came on March 4, when Franklin D. Roosevelt, smiling and waving, drove up Pennsylvania Avenue to the Capitol and took the oath as thirty-second president of the American Republic. He told his countrymen that they had nothing to fear except fear itself. Striking an anti-interventionist posture, he limited his remarks on foreign policy to a single sentence: in world affairs, he dedicated the United States to the policy of the Good Neighbor, a phrase that could mean everything and nothing at the same time. He then set in motion an unprecedented program, the New Deal, to relieve victims of the Depression and find a way to recovery.

Roosevelt entered the White House with an impressive record as a politician and administrator. A blue blood from the Hudson Valley who traced his ancestry to colonial times, he had been state legislator, assistant secretary of the navy, vice presidential candidate in 1920, and two-term governor of New York. Possessing a magnetic personality while turning vagueness into an absolute art, FDR saw leadership as a matter of continual compromise. Roosevelt's world was one of *problems*, some severe to be sure, but no *dilemmas*, which by definition could never be resolved.

The president's leadership style was strictly ad hoc. As noted by historian Wayne S. Cole, "Roosevelt was intuitive rather than systematic, artful rather than scientific, and innovative rather than doctrinaire. He was highly flexible, and shied away from rigid formulas or systems. . . . He kept his options open." Another historian, Warren F. Kimball, is a bit more stinging, writing, "Roosevelt often simply muddled through, sweeping obstacles under the rug in the hope that they would go away in time." As FDR himself confessed in 1934, "Frankly, I do not know how to effect a permanency in American foreign policy."

Roosevelt loved to keep matters in his own hands while at the same time administrating in an absolutely chaotic manner. Henry L. Stimson, who was to become FDR's secretary of war, would refer to the president's "happy-go-lucky snap of the moment style." The president often ignored his secretary of state, Cordell Hull, a Tennessee Democrat who had spent most of his career in the House, where he had crafted the first federal income tax law. Furthermore, FDR would continually pit subordinates against each other so as never to share the levers of power. He himself admitted to being disingenuous, deceptive, and devious, and one could add to these such labels as hard-boiled, intimidating, manipulative, self-centered, and ungrateful as well. Such qualities might produce some "payoff" in domestic policy but could be hazardous when issues of national interest are at stake.

Roosevelt did have one foreign policy aim: to establish diplomatic relations with the Soviet Union. On November 16, 1933, after negotiating with Maxim Maximovich Litvinoff, foreign commissar of the USSR, FDR announced recognition of the Soviet Union. Terms included Soviet pledges to refrain from propaganda or revolutionary agitation within the U.S. and to support freedom of conscience and religious liberty for Americans citizens within Soviet borders. Certain claims remained between the two countries, such as the debts owed the U.S. by the former Czarist government and provisional revolutionary government of 1917. These, however, would be subject to future negotiation.

Roosevelt's advisers dreamed of the sudden opening of the greatest available market in the world, and pundit Will Rogers jested, "We would recognize the Devil with a false face if he would contract for some pitchforks." The president personally focused on encouraging Russia as a counterweight against a resurgent Japan and Germany. His first ambassador, the dapper and urbane William C. Bullitt, departed for Moscow with much optimism, but his hopes were soon shattered. Americans found the Soviets refusing to moderate communist propaganda or repay long-standing debts, the Soviets insisting that an American loan must precede repayment. By 1936, the brutal show trials of the Old Bolsheviks had begun, followed a year later by the purges of the leading generals. In all, at least 800,000 people were shot, and some 8 million, about 5 percent of the population, were arrested.

Two other diplomatic matters demanded attention as Roosevelt took office: the World Disarmament Conference, which had been meeting at Geneva since February 1932, and the World Economic Conference, scheduled to open soon in London.

By the spring of 1933, the Geneva Conference had become mired in France's fears of Germany. The French remembered how in 1870, and again in 1914, German armies had pressed toward Paris. Therefore, they refused to consider disarmament without guarantees of support in event of attack. Roosevelt and Hull sympathized with France, but America's anti-interventionist mood prevented them from making adequate assurances. As for the new German chancellor, he seemed conciliatory, indicating that he would wait five years before insisting on equality in arms. When the British offered a plan for disarming that included clauses for collective action against aggressors, prospects for agreement appeared to brighten.

Then came one of the darkest days of the 1930s. On October 14, 1933, Hitler's government announced that it was withdrawing from the Geneva Conference and quitting the League of Nations. Without Germany there was no chance for disarmament.

Plans for American participation in a world economic conference had matured under President Hoover, and when Roosevelt entered the White House, the meeting was set for June 1933. In a statement issued May 16, FDR said the forthcoming meeting, scheduled to open on June 12, "must establish order in place of the present chaos by a stabilization of currencies, by freeing the flow of world trade, and by international action to raise price levels." The mention of international trade was much in harmony with the ideas of Secretary Hull, a tough Tennessee mountaineer who hid knowledge of tubercular lesions in both his lungs from even the president himself. Since 1916, Hull believed, as he noted in his memoirs, that "unhampered trade dovetailed with peace; high tariffs, trade barriers, and unfair economic practices with war." With goods flowing freely, so the secretary claimed, the living standards of all nations increase, thereby "eliminating the economic dissatisfaction that breeds war." Such notions were bound to conflict with the core of the early New Deal, which was based upon a highly nationalistic economic and monetary policy.

Disappointment awaited the new secretary. First, the delegation did not always conduct itself with distinction. For example, the drunken Senator Key Pittman (Dem.-Nev.), chairman of the Senate Foreign Relations Committee, would pop London streetlights with his six-shooter; he once chased technical adviser Herbert Feis down the corridor of the Claridge Hotel with a bowie knife.

Furthermore, the delegation itself was divided over trade and monetary policy, and by June Roosevelt himself was having second thoughts about the conference. Nothing, FDR believed, should interfere with his effort to raise domestic prices. Thanks to the inflation of the previous two months, the American economy had taken a sharp turn upward. Further tinkering with the monetary system might help it to recover more.

Only on the way to the conference did Hull learn that FDR sought no trade accords. Any loss of tariff barriers, the president feared, would result in a flood of cheaper foreign goods and loss of American jobs.

On June 16, four days after the conference convened, Roosevelt sent a special emissary to the conference, Assistant Secretary of State Raymond Moley. An economic nationalist, Moley was a member of the "Brains Trust," a group of university professors that had helped launch the New Deal. Moley believed that the U.S. should merely try to soothe gold bloc countries while stabilizing the dollar, a policy that would undercut Hull even further. He advanced a plan that would "baby" the conference, committing the U.S. to pious wishes concerning eventual accord while looking towards the time when gold would ultimately serve as the international medium of exchange.

FDR suspected Britain and France of seeking special advantages. In his "bombshell" message of July 2, 1933, he turned his back entirely on his recent position. He rejected the conference's ideas on stabilization, rapped delegates for giving currency questions a higher priority than other "fundamental economic ills," and proclaimed that planned national currencies were superior to international monetary agreements, which he referred to as "old fetishes of the so-called international bankers." "The sound internal economic system of a nation is a greater factor in its well-being," he said, "than the price of its currency in changing terms of the currencies of other Nations." In 1937 he told journalist Arthur Krock concerning the bombshell message, "I am prouder of that than anything else I ever did."

As Roosevelt had previously given foreign diplomats the decided indication he favored currency stabilization, they felt betrayed. British Prime Minister Ramsay MacDonald referred to FDR as "that person." Without American support discussion was useless, and the conference adjourned a short time later. The United States had announced in no uncertain terms that it would find its own exit from the Great Depression.

Historians still debate Roosevelt's action. Robert Dallek, examining FDR's intimations two and a half months before the conference met, finds it difficult to understand Roosevelt's action, though he notes a letter in which the president stressed the need for inflation. "The West is seething with unrest," FDR wrote his mother, "and must have higher values to relieve this distress." William E. Leuchtenburg stresses that the United States was both the world's most powerful nation and its leading creditor. Yet it took little action to redeem "the last opportunity of democratic statesmen to work out a co-operative solution to common economic problems"; the conference's collapse "sapped the morale of the democratic opponents of fascism." David M. Kennedy claims that Adolf Hitler was the ultimate beneficiary of the bombshell message, for the dictator henceforth assumed that the United States would play no role in checking German expansion. Arthur M. Schlesinger, Jr., sees failure inevitable, as one could not reconcile the fundamental national interests. Such countries as the U.S., for whom the domestic price level was the major problem, inevitably conflicted with such nations as France, for whom foreign exchange was crucial.

If the United States played any positive role, it lay in Latin American policy, where the Roosevelt administration sought to implement his Good Neighbor policy. The term "good neighbor" originally came from Herbert Hoover, who used it repeatedly when he had taken a ten-week tour of Latin America just after he had been elected president. In his first inaugural address, FDR said, "I would dedicate this nation to the policy of the good neighbor—the neighbor who respects his obligations and respects the sanctity of his agreements in and with a world of neighbors."

The policy was off to a shaky start. In 1933, Roosevelt named Sumner Welles as ambassador to Cuba. Soon to become FDR's leading foreign policy adviser, Welles, whose specialty was Latin America, had been a career diplomat since 1915. For the past nine years, Cuba had been ruled by Gerardo Machado, whose presidency combined stability and prosperity with ruthless crackdowns on dissenters. Once the U.S. adopted the restrictive Smoot-Hawley tariff in 1930, the all-important price of sugar plummeted, unemployment skyrocketed, and a general strike shook the nation. In August, Welles, now the most powerful figure in Cuba, was able to bring two U.S. destroyers to Havana harbor and chose Manuel de Céspedes, former Cuban ambassador to the United States, as Machado's successor. The inept Céspedes was bewildered by the tasks of government and lasted less than a month, being deposed by a palace coup of five noncommissioned officers led by Sergeant Fulgencio Batista. Welles sought U.S. troops, a suggestion vetoed by Roosevelt and Hull. The turmoil only ended in 1934 when Welles negotiated a treaty with a Batista puppet. The agreement abrogated the Platt amendment, a measure imposed on Cuba in 1901 that had turned it into a quasiprotectorate of the U.S.

At an inter-American conference in December 1933 held in Montevideo, Uruguay, Hull endorsed a declaration, introduced by Saaverda Lamas, Argentine foreign minister, that passed unanimously: "No state has the right to intervene in the internal or external affairs of another." The secretary himself remarked, "No government need fear any intervention on the part of the United States under the Roosevelt Administration." At the same time, he added a reservation saying the U.S. had a right to intervene "by the law of nations as generally recognized and accepted," that is under existing treaty rights. Within the year, the U.S. withdrew its troops from Haiti. They had been sent there in 1915 in the wake of the assassination of Haiti's president.

Although not until 1935 were genuinely comprehensive neutrality acts passed, the United States was already reflecting a strong anti-interventionist mood. In April 1934, Roosevelt signed the Johnson Debt Default Act, introduced by the acerbic Senator Hiram Johnson (Rep.-Calif.). The Senate passed the measure without a record vote, the House without dissent. The bill prohibited private loans to nations in default of obligations, contracted during World War I, to the U.S. government. Though France had just defaulted for the third time in a row and though Britain had offered $60 million in full settlement of its $8 billion debt, British ambassador Sir Ronald Lindsay could not resist a bit of Scripture, namely the passage that read "Forgive us our debts." The Johnson Act was popular among Americans, but it never succeeded in providing equitable settlements. Furthermore, it offered no allowance for partial remuneration, thereby making it easier for debtors to default. Of the borrowing nations, only Finland supplied further payment.

In late January 1935, Roosevelt met his second major defeat, for the Senate turned down American entry into the World Court by seven votes. The Permanent Court of International Justice (as the World Court was formally called) had been founded in 1921 and was closely tied to the League of Nations. The League Assembly and Council had to approve all nominations; the World Court's budget was underwritten by the League; the League Covenant required the Court to give "an advisory opinion upon any dispute or question referred to it by the Councilor by the Assembly." Not surprisingly, the League's major powers sought to turn the new judicial body into an instrument of their own interests. Furthermore, one could well argue that all too often the League itself did not really embody true internationalism, but instead reflected shifting political alliances.

A series of Court decisions levied between 1923 and 1925 showed the closest possible connection between the World Court and the League Council, something that made the U.S. Senate reservations of 1926 quite understandable. When in 1931, at the request of the League, the Court ruled against a proposed customs union between Germany and Austria, it appeared more partisan than ever. Yet, as noted by historian Michael Dunne, the 1935 defeat did not result from unscrupulous propaganda fostered by publisher William Randolph Hearst and radio priest Charles E. Coughlin. Rather it was due to Congress's hostile predisposition and Roosevelt's lack of leadership.

The darkening state of world politics led to demands for rigid neutrality legislation. Americans who sought to avoid "foreign war" wanted laws designed to prevent a collision with any belligerent. Above all, they feared a repetition of the years 1915–17, when ships carrying supplies to Britain and France became targets of German submarines. The prescription was alluringly simple: at the onset of war anywhere in the world, the United States should simply terminate trade with all contestants.

An economic boycott of this kind raised problems, however. Could the United States in good conscience deny food and medical supplies to civilians of belligerent countries? One must also consider the effect of a total embargo on the American economy. Aware of the complexities they faced, anti-interventionists concentrated on embargoes limited to arms and ammunition. The idea of an arms embargo held special appeal to Americans of the 1930s, many of whom were anxious to strike at munitions makers, those awful "merchants of death" who profited from war.

Anti-interventionist arguments met with sharp opposition. Some found embargoes that fell impartially on all belligerents, victims and aggressors alike, a cowardly policy and one that violated the spirit of the Kellogg Pact. Others thought that twentieth-century technology had made nineteenth-century ideas of isolation obsolete; therefore the United States could no longer escape a general war. Internationalists talked of drafting laws permitting the president to close American ports to nations that broke the peace. By putting aggressor nations on notice that only their victims would receive arms from America, such measures might deter conflict. Failing that, they would enable the U.S. to take collective action with other countries, perhaps the League of Nations, to nip aggression and prevent the spread of hostilities.

Anti-interventionists recoiled at the idea of discriminating between belligerents. How could the president be sure which side was the aggressor? War was complicated, and as scholarly debate over the World War had shown, even a generation later it was hard to allocate guilt. To make an accurate judgment amid the confusions of an exploding conflict probably would be difficult, and if the president erred, consequences might be tragic. Even if he did ascertain the guilty party correctly, might not the designated aggressor retaliate? Getting even would certainly lead to direct American involvement.

There was, one should add, a middle group that wanted no change in existing neutrality policy. Many proponents of the status quo represented business interests and opposed any interference, by embargo or otherwise, if an overseas war allowed for increased trade. Others, such as jurist John Bassett Moore and scholar Edwin M. Borchard, were individuals who felt strongly about the principles of traditional international law. The United States, they argued, would be shamefully abandoning freedom of the seas if, as certain leading anti-interventionists desired, it announced upon the outbreak of war that it was leaving the international waterways to belligerents. As for discriminatory embargoes, they were unduly provocative.

II

On December 5, 1934, troops from Italy and Ethiopia (also called Abyssinia) clashed at Walwal, a mere oasis 60 miles from Italian Somaliland. Even Italian maps located Walwal well within Italian borders. During the skirmish, which was a mere pretext for Italian aggression, 100 Ethiopians and 30 Italians died. Though pressed by Mussolini, the Ethiopian emperor, Haile Selassie, refused to apologize. The Italians, intent on conquest, refused a peaceful settlement, and the result was a quarrel that smoldered through the spring and summer of 1935.

One might point to several motives behind Italy's behavior, including the desire to revive the Roman empire, revenge for a defeat suffered in Ethiopia by forces of King Victor Emmanuel in 1896, Ethiopia's failure to grant major economic concessions to Italy, and the fear that Ethiopia might strike against Italian colonies on its border. As, however, the defeat at Adowa had taken place over forty years before and Ethiopia lacked valuable resources, glory was undoubtedly the main impetus. Successful conquest could return pride to the Italian people, compensate for hardship at home, and overshadow Hitler's rising star.

The European continent saw equally ominous disturbances. In January 1935, the people of the mineral-rich Saar Basin, acting under an internationally controlled plebiscite, voted for union with Germany. Two months later, Hitler renounced the disarmament provisions of the Versailles arrangement, putting the world on notice that Germany was planning to remilitarize.

In America, the neutrality debate had reached the Capitol. Before the summer of 1935 ended, Congress had passed new neutrality legislation. To understand the significance of this action, it is necessary to examine how U.S. policy evolved. In 1922, the Women's International League urged the Senate to investigate the trade in weapons. The WIL received support from other peace groups, and early in 1934 Senator Nye agreed to sponsor a resolution for an arms inquiry. While the resolution was pending, the monthly business magazine *Fortune* published a sensationalist article entitled "Arms and the Men," purporting to prove that arms makers were a major cause of war. In the same year, two books appeared, *Iron, Blood and Profits* by George Seldes, and *Merchants of Death* by Helmuth C. Engelbrecht and Frank C. Hanighen. According to the latter authors, "the arms maker has risen and grown powerful, until today he is one of the most dangerous factors in world affairs—a hindrance to peace, a promoter of war." Such ideas reached a national audience when *Merchants of Death* became a Book-of-the-Month Club selection and a condensed version of "Arms and the Men" appeared in *Reader's Digest*.

In August 1934, the Senate's Special Committee Investigating the Munitions Industry, chaired by Nye, had begun hearings. The bill creating the committee had been passed without a roll call vote and was supported by President Roosevelt. FDR's experience as assistant secretary of the navy during World War I led him to seek government controls over the armaments industry. Over the course of the next year and a half, the Nye Committee held ninety-three days of hearings, questioned over 200 witnesses, and gathered over 4,900 exhibits. Though Nye was far from being a docile chairman, Senator Bennett Champ Clark Dem.-Mo.) and chief investigator Stephen

Raushenbush played equally prominent roles. The result: seven reports that, in the words of historian Matthew Ware Coulter, offered an unmatched look at the American military-business establishment.

In the first series of hearings, which took place from August to December 1934, the committee focused on armament manufacturers. Special attention was given to the Du Pont Company, the nation's leading munitions maker, whose executives testified on over half the days the committee met. Though by no means the "merchants of death" of legend, Du Pont had clearly placed the financial interests of stockholders above all other considerations. An official of another firm, Federal Laboratories, Inc., mourned the fact that Bolivia and Paraguay had made peace before they could buy arms and poison gas. An agent of the Remington Arms company reported in 1933: "The Paraguay and Bolivia fracas appears to be coming to a termination, so business from that end is probably finished. We certainly are in one hell of a business, where a fellow has to wish for trouble so as to make a living, the only consolation being, however, that if we don't get the business someone else will. It would be a terrible state of affairs if my conscience started to bother me now." This document inspired another Engelbrecht book, *One Hell of a Business* (1934).

The committee found the American government by no means innocent, reporting that munitions companies had "secured the active support of the War, Navy, Commerce, and even State Departments in their sales abroad." In some cases, such as Argentina, outright bribery of foreign officials was involved.

From January to April 1935, the Nye Committee resumed hearings, examining the shipbuilding industry and focusing on collusive bidding for naval craft. In a report released in June, the committee described how shipbuilders were "allied in interest with naval suppliers and subcontractors, including the steel companies, the electrical manufacturing groups, the boiler producers, the instrument people." It noted ties as well with banking interests and the U.S. Navy. The industry, the committee concluded, should either "be policed" effectively or "be cut off entirely from the building of ships for the Navy."

In the spring of 1935, however, committee investigators began to gather material concerning American entry into the Great War. Nye in particular became outspoken on the need for America to isolate itself from foreign quarrels, and in April and May of 1935 he and his committee colleague, Bennett Champ Clark, introduced bills for an impartial arms embargo against belligerents, a prohibition on loans to belligerents, and denial of passports to Americans wishing to enter war zones. Both senators introduced the legislation strictly on their own behalf, not that of the Nye Committee. Yet the committee staff contributed much of the background work. Any neutrality bill would have had far more difficult sledding had not the Nye Committee pushed it.

The Roosevelt administration, opposed to "mandatory" isolation, countered with a bill that would permit discriminatory embargoes. The proposal found little response. Pittman told presidential secretary Stephen Early: "I tell you, Steve, the President is riding for a fall if he insists on designating the aggressor in accordance with the wishes of the League of Nations. . . . I will introduce it [a discretionary bill] on behalf of the Administration without comment, but he will be licked as sure as hell." There is no assurance, of course, that Roosevelt would have used the authority granted in the discretionary bill to co-operate with the League or punish aggression. Wishing to retain the executive's freedom to maneuver in foreign affairs, the president wanted legislation that would bestow such options as isolation, pun-ishment of aggressors, cooperation with the League, and doing abso-lutely nothing.

Matters stagnated until August 19, 1935, when dispatches from Paris revealed that negotiations between Ethiopia and Italy had collapsed. As gloom settled over Washington, Senate anti-interventionists threatened a filibuster, which would prevent Con-gress from adjourning unless an nondiscriminating measure passed. Exhausted by the summer's heat, members of the Foreign Relations Committee reported a joint resolution. The crux of the bill lay in a mandatory embargo of "arms, ammunition and imple-ments of war" to belligerents once the president declared the ex-istence of war. (FDR later defined "implements of war" to include airplanes, various chemicals, and armored vehicles but not such items as cotton, oil, scrap iron, and trucks). The bill also restricted use of American ports by belligerent submarines and gave the president discretionary authority to proclaim that Americans traveling on ships of belligerent registry did so at their own risk. Deferring to the country's anti-interventionism, the administration hesitantly permitted the bill to pass, although it did secure an amendment limiting it to six months. The legislation got by the Senate 77-to-2, the House without a record vote.

Hence, on August 31, Roosevelt reluctantly signed the bill, the first neutrality law in U.S. history designed not to observe international practices but to avoid war. He warned that "the inflexible provisions might drag us into war instead of keeping us out," though he appreciated the six-month deadline and the flexibility concerning timing and scope of certain restrictions. He did not want to jeopardize pending New Deal legislation, such as the regulation of the coal industry, over foreign policy matters. In addition, he thought the bill would probably injure Italy, on the verge of invading Ethiopia, far more than it would injure its victim.

When, on October 3, 1935, East Africa's rainy season ended early, Mussolini's armies attacked. Three days after the fighting began Roosevelt invoked the new Neutrality Act. No munitions could be sold to either side.

A fortnight later, the League showed more backbone than it had in Manchuria. With Roosevelt's private approval, it named Italy an aggressor and voted a partial ban of exports there. In fact, its list of banned articles was almost identical to those specified by the U.S. 1935 neutrality law. To some degree League sanctions were effective. They threw Italy's already failing trade out of kilter. Exports declined one-third within a year and the balance of trade was so unfavorable that the nation approached insolvency. Yet all-important oil shipments, not to mention coal and steel, were still permitted. Britain and France feared that a total embargo would simply drive Italy into the arms of the Germans.

Because of America's obsession with impartiality toward belligerents, there was little that Roosevelt and Hull could do to support the League action. Their only option was an expedient dubbed a "moral embargo." They announced that abnormal trade with belligerents in nonmilitary commodities, not covered by the Neutrality Act, violated the spirit of the recent legislation, and urged Americans to limit commerce with East Africa's belligerents to "peacetime levels." By such a move, the administration in reality was cooperating with League sanctions.

American business, however, refused to support the moral embargo, and through the winter of 1935–36, the Atlantic churned with freighters and tankers carrying scrap metal, oil, and cotton to Italian ports at three times their normal rate. As Walter Teagle, president of Standard Oil of New Jersey, saw the issue, his firm had been doing business with Italy for over forty years; it was not about to stop now. Historian Robert Dallek writes, "Roosevelt could not ignore the fact that American oil was fueling Mussolini's war machine." Historian Coulter argues that a U.S. embargo on oil exports alone would have crippled Italian forces.

There could, however, have been a domestic price. Further restrictions on Italy would have given the Republican party an opportunity to encourage anti-interventionist sentiment in general and with Italian Americans in particular, thereby jeopardizing Roosevelt's ability to lead. An abortive agreement made between British Foreign Minister Sir Samuel Hoare and French Prime Minister Pierre Laval infuriated Americans, particularly those who were already suspicious of Europe, for it would have turned two-thirds of Ethiopia over to Mussolini. In the long run, the entire crisis discredited collective security, led to further appeasement, and showed Hitler that the West was indecisive.

Congress reconvened in January 1936 and the Nye Committee resumed activity. In the third and last series of hearings, which took place in January and February 1936, the committee investigated the role of major investment banks in pulling the United States into World War. It focused on the firm of J.P. Morgan & Co., agents for Britain's purchase of war supplies. Nye and committee counsel Raushenbush accused the U.S. Treasury Department of continually rescuing private bankers, an imputation Morgan officials strongly denied.

By now, Nye's committee was spotlighting the general neutrality issue. Anti-interventionist members sought to win support for total embargoes, claiming that business with the Allies had taken the United States into the Great War. They hoped in vain. Though the committee exhibited strong evidence that trade with the Allies in 1914–17 had made the United States an object of German hostility, most members of Congress refused to go beyond arms embargoes. Threats of filibuster could not move them. President Roosevelt wanted the new legislation to leave some room to discriminate between belligerents. His neutrality proposal included cleverly worded sections designed to give the president limited control over export of nonmilitary commodities. But he got nowhere.

As the 1935 neutrality law was due to expire on February 29, 1936, a move began for reenacting the original legislation. The administration fell in line. The result was the Neutrality Act of 1936, almost identical to the 1935 law. The House voted 353 to 27; the Senate adopted the measure without a roll call. As a concession to the Nye group, it forbade Americans to lend money to belligerents though exceptions were made for wars in Latin America. It did not, as Roosevelt had hoped, prohibit any trade with the belligerents beyond peacetime levels. Like the previous act, the new one was temporary; it would elapse on May 1, 1937.

Though the bill imposed more restrictions upon a president already opposed to mandatory legislation, Roosevelt signed it without comment. He feared that a fight would risk further stripping of his power, produce debate that could only comfort Mussolini, and risk votes in the impending presidential race.

As far as the Nye committee is concerned, historian Coulter finds it playing a genuinely positive role. Coulter denied that the inquiry blocked a realistic American response to aggression; rather it held culpable American businesses that sold to aggressors. Far from simplistically blaming U.S. entry into World War I on "merchants of death," the committee stressed that bankers and munitions profiteers, though major players, were only part of the story. Farmers, laborers, indeed nearly all occupations had been "monetized" (to use a term of committee member Arthur Vandenberg [Rep.-Mich.]), that is, had become massive beneficiaries of war trade. Nye himself commented, "It was the commercial activity as a whole, in which bankers had a hand, which finally did break down our neutrality." Even if the investigators were often mistaken, writes Coulter, they deserve credit for providing the first critical examination of the nation's modern military establishment.

III

Overseas the situation continued to worsen. In March 1936, in violation of the Versailles Treaty, Hitler's troops entered the demilitarized zones of the Rhineland. Two months later, after the fall of Addis Ababa, Italy annexed Ethiopia and quit the League of Nations. In July civil war broke out in Spain between the Republican forces, called Loyalists, and its opponents, called Rebels or Insurgents. That autumn Germany and Italy announced the "Rome-Berlin axis," and in November Germany and Japan signed the Anti-Comintern Pact against Russia, which Italy joined the next year.

Meanwhile the State Department set out to broaden the Good Neighbor policy. To be concrete, it sought to strengthen the New World against outside aggression by committing every country in the Western Hemisphere to the noninterventionist principle of the Monroe Doctrine. In pursuit of this goal, in 1936 Washington engineered a special Inter-American Conference "to determine how the maintenance of peace among the American Republics may best be safeguarded." It desired a permanent Inter-American Consultative Committee, compulsory consultation in case of war, and a common neutrality posture.

To encourage the conference, Roosevelt himself, shortly after winning reelection, sailed to Buenos Aires as "a traveling salesman of peace" and addressed the opening session. He told the delegates that non-American states seeking "to commit acts of aggression against us will find a Hemisphere wholly prepared to consult together for our mutual safety and our common good." The conference responded by adopting a pact that pledged consultation whenever war threatened. Furthermore, it gave unqualified endorsement to the principle of nonintervention. At the same time, under the prompting of Argentine diplomat Saaverda Lamas, Hull's proposal for a permanent committee that would give some teeth to consultation went unheeded.

A stronger statement was adopted on December 24, 1938, the Declaration of Lima, in which the inter-American delegates expressed their determination to resist "all foreign intervention or activities that may threaten them." Hull sought an unmistakable warning aimed squarely at Europe's totalitarian powers but again found himself blocked by Argentina.

A more urgent matter was the Spanish Civil War. In 1931, a rather mild revolution had overthrown King Alfonso XIII and created a republic. This republic was always unstable, polarizing the population because of its efforts to parcel out the landed estates, curb the power of its army, and confiscate the massive holdings of the Roman Catholic Church. When, in February 1936, the left won a victory at the polls, a host of its enemies—monarchists, clergy, army officers, and local fascists (called the *Falange*)—started to organize resistance and, on July 18, General Francisco Franco launched a rebellion from Spanish Morocco. It spread rapidly to such garrison towns as Cadiz and Seville though Madrid and Barcelona remained republican strongholds.

Immediately the conflict drew in foreign forces. On July 26 Adolf Hitler started sending planes and tanks to the Rebels. By the end of the month Mussolini had followed suit. Soon they were supplying pilots and ground troops as well. For both, ideological affinity was crucial. So was the desire to weaken the democracies.

In mid-September the Soviet Union began shipping massive military aid to the republic. In November the first Russian-sponsored international brigade arrived in Madrid. Soon the Soviet ambassador was one of the most important figures in the capital. Dictator Josef Stalin had several reasons to participate. He feared the general spread of fascism in Europe, hoped to extend his own political influence, and sought to maintain existing popular front governments (coalitions of liberals, socialists, and communists) in both Spain and France.

During this time Britain and France denied the Spanish republic the right to buy war materials. Britain took the initiative, acting out of a variety of motives: fear that the conflict would spread throughout Europe, that France was too weak to support intervention, that Italy still might be won over to an anti-Hitler coalition, that the Spanish republic was too radical, and that a huge rearmament program would make domestic reform impossible.

On August 15, a Non-Intervention Committee was established in London. Hence, all the European powers agreed to remain strictly neutral. No one, however, was fooled. Certainly Germany, Italy, and Russia continued to be quite brazen in supplying overt military aid.

That very month, the American government reinforced the Non-Intervention Committee by announcing a "moral embargo" on arms shipments to either side. In the U.S., the State Department, lacking the authority to do otherwise, reluctantly granted Robert Cuse of Jersey City, a major dealer in secondhand aircraft and plane parts, a license to sell $2.7 million worth of aviation equipment to the Spanish Loyalists. In January 1937, on Roosevelt's recommendation, Congress passed a nondiscriminatory arms embargo, the Senate voting 81-0 and the House 406-1. By keeping the United States totally aloof from the conflict, the policy pleased anti-interventionists, and by permitting cooperation with France and England, it satisfied internationalists.

American public opinion was split over the matter. Political liberals (some of them, like Senator Nye, ardent anti-interventionists) suddenly saw the war as a struggle between democracy and fascism and therefore urged Congress to lift the arms embargo for the legal government. Other Americans opposed any change in policy. Many Roman Catholics deplored the anticlericalism of Spain's Loyalists and, pointing to Soviet military support, also denounced the Spanish Republic as a hotbed of communism. According to the polls, pro-Loyalist sentiment at its peak was only 51 percent; no more than 25 percent of the American public ever wanted the embargo lifted.

Roosevelt wavered. He considered a recommendation that Congress permit arms shipments to the Spanish government, but in the end decided to leave the policy unchanged. For months, in fact, Roosevelt blocked efforts to repeal the arms embargo, though in January 1939 he admitted that the U.S. had made a great mistake. "The policy we should have adopted," he told his cabinet, "was to forbid the transportation of munitions in American bottoms [ships]. This could have been done and Loyalist Spain would still have been able to come to us for what she needed to fight for her life against Franco—to fight for her life and for the lives of some of the rest of us as well, as events will very likely prove." Early in 1939, debate over American policy became academic, for Franco's forces captured Barcelona and Madrid.

United States policy toward Spain's civil war was long debated. In his memoirs, Harry S Truman, then a senator from Missouri, lamented his own support for the arms embargo against "the democratic forces in Spain." The embargo, he said, "was partly responsible for our losing that country as a potential ally in World War II." Roosevelt's defenders claim that a mere lifting of the embargo would not have changed events in Spain, could have escalated the conflict into a general European war, and might well have encouraged the spread of communism.

What determined American policy? When the conflict first broke out, Roosevelt sought above all to align himself with Anglo-French policy. But as the war continued, political factors soon emerged. In May 1938, Interior Secretary Harold L. Ickes recorded that Roosevelt told him that lifting the arms embargo for the Loyalists "would mean the loss of every Catholic voter next fall."

Historian Robert Dallek, while not denying the Catholic factor, finds Roosevelt's motives more complicated. In July 1937, FDR launched a major battle against a Supreme Court that had declared unconstitutional essential parts of his domestic program, including the very linchpin of the New Deal, the National Recovery Administration. Pro-union labor legislation, social security, the Tennessee Valley Authority—all appeared in jeopardy. Further presidential battles would include reorganizing the executive branch, wages-and-hours legislation, and probing monopolies. It was no time, the president believed, to further split the country over foreign policy.

In the fall of 1938, Roosevelt received a serious setback in the congressional elections. Now, he believed, there was no way to compel action on any major matters, much less foreign policy ones. He had been unable to purge conservative Democrats, and it was unlikely he would run for reelection in 1940. Furthermore, he did not want to jeopardize his chances for revising general neutrality legislation. Besides, by 1939, he estimated—quite correctly, it turns out—that it was too late to save the Spanish Republic. Had he decided to cancel the embargo on his own, he would have been on dubious legal grounds, antagonized the Congress, and still have faced the problem of getting the munitions into Loyalist hands.

Historian Douglas Little stresses another factor: continued State Department hostility toward Republican Spain. Even at the outset of the conflict, the Department feared that communist subversion there was strong enough to endanger American economic interests and contaminate Europe as a whole. Moscow's mounting involvement in the Madrid government appeared to be proof that a Republican victory would result in the outright Bolshevization of Spain.

In the spring of 1937, keeping an eye on the barbaric combat in Spain, America again turned its attention to neutrality, for on May 1 the Neutrality Act of 1936 would expire. Anti-interventionist sentiment remained strong, and it was clear that Congress would retain the arms embargo and loan prohibition. But what about trade in nonmilitary commodities? Munitions composed only part of the needs of belligerents, and so long as American ships could carry nonmilitary cargoes to belligerent ports, there still was danger of involvement in war. Yet, as a total embargo would hurt the national economy, Americans sought a magic formula, one that could preserve both peace and prosperity. Only a few anti-interventionists would follow Nye's theory to its logical conclusion and embargo all goods to belligerents.

A solution appeared in "cash-and-carry," a plan whereby prospective purchasers would collect the goods in U.S. ports and pay for them on the spot. The scheme was advanced by financier Bernard M. Baruch in the June 1936 issue of the magazine *Current History:* "We will sell to any belligerent anything except lethal weapons, but the terms are 'cash on the barrel-head and come and get it.'"

Critics claimed that cash-and-carry would amount to benevolent neutrality in favor of wealthy countries. Hiram Johnson, part of a decided Senate minority who linked neutrality to traditional international law, asked: "What sort of government is this and what sort of men are we to accept a formula which will enable us to sell goods and then hide?" More important were the views of the president. Roosevelt offered no objection, undoubtedly because he realized that cash-and-carry would favor Great Britain and France, nations that controlled the sea, rather than Germany and Italy.

When cash-and-carry reached Congress, a dispute arose over presidential discretion in applying the provision. Anti-interventionists wanted its application to be mandatory; supporters of the administration desired to let the president decide whether and under what circumstances it should be imposed. A compromise emerged. In return for sections forbidding Americans to travel on belligerent ships and prohibiting the arming of American merchantmen, anti-interventionists accepted discretionary authority on cash-and-carry. The cash-and-carry provision would remain in force until May 1, 1939. The president could also ban shipment on American vessels of commodities that he might specify, close American ports to belligerent warships, and declare American territorial waters off-limits to belligerent submarines and merchantmen. The measure retained the arms embargo and loan prohibition of the old law, and it applied to civil strife as well as international war. Given the obvious efforts to avoid repeating the steps by which the U.S. was perceived to have entered World War I, the *New York Herald Tribune* labeled the bill "an Act to preserve the U.S. from intervention in the War of 1914–18."

On April 29, 1937, the new bill was passed, and now a bit of drama was involved. To prevent a lapse in neutrality, it was necessary to have the presidential signature before May 1, when the old law expired. This created a small problem, for Roosevelt was on a fishing cruise in the Gulf of Mexico. To beat the April 30 deadline, an airplane carrying a copy of the bill took off from Washington. At Galveston, the document was hurried aboard a navy seaplane that roared out over the Gulf and landed alongside the presidential yacht. On May 1, at 6:30 A.M., Roosevelt signed it. Engrossed in the Supreme Court struggle, Roosevelt sought no additional conflict. By remaining aloof from debate while quietly backing the congressional moderates, he was able to maintain some flexibility.

IV

While world attention was fixed on the uneasy situation in Europe, Far Eastern matters were again reaching to a crisis. In July 1937, at the Marco Polo Bridge in North China, a railway junction ten miles west of Beijing, the first shots were fired in a conflict that would continue for over eight years, in fact until the representatives of Imperial Japan surrendered unconditionally on the deck of the *U.S.S. Missouri*.

For several years Japan had focused on consolidating its triumph in Manchuria. The Tangku truce of May 1933, however, had not weakened its ambitions. Leaders in Tokyo continued to anticipate the day when they would control China and extend hegemony over what they later termed "Greater East Asia." In the spring of 1934, Amau Eiji, a spokesman for the Foreign Ministry, claimed that Japan alone possessed the mission of maintaining peace and order in East Asia. By excluding Western economic and political activities, the Amau Doctrine directly challenged the Washington system of 1921–22.

As historian Akira Iriye notes, Japan's leaders believed that the pattern of peaceful expansion that earmarked the twenties had failed. Only force, therefore, could assure the nation's growth. More and more, Japan perceived that its security and prosperity, indeed its very survival, were contingent upon dominating East Asia. This dominance in turn, they believed, depended upon its ability to fight the Soviets and the Americans and to conquer Nationalist China.

In 1935, the Japanese used nonmilitary methods against China, hoping that persuasion, bribery, and intimidation would enable them to divide and conquer that loosely knit nation. In fact, the Chinese Nationalist government was so weak that warlords ran rampant amid the absolute anarchy. During the next two years, the Japanese undermined Jiang Jieshi's authority in North China, dealing with local warlords and thereby excluding Goumindang military forces.

American economic practices did little to alleviate China's predicament. By making massive silver purchases in China, it so raised the world price that large quantities of silver began to flow out of the country. In November 1935 the U.S. forced the Chinese *yuan* off the silver-based currency system, thereby derailing Nanjing's efforts at economic rehabilitation.

If, however, East Asia appeared quiet in the years after the Tangku truce, Americans remained keenly interested in what happened in that area. First of all, there had long been extensive Protestant missionary activity in China. Second, ever since the turn of the century, when Secretary Hay announced the Open Door policy, many Americans had felt a curious attachment to China, seeing themselves as self-appointed guardians of that country. Conversely, as noted by historian and diplomat Edwin O. Reischauer, "our compulsive desire to believe the worst about the Japanese pushed us toward believing only the best about the Chinese." As a result, he claims, "we gradually built up in our minds an idealized picture of China."

During the mid-1930s, Washington kept a wary eye on the Far East, and the Roosevelt administration seemed to follow the course charted by Secretary Stimson. There was no recognition of Manchukuo, and when the Japanese disregarded the Open Door there, Secretary Hull lectured them on the virtue of keeping promises. As during the presidency of Hoover, there was little American military presence in the Pacific.

Continuity of policy was more apparent than real, however, for America's diplomacy in the Far East underwent a subtle change in those years. Instead of protest and moralizing, the idea was to build China as a counterweight to Japan, mainly by financial and technical assistance. Unfortunately protest by Japan, the Great Depression at home, and Jiang's inability to achieve China's reconstruction all caused the new policy to fail.

Throughout most of the 1930s, Roosevelt dealt with Japan in ad hoc fashion. Hoping to make sure that Japan's naval predominance in the western Pacific would not threaten the status quo in the rest of that ocean, he adamantly opposed naval equality. At the same time, FDR sought to build up the American fleet to the limits set by the London treaty of 1930. Using funds from a major New Deal agency, the Public Works Administration, in 1933 he initiated construction of four cruisers, two aircraft carriers, sixteen destroyers, four submarines, and a number of auxiliary cruisers. The number marked the greatest batch of warships yet ordered in a single day. During this time, Japanese appropriations for new ships had been declining from $40.8 million in 1930–31 to $33.5 million in 1931–32 and $26.9 million in 1932–33.

Critics charged that the American program was initiating a naval race, with one of Japan's least chauvinistic papers, *Osaka Asahi,* claiming FDR's policy "betrays the spirit of the London treaty." Japanese naval expansionists countered by securing over $100 million dollars from their Diet. Even the British Foreign Office sought curtailment of the American plans.

In response FDR wrote a friend in August 1933 that the Japanese had built up to treaty limit and that the British had done so partially but that the U.S. had not acted so at all. "The whole scheme of things in Tokio [sic] does not make for an assurance of non-aggression in the future," he continued. "As a matter of fact our building program, far from building us up to our Treaty quotas, will barely suffice to keep up almost up to the ship strength of the Japanese Navy and still, of course, far below the British Navy. I am not concerned about the latter, but I am concerned about the first."

All during the early thirties, Japan made no secret of its desire to expand in East Asia. Not surprisingly, naval accords created at Washington in 1922 and at London in 1930 disintegrated. The Japanese were no longer content with the Washington agreements of 1922, as they limited its construction in battleships and aircraft carriers to 60 percent of American and British craft, or with the London agreements of 1930, as they assigned Japan a 60 percent ratio in heavy cruisers and 70 percent in light ones. With ranges of ships and planes steadily increasing, the Japanese continually called for absolute equality.

As the U.S. objected to such expansion, on December 29, 1934, Japan gave the stipulated two-years notice concerning the Washington agreement, after which it could legally build as much as it wanted to. On that very day, the U.S. announced that it would hold naval maneuvers west of Hawaii. After the failure of the London Naval Conference, which convened in December 1935, Japan abrogated the arms limitation agreements and launched an ambitious building program.

A naval race was again in the offing. Roosevelt would not even promise a naval freeze in the Pacific, even when Admiral William H. Standley, chief of naval operations, told Roosevelt that such a promise would not hurt the United States, for Japanese strength would still be inadequate outside Asian waters. Roosevelt refused to give in to the very idea of parity with Japan. Although the Japanese originally tried to scale down the American and British navies, all their disarmament proposals kept Anglo-American superiority intact while saving their all-important pride.

In the election year of 1936 FDR's own naval agenda went through easily. Indeed, one could talk of a renaissance of naval building, one that included three aircraft carriers, eleven cruisers, sixty-three destroyers, and eighteen submarines. The Japanese were not slow in responding, though they did not make their program public. Yet, at least until 1939, Roosevelt did not think that Japan threatened American security or sought war with the United States.

Such "navalism," as it was called, took place amid renewed fighting in China. On July 7, 1937, at Marco Polo Bridge, Japanese soldiers, stationed in the Beijing area in accordance with the Boxer Protocol of 1901, clashed with the Chinese. According to the Chinese, a Japanese unit on night maneuvers had demanded entry into the village of Wanping to search for a missing soldier and, when turned away, had shelled the village. The Japanese accused the Chinese troops of initiating hostilities by firing on them just north of the bridge.

Neither Japan's Guandong Army in North China nor the civilian government in Tokyo had sought the confrontation; in fact, the army general staff was beginning to accept the lasting tenacity of Chinese nationalism in the area and had considered withdrawing forces from northern China. Just as it seemed as if the conflict was subsiding, fighting broke out again, and on July 25 Japanese troops had seized Beijing and Shanghai. The Tokyo cabinet had decided upon a war of chastisement, then annihilation. Hence, unlike the Manchurian incident, Japanese policy did not result from any independent military action; it was ordered by the civilian government, which saw its hegemony in North China threatened by a resurgent Goumindang.

In Washington there was hope that the fighting would be contained, with the commanders on the spot working out a truce. Such sentiments faded a few days later when U.S. Ambassador Joseph C. Grew reported that Japan was sending fresh troops to North China. Then came another "incident," followed on July 26 by a Japanese ultimatum that Chinese soldiers evacuate the town of Langfan. Chinese rejection of the ultimatum signaled full-scale fighting, and the Nanjing government sent four divisions into North China. Within weeks the Japanese were in control of the entire Beijing-Tianjin area.

Then the struggle shifted 650 miles southward to Shanghai. Early in August 1937, fighting broke out at China's largest port, and in a fortnight the city was shaking under the crash of shells and bombs. The Chinese managed to hold on until November, when a

Japanese flanking movement compelled them to withdraw up the Yangtze toward Nanjing, Jiang Jieshi's capital. In pursuit of the retreating Chinese, the Japanese unleashed air squadrons, and reports of bombs falling indiscriminately on soldiers and civilians shocked the world. At Nanjing, the Chinese turned to give battle, but in less than a month the Japanese sent them fleeing. Although the Japanese had won acclaim in the past for their discipline and generosity toward the vanquished, that December they gave themselves over to an orgy of looting and murder. Their entry reinforced a newly acquired reputation for brutality, so much so that for years Americans would refer to the "rape of Nanking," as the city was long called.

Japan now found itself in a bind of its own making. Even though Jiang Jieshi at times appeared willing to negotiate, he would not recognize Japan's control of Manchuria, its economic primacy in North China or Inner Mongolia, or the special relationship with Japan implicit in the Amau Doctrine. Japan therefore continued its push, always hoping that one more victory would allow it to abandon the Chinese imbroglio. Not only did the Japanese want to avoid the permanent occupation of China; their drive southward was really part of an effort to withdraw from the China war.

The "China incident," as the Japanese persisted in calling the new war, reopened debate in America between anti-interventionists and their opponents. Anti-interventionists recalled that Roosevelt had invoked the Neutrality Act in 1935, when Italy and Ethiopia went to war without formal declaration, and they urged him to do so again. Interventionists wanted pressure on Japan. The debate took on a new dimension when news of the agony of China's civilian population reached the United States, accompanied by such headlines as "AMERICAN SCRAP IRON PLAYS GRIM ROLE IN FAR EASTERN WAR. JAPANESE RAIN DEATH WITH ONE-TIME JUNK." In the name of humanity, many felt, should not the U.S. impose an embargo on the "sinews of war"—scrap metal, oil, cotton? But talk of an embargo raised the old question: would the Japanese retaliate?

China was in a most unfavorable position. In America anti-interventionist sentiment remained intense. Anxieties over German rearmament prevented strong action by Britain and France. Jiang's chances of beating the Japanese were nil. At best, Japan might limit its ambitions in China, and China in turn might officially recognize a permanent Japanese presence there. Such optimism did not seem vain. Ambassador Grew, thinking that there was a chance of a negotiated settlement, pleaded with his superiors to take no action that would further excite Japanese nationalism.

Grew's estimate was well-founded. In fact, in October 1937, Japan put out peace feelers. Its leaders still found the Soviet Union the real menace and therefore opposed draining the nation's resources in a China quagmire. One might well reason that Japan's security could be satisfied by increased influence in Inner Mongolia, a buffer zone in the Beijing-Tianjin region, and another protecting its interests in Shanghai. Elsewhere Nanjing, not Tokyo, should preserve order. Jiang, however, was in no mood to come to terms.

For the United States, neutrality and avoidance of provocative action remained crucial. The president and his secretary of state did share the national sympathy for China, viewing Japan as a brutal aggressor. Roosevelt knew that China needed foreign arms and Japan did not. Furthermore, any embargo would favor Japan, a nation in better condition to conduct a "cash-and-carry" trade with the U.S. Roosevelt declined to invoke the 1937 Neutrality Act, though he did forbid some thirteen merchant vessels owned by the U.S. government to transport arms to either belligerent. He skillfully put off anti-interventionists with the argument that officially labeling the Far Eastern affair a war would stir passions and reduce chances for peace. While operating within the letter of the law, he could permit the flow of American munitions to China.

Meanwhile Hull had set out to rally moral pressure against Japan. His device was a highly publicized statement, made on July 16, 1937, outlining American affirmation of "international self-restraint," "sanctity of treaties," and "orderly processes." The pronouncement went out to all capitals with the request that the governments express their opinions. Since "everybody was against sin," favorable responses were soon streaming into Washington. Unfortunately the climax of Hull's maneuver coincided with the beginning of hostilities at Shanghai. Sensational news from the battle area kept reports of the general acceptance of Hull's principles off the front pages, undercutting the attempt at moral suasion and demonstrating that the pressure of world opinion had scant influence on the Japanese.

V

The attention of diplomats next turned to Geneva, where early in October 1937 the League censured Japan as a violator of the Nine-Power and Kellogg-Briand treaties. It recommended a conference of signatories of the Nine-Power agreement and "other States which have special interests in the Far East." Hull endorsed the League action and advised officials at Geneva that the United States would take part in the conference.

Meanwhile, to mend political fences after his attempt to "pack" the Supreme Court, Roosevelt undertook a speaking tour of western states. On October 5, in Chicago, the president gave one of the most memorable addresses of his presidency, his "quarantine speech." He announced that "the peace-loving nations must make a concerted effort in opposition to those violations of treaties and those ignorings of humane instincts which today are creating a state of international anarchy and instability. . . . It seems to be unfortunately true that the epidemic of world lawlessness is spreading. When an epidemic of physical disease starts to spread, the community approves and joins in a quarantine of the patients in order to protect the health of the community against the spread of the disease. . . . War is a contagion, whether it be declared or undeclared." Except for the most staunch anti-administration newspapers, press reaction was favorable, not—as FDR feared—overwhelmingly negative. The term "quarantine" itself came from Interior Secretary Harold Ickes.

Roosevelt himself was quick to say that his speech conveyed "an attitude and it does not define a program; but it says we are looking for a program." There were, he went on, many methods that had not yet been tried, though he mentioned none. Almost immediately, the president drew back from the idea that the address had suggested sanctions against Japan. The day after the speech he told reporters: "Look, 'sanctions' is a terrible word to use. They are out the window." He hinted that he was thinking only of a general treaty guaranteeing "lasting peace."

Why did FDR insist upon walking cautiously in East Asia? Howls by anti-interventionists and a general lack of enthusiasm for a "tough" line were partly responsible. The president complained privately that "it's a terrible thing to look over your shoulder when you are trying to lead—and to find no one there." The response in Tokyo also was a factor. Ambassador Grew warned that Japan's temperature was rising, and if American policy hardened, there would be less chance of Japanese moderation in China.

Proof that America's policy had not changed came in November 1937, when a League-sponsored conference of the Nine Power Treaty signatories and "others" met at Brussels. American delegate Norman H. Davis learned that European representatives were willing to consider sanctions against Japan. Unmoved, the State Department cabled that coercive measures did not fall within the scope of the conference—that the purpose of the Brussels meeting was to arrange a settlement between Japan and China. As discussion continued, American diplomats became nervous over newspaper stories that the United States was talking surreptitiously about punitive measures. Lest America be an object of Japanese wrath, as had occurred in the Manchurian affair, Secretary Hull sought adjournment of the conference. The futile deliberations ended on November 24, when delegates accepted a report mildly rebuking Japan as a violator of the Nine-Power Treaty.

The powers, however, made it clear they would take no risks to stop Japan's advance. Ambassador Grew probably made the best appraisal of the conference when he wrote in his diary that the meeting should never have been convened. It had been evident from the start that delegates "could never in the world agree to take *effective* measures" and would only encourage Japanese militarists by exhibiting the "lack of unity and impotence of the Powers (emphasis his)." Grew then asked: "Why can't statesmen think through things?"

In May 1937, Neville Chamberlain replaced Stanley Baldwin as Britain's prime minister. Soon afterwards, he spurned FDR's effort to establish personal contact, turning down an invitation to visit the White House. Always mistrustful of American commitment, at the end of the year Chamberlain confided, "It is always best & safest to count on *nothing* from the Americans but words" (emphasis his). His sister simply remarked: "Hardly a people to go tiger shooting with."

Three weeks after the debacle at Brussels, the *Panay* incident occurred.

Since 1858, in accordance with a treaty with China, the United States had maintained a naval squadron on the Yangtze to protect

American nationals and their interests. In December 1937, one of the gunboats, the *Panay* (named for an island in the Philippines), was trying to perform its safeguarding mission and at the same time stay clear of the Japanese and Chinese armies fighting along the river. Built expressly for patrol purposes, it was armed with two three-inch guns and ten .30-caliber machine guns.

On December 11, to escape Japanese artillery fire, the *Panay* left its anchorage near Nanjing and steamed upriver. En route it joined three tankers belonging to the Standard Vacuum Oil Company. The next day the four ships dropped anchor twenty-seven miles from Nanjing. Through the American consulate at Shanghai, they radioed the Japanese of their new location. The sun was shining brightly, freshly painted American flags were visible on the *Panay*'s awnings, and the Stars and Stripes were flying from every mast. At 10 A.M. a Japanese officer and several soldiers boarded the ships, asking the captain to disclose the movement of any Chinese troops in the area. The captain refused, telling the boarding party that the U.S. had to be strictly neutral in the matter.

Suddenly, about 1:30 in the afternoon, a squadron of twin-motored Japanese planes appeared. A *Collier's* reporter later recalled that the planes "zoomed over, reconnoitering . . . , wheeled and began lining up for the bombing." Moments later the first bomb crashed down on the gunboat, ripping a hole in the roof of the bridge and putting the ship's only antiaircraft gun out of action. In relays the planes kept up the attack, a United Press correspondent writing that "bombs rained like hailstones and churned the water all around the ships like geysers." When survivors tried to scramble ashore in lifeboats, the Japanese planes swooped toward them, machine guns blazing. After thirty minutes, the *Panay* rolled to starboard, and with colors still flying, sank in fifty feet of water. Three Americans were dead and forty-three injured. The tankers, also under attack, reached shore before settling to the bottom, and their crews managed to escape. Elsewhere on the Yangtze that day, several British boats met with similar attacks.

Reaction in America was mixed. When the flag-draped coffin of one of the *Panay*'s crew flashed on a New York movie screen, a man jumped from his seat and commanded: "Everybody stand up!" The audience obeyed. Most people remained calm, however, the *Christian Century* finding hardly "the slightest trace of such frenzied excitement as followed the sinking of the *Maine* and of the *Lusitania*." Most Americans seemed to agree with Senator Borah that "it was just one of those regrettable things," or with Senator Henrik Shipstead (Farmer-Labor-Minn.) that Americans should "get the hell out of China war zones."

In the State Department, there was shock and outrage. Hull sent off messages to Tokyo indicating the gravity of the attack. He soon learned that the Japanese Foreign Office was almost as upset as the State Department. To demonstrate Tokyo's good intentions, Japan's foreign minister took the unusual step of going to the American embassy to offer a "profound apology." According to the Japanese, the affair had been a case of mistaken identity. Skeptics in the State Department were not convinced, but it was clear that Japan was not looking for a fight with America; the *Panay* attack had been the doing of irresponsible aviators who suspected the presence of Chinese military personnel and weapons on board. The Tokyo government agreed to major American demands: official apologies, indemnities for the injured and relatives of the dead, and assurances against future attacks. Japan dismissed the rear admiral who ordered the attack of the pilots but it did not remove the officer who gave the command to the machine gunners, as he was too powerful.

By the end of 1937, the *Panay* affair was nearly forgotten, Japan's aggression in China was continuing, and America's Far Eastern policy had retreated to inaction. Yet both the United States and Britain remained alarmed. British Foreign Secretary Anthony Eden sought a joint Anglo-American naval demonstration, one in which eight or nine capital ships would be sent to the Far East if Japan provoked the two nations further. Roosevelt suggested an alternative, namely that both countries rely on their cruisers to halt Japanese shipping, thereby cutting Japan off from all raw materials. Within eighteen months, he predicted, Japan would be helpless and no blood would have been shed. In January 1938, Roosevelt sent Captain Royal E. Ingersoll, chief of the U.S. Navy's War Plans Division, to London. Although neither Britain nor America would accept each other's scheme, the conversations led directly to the open naval staff meetings so crucial in 1941.

There was, moreover, the possibility that other forms of pressure might work. Some, such as Roosevelt and Hull, hoped that world-wide condemnation of Japanese policies would bring Japan back to its senses. Hence Hull would frequently lecture the Japanese ambassador on the "sanctity of treaties," "orderly processes" in international relations, and the Open Door in China.

Then there was the solution first advanced during the Manchurian crisis: economic pressure. Five-and-dime stores refused to carry Japanese goods. College students discarded silk stockings and ties. The reasoning was simple. If Japan could not sell overseas, it would lack the foreign exchange needed to fight the China war. An effective boycott, proponents argued, would trim Japan's exports 40 percent, requiring a parallel cut in imports and hampering the war effort. Arguing that Japan was too weak to withstand serious economic pressure, Freda Utley, a British journalist soon to be naturalized as an American citizen, wrote a book entitled *Japan's Feet of Clay* (1937).

Some Americans opposed any pressure. The belief existed, as in the days of Theodore Roosevelt, that Japan served as a needed check on Russian ambitions going back to the days of the czars. Furthermore, because of the recent Soviet Five-Year Plans, the ideological appeal of communism now had military strength behind it. In the words of John V. A. MacMurray, former chief of the State Department's Far Eastern Division, "Nobody except perhaps Russia would gain from our victory in a war against Japan."

Others feared an increasingly truculent Chinese nationalism. By 1931, China had given ample proof of its desire to cast off Western domination of its life—political, economic, and cultural. MacMurray again spoke to the issue, saying that "If we were to 'save' China from Japan and become the 'Number One' nation in the eyes of her people, we should thereby become not the most favored but the most distrusted of nations." In other words, any American rescue would not long be appreciated.

Economic motives were important. For some years, Japan had been America's best customer in Asia and the third largest purchaser of American products in the world. Indeed, American sales to Japan were four to seven times as large as those to China.

Besides, voices of caution argued, the United States lacked the strength to fight any war in Asia. The Philippines were due for independence within the decade, leaving far-flung Samoa and Guam as the only U.S. bases west of Hawaii. And even if the Philippines allowed American bases on their islands, a major Pacific war would require still more bases, a massive navy, and many thousands of troops.

If Americans have long since decried the country's failure to meet its responsibilities, at the time few felt pangs of conscience. They saw the aggression of Japan, Italy, and Germany as a new manifestation of the Old World's habit of treaty-breaking and war and were satisfied to be following the advice of George Washington. Reinforcing such ideas was a corps of anti-interventionist writers who were busy demonstrating that the United States had had no business in the war of 1914–18. An Allied victory had been no more preferable than a German one, and certainly not worth American involvement. If, they argued, the United States had isolated herself in 1914–17 with laws akin to the neutrality measures of 1935–37, it could have avoided the Great War and the resulting calamities of debt, default, and depression.

The problem of staying out of war was, of course, bigger than anti-interventionists thought, and their victories would prove transitory. It was just after the *Panay* incident that the Ludlow war-referendum amendment was almost called out of a House committee. Congressman Louis Ludlow (Dem.-Ind.) sought an amendment to the U.S. Constitution by which Congress's power to declare war would be restricted to cases of actual or imminent invasion of the United States or its territories or attack by a non-American nation on a state in the Western Hemisphere. In any other case, Congress must allow voters to choose, by means of a national referendum, whether they wished to go to war. In Ludlow's words, "my war-referendum peace resolution . . . is intended to prevent our precious boys—the flower of American manhood—from being drawn into another world war which appears at the moment to be looming over the world horizon." Seeing his proposal as a venture in international cooperation, he hoped other nations would adopt a similar policy. A majority in Congress, however, agreed with Senator Arthur H. Vandenberg (Rep.-

Mich.) that "it would be as sensible to require a town meeting before permitting the fire department to put out the blaze."

Even so the tally was perilously close. On January 10, 1938, the House voted 209 to 188 to return it to committee. Just before the vote, House Speaker William Bankhead (Dem.-Ala.) read a public letter from FDR, claiming that the amendment would "cripple" the president's ability to conduct foreign policy and encourage other nations to "violate American rights with impunity." For the Roosevelt administration, the tide was just beginning to turn.

For FDR, however, domestic politics remained the priority. The economy had taken a such a sudden drop in the fall of 1937 that many Americans were approaching starvation. The president successfully fought for emergency relief appropriations and a wages-hours bill but was stymied in his efforts to reorganize the executive branch of the government and purge opponents of the New Deal from the ranks of his own party. When the Republicans gained markedly in the 1938 congressional elections, FDR realized that further domestic reform and foreign policy initiatives were thwarted. The power he had wielded just two years earlier had apparently vanished. Hence, for the time being, the United States made no overt challenge.

CHAPTER FOUR

Toward War in Europe

In the year 1937, apart from the civil war in Spain, a relative calm seemed to settle over Europe. Hitler, however, was plotting the destruction of independent government in his native Austria, doing so with assurances of considerable internal support. Since the end of the World War, many Austrians had been anxious to set aside the Treaty of St. Germain (1919) forbidding the nation ever to unite with Germany. They wanted their country, German in language and culture, to be part of a "greater Reich." On taking power in Berlin, Hitler encouraged this attitude, and in the mid-1930s the Austrian section of the Nazi party became a force. For a time the Austrian government had the support of Mussolini, who was nervous about Germany's border suddenly reaching the Brenner Pass. By the end of 1937, however, Italy's dictator had reconciled himself to a German takeover.

As a last resort, Austrian chancellor Kurt von Schuschnigg called for a plebiscite to let his people decide their own political future. But, in March 1938, before the Austrians could speak out, Hitler sent troops across the frontier, and news photographs released by the Nazis showed throngs of Austrians smiling and cheering while pretty *Fraülein* garlanded German soldiers with flowers. After silencing opposition, the Germans staged their own plebiscite, which—according to Nazi accounts—brought a nearly unanimous vote in favor of *Anschluss*, or union with Germany.

All Europe experienced shock at this latest violation of the Paris peace settlement, but there was no talk of action. France had no desire for war, and Britain had begun a policy of "appeasement," that is heading off conflict by "reasonable" concessions. As for the United States, Austria was quite distant, and the Washington government kept its show of displeasure in bounds. It refused to recognize the Anschluss and suspended the commercial treaty with Austria.

Hitler had taken his boldest step to date. After parading through Vienna, he began to plan his next step.

I

This time, Hitler's object was Czechoslovakia, and his first tactic was to stir trouble in the Sudetenland, a mountainous fringe along the German-Czech border containing a million and a half Germans. Invoking the principle of self-determination, the dictator insisted that this region should have the right to decide its own future, meaning the right to secede from Czechoslovakia and join the Reich. Loss of the Sudeten territory would deprive Czechoslovakia of its natural defensive barrier, seen by Winston Churchill, Chamberlain's strongest critic in Parliament, as "the strongest fortress in Europe."

When, in September 1938, Hitler brought the Czech dispute to the point of crisis, British Prime Minister Neville Chamberlain assumed leadership in the Anglo-French attempt to head off war. Meeting Hitler at Berchtesgaden on September 15, Chamberlain agreed to cede 8,000 square miles to Germany over the following six months. In addition to the Sudeten minority, some 800,000 Czechs would be transferred to Germany. Upon returning to Britain, Chamberlain had gained French and Czech concurrence, the Czechs realizing they had no option.

The prime minister and the Führer met again at Godesberg on September 22–23, Chamberlain informing Hitler of his success in securing French and Czech agreement. At this point, Hitler shocked Chamberlain by insisting upon an additional 1,000 square miles, the triumphal entrance of German forces, the withdrawal of all Czech troops, and limiting the plebiscite to those people—obviously Germans—who had lived in the affected area before the end of World War I. He softened Chamberlain by pledging that "this is the last territorial claim I have to make in Europe." Hitler, however, set a deadline of October 1, thereby giving the Czechs insufficient time to dynamite the fortifications and factories they had constructed.

Not surprisingly, France and England balked, not to mention Czechoslovakia, and for several days war appeared inevitable. France mobilized a million men, while the British Home Fleet, stationed in the North Sea, prepared for battle. In London's Hyde Park, people were trying on gas masks.

Yet, on September 28, as the deadline neared, Hitler responded to last-minute urgings of Benito Mussolini and accepted Chamberlain's appeal for a four-power conference. The German leader had been warned by his generals that the Wehrmacht was unready for a major war, noted that Britain had mobilized the Royal Navy, and heard Mussolini, with whom he had a military alliance, deny he would enter any conflict. Soon the British, French, Germans, and Italians were meeting at the Bavarian city of Munich. Conversations began at noon on the 29th and ran until two o'clock the following morning. The negotiators agreed that much Sudeten territory should pass to German control, to be concrete, 10,000 square miles without plebiscite by October 10 and a possible 2,000 more later by plebiscites. Military installations erected by the Czechs were not to be destroyed. The four powers agreed to guarantee Czechoslovakia's new frontiers.

After the meeting Chamberlain flew back to England and on September 30, before an excited crowd at the London airport, he waved the declaration that Hitler had signed. As he was driven through the streets of the city, throngs of Britons cheered, and from a window of his residence he again brandished his piece of paper, announcing: "This is the second time there has come back from Germany to Downing Street peace with honor. I believe it is peace in our time." Similarly French premier Edouard Daladier enjoyed the greatest ovation in modern French history.

For the Czechs, surrender appeared the only option, although Churchill later wrote that they should have stood firm. In event of a German attack, he argued in 1948, France and Britain would have honored their commitment to Czechoslovakia. Moreover, the Western powers would have possessed sufficient strength to repulse German attacks.

What role did the United States play in this crisis? Late in May, when the Czech problem first appeared critical, Secretary Hull issued an innocuous statement stressing America's hope for peace. As the affair neared a crisis in August, the secretary warned of "dangerous developments." In an address that month at Kingston, Ontario, Roosevelt himself pledged United States support if Canadian soil were "threatened by any other empire." It was rumored that FDR might act as arbiter in the dispute; when that idea drew no response, the president sent messages urging peaceful settlement to Hitler, Mussolini, Chamberlain, Daladier, and the Czech president Eduard Beneš. Britain and France, he feared, would be defeated in any war. Roosevelt suggested that Hitler widen the conference to include all interested nations, but the president displayed no interest in passing on the merits of the controversy or undertaking any responsibilities. Throughout the crisis, FDR made it plain that the U.S. had no intention of getting embroiled: "The Government of the United States has no political involvements in Europe, and will assume no obligations in the conduct of present negotiations."

France and Britain both realized that the Americans counseled no resistance to Hitler. In fact, when Chamberlain accepted Hitler's invitation to Munich, Roosevelt cabled the British prime minister. "Good man" was all he said. Historian Arnold A. Offner claims that "By and large Roosevelt had convinced himself that Munich had opened the way to a new and better world." On October 5, within a week after the conference was held, he telegraphed Chamberlain, "I fully share your hope and belief that there exists today the greatest opportunity in years for the establishment of a new world order based on justice and law." During those crucial weeks of September 1939, so Offner notes, he never raised such matters as the first-class status of the Czech army, Germany's weak western fortifications, Britain's clear naval supremacy, Britain's and France's air parity with Germany, or the possibility of Soviet intervention.

Another scholar, Barbara Rearden Farnham, sees FDR initially encouraging Chamberlain to resist Hitler's demands. True, Roosevelt did back continuation of negotiations after the Chamberlain-Hitler

Europe, 1939

meeting at Godesberg, for the alternative appeared to be an all-out European war. After Munich, however, Roosevelt became committed, even eager, to check Hitler. According to Farnham, the president feared that Brazil, whose 1.5 million Germans might engage in insurgency, would serve as Germany's launching pad within the Western Hemisphere. In talking confidentially with Sir Ronald Lindsay, British ambassador to the U.S., FDR spoke of a general international conference to rectify unjust boundaries. If, however, war still came, the Allies should fight a defensive conflict, based on naval blockade, until the neutrality act was weakened enough to permit American aid.

Sixty percent of the Americans polled favored the agreement. Roosevelt obviously had no control over the crisis, which was solely in European hands, and given anti-interventionist sentiment at home, he could not have committed American power to resisting Hitler. Yet to the degree that his administration participated in the events surrounding Munich, it was tacitly on the side of appeasement.

Whatever the president's estimate of the situation, such optimism inside the government was short-lived. Less than a week after the Munich conference, William C. Bullitt, American ambassador to France, reported that Daladier predicted a new German demand within six months. Unlike Chamberlain, the French premier saw Munich as a colossal defeat. A few days later came a thunderclap from Berlin. Declaring that Germany could not rely on Chamberlain's promises, Hitler called for new German armament. By then Roosevelt had lost all his illusions and announced that the United States would spend an additional $300 million on national defense.

Five weeks after Munich, in the infamous *Kristallnacht* of November 9–10, 1938, the Nazis looted 7,500 Jewish shops, burned 195 synagogues, and transported over 20,000 Jews to concentration camps. Numerous Jews of both sexes were beaten by mobs throughout the entire Reich. Roosevelt recalled Ambassador Hugh Wilson from Berlin and permitted some 15,000 refugees from Germany and Austria to remain in the United States on visitor's permits. He sought without success to amend the 1924 immigration law so as to allow the entrance of refugee children from Germany. He also futilely attempted, through intermediaries, to prod Hitler to allow 150,000 Jews to emigrate by means of a massive international loan.

One thing, however, should be noted. Beyond these efforts, FDR would not go. Not only did immigration quotas remain rigid, but the State Department bureaucracy blocked the admission of over 1 million Jews who might legally have entered the nation. In the words of historian Offner, the department was "timid, rigidly legal, and without innovation." In late May 1939, the Hamburg-American passenger liner *St. Louis,* containing 930 German-Jewish refugees, sought refuge in the United States. Bound first for Havana, then for Miami, it was forcibly returned to Europe. The captain managed to distribute his passengers among Britain, France, Belgium, and the Netherlands, but most of these nations fell under German rule within two years. Said the *New York Times,* "The cruise of the *St. Louis* cries to high heaven of man's inhumanity to man."

When an international refugee conference was held at Evian-les-Bains in July 1938, the U.S. participated but it was no more willing than the thirty-one other nations to permit large-scale Jewish immigration. In mid-1940, and again in July 1941, refugee immigration was first cut in half, then by 25 percent. Between March and December 1938, public support for the prevailing immigration restrictions actually rose from 75 to 83 percent. Writes historian Irwin Gellman, "Americans were far more concerned about protecting their jobs from unwanted immigrants than about granting them safe harbor."

Early in 1939, the Nazi dictator prepared for the destruction of Czechoslovakia. After encouraging the Slovaks to separate from the Czech Republic, Hitler alleged that "disturbances" existed inside the country, and at 6:00 A.M., March 15, ordered troops across the Czech frontier. The German move came as a surprise, causing George F. Kennan, second secretary of the American legation in Prague, to report a few days later: "No one understood . . . that a trap was being prepared which was designed to bring about the end of Czechoslovakia." Pushing through howling wind and snow, German mechanized columns completed the occupation in one day. That same evening, Hitler arrived in Prague and proclaimed a protectorate. Britain and France did nothing, Chamberlain explaining that disruption of the Czech state by the Slovak secession had nullified the Munich agreement. A few days later Hitler's troops entered Memel, a German city along the Baltic that had passed to Lithuanian control after the World

War. The following month, on Good Friday, Mussolini sent troops across the Adriatic to seize Albania.

The United States condemned the Axis aggression, continued to recognize the Czech and Albanian ministers, and suspended its reciprocal trade agreement with Czechoslovakia. Roosevelt enabled a French military mission to purchase American planes, an event that proved embarrassing on January 23, 1939, when a French military observer crashed in a new Douglas twin-engine bomber outside of Los Angeles. Late that month the president told the Senate Military Affairs Committee that Germany, Italy, and Japan were working together to seek world domination. Hence America's line of defense rested in part on "the continued independence" of countries from Finland to Turkey. (When his critics quote him as saying that "the frontiers of the United States are on the Rhine," he called the leak "a deliberate lie.") On April 15, 1939, the president made his "Saturday surprise" appeal to Hitler and Mussolini, requesting that the two dictators pledge not to attack any of thirty-one specified European and Near Eastern countries for ten years, He also promised to support international conferences on trade and disarmament.

Roosevelt did not expect favorable responses from the Axis capitals, and he received none. Indeed, the appeal brought only scorn. Leading Nazi Hermann Goering told Mussolini that the president's proposal revealed "an incipient brain disease." Mussolini privately suggested that some malady, perhaps a creeping paralysis, had affected FDR; the Italian dictator announced his refusal to be guided by "Messiah-like messages." In a Reichstag address that delighted Nazi listeners, Hitler responded most sarcastically. The dictators had succeeded in portraying FDR as an ignorant and inept fool, and the more rabid anti-interventionists took furtive satisfaction in this foreign insolence. "He asked for it," said Senator Nye.

Meanwhile the president sought revision of the neutrality law. As the cash-and-carry provision of the 1937 Neutrality Act was due to expire on May 1, 1939, the administration wanted a new bill, one that would retain cash-and-carry while repealing the arms embargo. Secretary Hull claimed that the embargo "conferred gratuitous benefit on the probable aggressors." At the end of June the House, by a vote of

200 to 188, passed an amended bill that included cash-and-carry. It also added, however, an arms embargo introduced by Congressman John Vorys (Rep.-Ohio).

FDR hoped the Senate would be more amenable to his wishes. On July 18 senators of both parties gathered in the Oval Room of the White House for an evening conference with Roosevelt, Hull, and Vice-president John Nance Garner. After sandwiches and a display of the Rooseveltian charm, the gentlemen got down to business. The president explained that he wanted to be able to act if war broke out in Europe. Therefore he sought repeal of the arms embargo and placing all trade with the belligerents on a cash-and-carry basis. (Bans on loans and travel would be retained). Turning to Hull, he asked: "Cordell, what do you think about it?" While the secretary was reinforcing FDR's argument, Senator Borah interrupted: "I do not believe there is going to be any war in Europe, between now and the first of January or for some time thereafter." His temper rising, Hull spoke out: "I wish the Senator from Idaho would come down to the State Department and read the dispatches which come in from all over Europe from day to day and I am sure he would change his opinion." "I don't give a damn about your dispatches," Borah retorted, claiming that his private sources of information were more dependable than those of the State Department. (In fact, his sources consisted of an obscure left-wing mimeographed journal, *The Week*, published in London.) Tears came to Hull's eyes, and Garner finally turned to Roosevelt: "Well, Captain, we may as well face the facts. You haven't got the votes, and that's all there is to it." Because the Senate did not act, most of the 1937 law, including the arms embargo, remained in effect.

Hitler now set his eyes on Poland. The pretext for Hitler's latest war of nerves was the alleged inequities of the Versailles Treaty, which had carved the "Polish corridor" from German territory. It had also made the Baltic port of Danzig, whose population was overwhelmingly German, an international "free city." This time the British and French resolved to stand firm. On March 31, in the wake of Hitler's entry into Prague, Chamberlain gave an all-embracing guarantee to support Poland if Germany attempted to undermine its independence. The United States strongly welcomed the "blank check," Roosevelt believing it would have "a very great effect."

In the spring and summer of 1939, the decisive factor in the European equation increasingly became the Soviet Union. When leaders of Britain, France, and Poland hesitated to accept an alliance with the Russians, Josef Stalin turned to Hitler. The Soviet dictator warned the Russians "not to allow our country to have others pull the chestnuts out of the fire for them." Hitler, on his part, sought to avoid the mistake of both Napoleon and Kaiser Wilhelm I by steering clear of any conflict with Russia.

Negotiations proceeded, reaching a climax on August 23. On the surface, the so-called Nazi-Soviet Pact was simply a nonaggression agreement. A secret protocol, however, divided much of Eastern Europe as spheres of influence between the two powers. Poland was split, Hitler received Lithuania, and the Soviets gained Latvia, Estonia, and the Rumanian province of Bessarabia. Once Hitler heard that Stalin had agreed to a general settlement, he said confidentially, "I have the world in my pocket." Yet Stalin felt himself the real winner, similarly remarking of Hitler in private, "He thinks he's outsmarted me—but actually I have outsmarted him."

Following the agreement, Hitler completed preparations for his strike on Poland, and on September 1 commenced his attack. It was in the middle of the night when the news first broke in America, and possibly the first person in the country to be alerted was the president, roused at 2:50 A.M. by a telephone call from Ambassador Bullitt in Paris: "Mr. President, several German divisions are deep in Polish territory, . . . There are reports of bombers over the city of Warsaw." Roosevelt replied, "Then it's happened!"

Within hours nearly every American knew, for millions huddled around radio receivers to hear the bulletins. Later in the day, Roosevelt appealed to belligerents to renounce air attacks on civil populations. With few exceptions, Americans blamed Hitler and hoped that he would be defeated on the plains of Poland.

Two days later, after the dictator refused appeals to pull back, the British and French declared war. Within hours, Roosevelt gave one of his famous fireside chats: "I hope the United States will keep out of this war. I believe that it will. And I give you assurance and reassurance that every effort of your Government will be directed toward that end." But unlike President Wilson in August 1914, he did not request impartiality: "I cannot ask that every American remain neutral in thought. . . . Even a neutral has a right to take account of facts. Even a neutral cannot be asked to close his mind or his conscience." Meanwhile efforts were underway to repatriate several thousand Americans caught in Europe by the outbreak; the State Department had gone on a round-the-clock schedule, setting a system for monitoring broadcasts from Europe to speed news of military and diplomatic developments. Then on September 5, the president invoked the Neutrality Act, closing American arsenals to belligerents.

II

Even as he applied the arms embargo, Roosevelt hoped to repeal it, and with the outbreak of war in Europe, his cause took on new urgency. The president was about to launch a debate over intervention in the war that would last slightly over two years and would be among the most bitter in the history of the entire nation. No mere clash between action committees or reflecting a casual public opinion, the conflict centered on matters of life-or-death. As historian Gerhard L. Weinberg notes, the fate of the world lay "in the balance," and it is hardly surprising that Weinberg uses that very phrase to introduce one of his studies. Late in 1939, the *Saturday Evening Post* editorialized, "The decision we make may alter the history of the world for a thousand years." Rhetoric grew so harsh that the two sides ended up accusing each other of being actual traitors.

As Roosevelt was formulating his proposal, Polish armies scattered like sheep before German tanks; they clearly would be defeated before France and Britain could bring up forces. Whether Anglo-French arms could ever stop the Germans seemed questionable. Underscoring such doubt was a mid-September communication from Ambassador Joseph P. Kennedy in London: Chamberlain believed that unless he secured American munitions, England and France faced "sheer disaster."

Roosevelt composed his plans with care. He had to end the embargo while allaying fears that this step meant war. The result: a clever proposal designed to disarm anti-interventionists while opening arsenals to the Allies. On September 21, 1939, the president placed his neutrality package before a special session of Congress. According to FDR, the current legislation threatened peace. Why? Because existing law permitted American merchantmen to enter belligerent waters with nonmilitary cargoes and hence could not prevent the kind of "incident" most likely to involve America in war. American ships, he continued, must be banned from entering "danger zones." Furthermore, belligerents must pay cash for supplies secured in the United States and carry them away in foreign vessels. Privately FDR told aides, "foreign orders mean prosperity in this country, and we can't elect the Democratic party unless we get prosperity." The president never mentioned that revision of the neutrality law would help Britain and France; rather, so he stressed, his scheme would keep America out of the conflict.

Roosevelt's charade fooled no one. He was clearly seeking a "horse trade"—repeal of the arms embargo as a swap for provisions to keep American ships out of war zones. Anti-interventionist members of Congress were not interested; they announced that they would resist "from hell to breakfast." In the words of Senator Borah, the demand for repeal had come from the "war hounds of Europe." The next step would be extension of credit, even outright gifts, and after that American armies would sail to Europe. Said one member of the House, "If a man doesn't take the first drink of liquor, he will never get intoxicated."

Moreover, so anti-interventionists feared, depression and inflation would invariably follow in the wake of any war boom. Once government credit fell, the administration would be forced to declare an emergency, one that would involve the seizing of factories and farms. In addition, cash-and-carry seemed immoral, involving profits from the tragedy of others. Terms were used like "unholy business," "blood money," "international sadism," and Roosevelt's own phrase of an earlier day—"fool's gold." One foe even found the sale of toothpicks dangerous: they were "merely celluloid in splinter form," and would therefore be put to military use.

The matter of international law was raised. A nation, said legal scholar Edwin M. Borchard of Yale, could not legally relax its neutrality in order to aid one belligerent. Congressman Hamilton Fish (Rep.-N.Y.), former All-American tackle for Harvard, compared FDR's proposal to "changing the rules after the kick-off."

But such criticism was not in harmony with national thinking. Roosevelt's proposal, with its blend of isolation and intervention, had caught a popular mood. Most Americans sought to stay out of war while helping the Allies. The legislative battle lasted four weeks minus one day; it comprised over a million words in the Senate alone. As a result of it all, Congress passed the administration measure by large margins, the Senate voting 63 to 30, the House 243 to 181. Sixty-two percent of those polled favored the measure. Freda Kirchwey, editor of the liberal weekly *The Nation,* commented aptly, "What a majority of the American people want is to be as unneutral as possible without getting into war."

Repeal of the arms embargo came too late to rescue Poland. German panzer divisions caught the Polish army in giant encircling maneuvers and by mid-September had sealed Poland's fate. On September 17, the Soviets began to claim their share of the recent deal with Hitler and invaded from the east. Eleven days later, Germany and Russia agreed to the partition of Poland.

Hitler looked westward. Seeking only minor territory in western Europe, he wanted British and French acknowledgment of his new eastern conquests. He hoped in vain. The governments in London and Paris were confident that the Germans could not breach the famous Maginot Line, a chain of fortifications between France and Germany of unprecedented size and design, and therefore rejected the dictator's overtures. The result was the pause that extended through the winter of 1939–40—the "phony war"—an appellation taken from Senator Borah's remark of October 1939 that "there is something phony about this war." Went one American limerick: "A elderly man with gout/ When asked what this war was about/ Replied with a sigh/ My colleagues and I/ Are doing our best to find out."

Roosevelt briefly toyed with the idea of mediation. In February 1940, he sent Sumner Welles to the various European capitals on a fact-finding mission, but the undersecretary of state soon found himself stymied. In forty-one days, Welles covered 1,400 miles, meeting every major leader but Hitler. As noted by Welles' biographer Irwin Gellman, the mission was "poorly conceived, planned, and prepared." Welles in turn exceeded his orders, naively believing that he could personally mediate the conflict and possessing a strangely high opinion of Mussolini, whom he called "a man of genius."

FDR could well have had several motives, among them the postponement of a German spring offensive and an effort to convince the American public he was doing all possible to broker a peace. Certainly, as historian Wayne S. Cole notes, even a failed mission strengthened the president's hand, for he would have appeared to have made efforts to negotiate a settlement. As historian Warren F. Kimball ably argues, however, any chances of Adolf Hitler backing any compromise made by FDR would have been slim indeed.

Ironically the Allies asked for few American supplies, being particularly parsimonious concerning aircraft orders. The standstill in fighting and the belief that the conflict could last three years, they believed, gave them sufficient time to produce their own arms. So did the desire to protect their own gold and dollar reserves. The American neutrality laws prohibited them from raising any private or governmental loans in the U.S. Believing most incorrectly that the German economy was overextended, Chamberlain banked on an internal collapse, followed by negotiations with a non-Nazi regime. As Kimball notes, the Roosevelt administration assumed that Hitler would get so bogged down on the European continent that British naval strength would remain able to quarantine Germany.

In the meantime, Roosevelt pushed measures for hemispheric defense. Early in October 1939, the inter-American foreign ministers, acting under U.S. prompting, drafted the Declaration of Panama, proclaiming a "security belt" reaching several hundred miles from the shores of the neutral American republics. Almost immediately the measure proved unenforceable. Towards the end of 1940, FDR accepted Hull's proposal for a more flexible zone, which was privately honored by all belligerents.

In July 1940 another such meeting of foreign ministers was convened in Cuba. Here the delegates, led by Secretary Hull, unanimously declared an attack on one as an attack on all. In case of a threatened strike, any American republic could move unilaterally in seizing any European colony in the hemisphere. The assemblage signed the Act of Havana, which provided for an Inter-American Commission for Territorial Concessions in the New World. The new body would assume temporary control of any European possessions facing transfer to another sovereignty.

Within the year the U.S. sought to cover its flank south of the border. It came to terms with Mexico, which had expropriated the property of all foreign oil companies in 1938. British nationals owned 70 percent of the industry, but U.S. citizens controlled most of the remaining fields. To the Roosevelt administration, acutely sensitive to Axis penetration, hemispheric solidarity could not be put at risk in order to protect the massive profits of major petroleum firms. Once Mexico agreed to pay for the seized properties, the U.S. extended a $30 million loan, stabilized the dollar-peso ratio, pledged to purchase newly minted Mexican silver, and promised to finance Mexico's portion of the Pan American highway.

On October 11, 1939, the Soviet Union proposed moving the Soviet-Finnish border northward, twenty-five miles up the Karelian Isthmus into Finland, so as to take it well out of artillery range of Leningrad. It also proposed to take the Rybachi peninsula, which commanded the approaches to Murmansk, and to lease Hangö harbor, which lay at the entrance to the Gulf of Finland. In return, it offered territory along the central portion of the Russian-Finnish frontier.

When, on November 30, Finland refused, the Russians invaded. Roosevelt strongly condemned the Soviets, released forty-four pursuit planes, and granted $10 million in nonmilitary credits. Although the American people cheered the Finns on, the government in Washington knew that they were fighting a lost cause. After long debate, Congress appropriated the paltry sum of $20 million and limited its use to agricultural and other civilian supplies. Hence the Finns could not obtain what they really needed, U.S. arms.

The administration calculated that the alliance between Hitler and Stalin was shaky, and it looked to the day when the Russians, as Hull later recalled, "would come over to the side of the Allies." Roosevelt also proclaimed a "moral embargo" on aircraft sales and ordered the Treasury to block Soviet purchases of selected raw materials. But seeking to avoid a permanent break with the Soviets, he did not close the door completely. For several months, the Finns fought ably against far greater numbers of Russians, but on March 12, 1940, they were forced to sign a surrender. Finland retained its independence, but ceded strategic parts of its territory, rich forest preserves, 10 percent of its arable land, and 625 miles of railroad.

A month later, on the dawn of April 9, the Germans invaded Denmark and Norway. On May 10, Germany turned southward to the Netherlands, Belgium, Luxembourg, and the main prize: France. When Hitler launched his French offensive, it appeared that he was following the same route as the Kaiser's armies in 1914. While everyone focused on the German "right wing," the dictator sent his main force crashing through the Ardennes Forest. Within a fortnight, German arms had shattered French defenses and were sweeping behind the Maginot Line toward Paris. Hitler was about to accomplish in a few weeks what the Kaiser had been unable to do in four years of the First World War. In those terrible spring days only one event was reassuring: in late May, about 340,000 British soldiers were evacuated from the beaches of Dunkirk, a move that saved a seasoned fighting force.

As Allied armies fell back, the new French premier, Paul Reynaud, appealed in vain to America for a declaration of war against Germany. Unfortunately for France, the United States could contribute little other than its productive capacity, something already at the Allies' disposal. Lack of planes, guns, and ammunition ruled out substantial shipments. The most the U.S. could do was to urge Italy to stay out of the war. Mussolini attacked southern France, provoking Roosevelt's famous utterance that "on this tenth day of June 1940, the hand that held the dagger has struck it into the back of its neighbor." All was over on June 22, when the French leaders surrendered in the same railway carriage in which the Germans had signed the armistice of November 11, 1918.

According to the surrender terms, three-fifths of France was to be directly occupied by German troops. The rest of France, the southern inland region, was to remain unoccupied and under French administration. After much soul-searching, the Roosevelt administration established diplomatic relations with the Vichy government, an authoritarian and collaborationist regime, doing so in the hopes that a U.S. diplomatic presence could minimize Nazi influence, keep Vichy from declaring war on Britain, and prevent French naval and colonial assets from passing onto Hitler .

Now with the fall of France imminent, America suddenly felt defenseless. *Time* noted, "To many a U.S. citizen, the screaming headlines of the German smash through Belgium and down into France came like an unremitting seven-day Orson Welles broadcast of an invasion from Mars." In the town of Jeannette, Pennsylvania, a gun club got ready to shoot any Nazi parachutists descending from the skies. In Manhattan and Seattle, two men killed themselves.

The ensuing three months witnessed America's first, halting response to Hitler's domination of Europe. The U.S. regular army consisted of 245,000 men, a tally that put it twentieth in the world, in fact just behind Switzerland. In any real crisis, only five divisions could be available. In addition, the president had not appointed the most able figures to crucial defense slots. Harry Woodring, secretary of the army when war broke out in Europe, was a former Kansas governor who fought bitterly with undersecretary Louis Johnson. His counterpart in the Navy Department, Charles Edison, had served in various New Deal bureaucracies; he was told his position was only temporary.

Just as France was falling, two staunch conservatives, Senator Edward R. Burke (Dem.-Nebr.) and Representative James S. Wadsworth (Rep.-N.Y.) introduced a bill calling for America's first peacetime draft. Roosevelt feared domestic repercussions, for 1940 was an election year. He had therefore hoped that the bill would pass without his unqualified endorsement. To General George C. Marshall, army chief of staff, there was no other conceivable way to secure "trained, seasoned men in adequate numbers." Marshall went on: "You cannot get a sufficiently trained force of all kinds at the front, in the navy yards and the arsenals, transportation supply system, and munitions output just by passing an Act of Congress when war breaks out, and you cannot get it by the mere volunteer system."

Anti-interventionists questioned Marshall's assumptions. So far, they said, the volunteer system had worked and worked well. Every army quota had been filled, and in June and July 1940, quotas had been met in advance. Furthermore, so reasoned the foes of the draft, the recent Nazi victories proved that mass conscript armies were simply outmoded. The fate of Belgium, Holland, and France showed the effectiveness of small, well-trained units. Anti-interventionists also found the Burke-Wadsworth program leading to militarism, exploitation of conscripts, and the death of civil liberties. Said Senator Burton K. Wheeler (Dem.-Mont.), "If you pass this bill, you slit the throat of the last democracy still living; you accord to Hitler his greatest and cheapest victory to date."

Where, asked the anti-interventionists, was the danger to America? The United States had the largest navy in the world, indeed one seven times the strength of Germany's, and an air force expanding at the potential rate of 8,000 planes a week. The weekly Jesuit magazine *America* offered an analogy: "It is a good deal like calling out the militia in California when the wild beast is somewhere in the neighborhood of the circus quarters at Bridgeport, Conn." Even if Hitler captured the British fleet, he would be unable to gain naval and air bases in the Western Hemisphere, destroy the U.S. Navy and Air Force, cripple coastal defenses, land an expeditionary force, and wipe out the American army. Would "a murderous marauder, baffled by the English Channel, . . . find the Atlantic Ocean a duck pond?"

But by September 8, both houses of Congress, backed by public opinion polls, had passed the bill by close to a two-to-one margin. All males between the ages of 21 and 36, totaling some 16.5 million, were required to register. Those inducted would serve in the armed forces for twelve months, then enter the reserves, although they could not be sent outside the United States and its territories. General Marshall was now authorized to call upon 900,000 men annually. His biographer, Forrest C. Pogue, notes that the bill, by providing a pool of 16.5 million men, "made possible the huge United States army and air force that fought World War II." Without this trained manpower, argues Pogue, American forces could not have taken the offensive in North Africa and in the Pacific in 1942, and hence the entire outcome of the war might have been different. At the outset, however, establishing a mass army was not easy. Many draftees had to use broomsticks for rifles, wooden sawhorses for machine guns.

Several weeks before the collapse of France, Roosevelt had directed the State Department to seek legal ways of supplying Britain with guns, ammunition, and planes from stock belonging to the U.S. government. The recent neutrality legislation coincided with international law: private agents could sell munitions to a belligerent, but the government itself could not. The solution was to sell government-owned armaments to private interests for resale to the British. After making sure that Congress would make no major objection, Roosevelt threw open the government's arsenals, and within weeks guns and planes began to arrive in Atlantic ports for shipment to Britain. On June 10, 1940, in a speech at Charlottesville, Virginia, he advised the country of his intentions, saying that "we will extend to the opponents of force the material resources of this nation." With those words, the president abandoned all pretense of neutrality.

Also in June, Roosevelt sought to give his foreign policy a bipartisan flavor by bringing two prominent Republicans into his cabinet, Henry L. Stimson as secretary of war and Frank Knox as secretary of the navy; Stimson had not only been Hoover's secretary of state but two decades earlier had served William Howard Taft as secretary of war. Knox, ex Rough Rider and publisher of the *Chicago Daily News,* had been the Republican vice-presidential candidate just four years previously. Stimson and Knox were strong interventionists: the seventy-two-year-old Stimson favored compulsory military training and U.S. naval convoys to Britain; the sixty-six-year-old Knox sought an army of a million men, the largest air force in the world, and prompt shipment of the latest planes to Britain.

III

Meanwhile Hitler was experiencing frustration. Relations with the Soviet Union had become troubled, causing the Nazis to fear for their eastern flank, and the British were giving no sign that they accepted defeat. "Operation Sea Lion," the invasion of the British Isles, had run into delay, chiefly because the Royal Air Force was denying the Germans mastery of English skies. In August 1940, to eliminate British air power, the Germans launched massive air strikes against British airfields and planes. After a few weeks, however, the *Luftwaffe* became so discouraged by losses that it changed tactics. The Germans turned their bombing planes on Britain's cities, hoping to bring the British to terms by terrorizing the civil population. Night after night through the autumn, warning sirens howled, people scurried to shelters, searchlights pierced the darkness. Then came the din of airplane motors, antiaircraft guns, and exploding bombs. When the bombers left, there was the task of putting out fires and digging through the rubble for victims. But the morale of Britain's people did not crack.

On May 10, 1940, Winston Spencer Churchill, who been appointed first lord of the admiralty the previous September, replaced Chamberlain as prime minister. Only now are we beginning to learn vital details concerning the complicated Roosevelt-Churchill relationship. We are finding, for example, that Churchill had long been suspicious of American ambitions. Certainly he had never been a close friend of FDR's. Though the two men had met briefly in 1918, when FDR was assistant secretary of the navy, Churchill later confessed that he did not recall the encounter. Moreover, he had never been an ardent social reformer and was strongly critical of the New Deal.

At first, Washington was suspicious about Britain's chances for survival, estimating them to be about one in three. Roosevelt initially doubted the sobriety and judgment of the hard-drinking prime minister, and feared that he might surrender the British fleet to Germany. (Indeed, Churchill did toy with the idea of a negotiated peace, though he first wanted to show Hitler that Britain could not be beaten.)

As the Battle of Britain began, Roosevelt was wrestling with a major British request. On May 15, the day after the Germans had pierced French defenses near Sedan, the prime minister sent FDR a gloomy message. "The scene," he said, "has darkened swiftly. . . the small countries are simply smashed up, one by one, like matchwood." He requested several hundred modern aircraft; antiaircraft guns, ammunition, and steel; and efforts to "keep that Japanese dog quiet in the Pacific, using Singapore in any way convenient." He also wanted the United States to lend part of its destroyer fleet to the Royal Navy.

The American military strongly opposed any such transfer. On June 22, army Chief of Staff George C. Marshall and Chief of Naval Operations Harold R. Stark asked FDR to ban further arms sales to Britain. Major General Walter Bedell Smith commented in June, "If we are required to mobilize after having released guns [to Britain] . . . and were found to be short in artillery material . . . everyone who was a party to the deal might hope to be found hanging from a lamp post." Congress cooperated to the extent of prohibiting sales of American equipment unless Marshall and Stark declared it was "not essential for U.S. defense."

The leading interventionist group, the Committee to Defend America by Aiding the Allies (CDAAA), claimed that Britain had begun the war with 176 destroyers but had only 70 left. Yet, it continued, Britain had a huge task: deterring invasion of its own isles, providing for the defense of Gibraltar, preventing Axis shipping from leaving continental Europe and the Mediterranean, and protecting convoys on which imports and exports depended. By contrast, the United States had 240 destroyers in commission and another 57 under construction. Britain maintained that even World War I holdovers could be fitted with modern sound-detection devices, radar, and late model antiaircraft guns, measures that could thereby convert these rusty old vessels into effective U-boat hunters. On June 15, Churchill called Britain's need for destroyers "a matter of life or death."

Roosevelt wanted to answer Churchill's appeal, but delayed any response to the prime minister for six weeks. Significant questions remained. Even with the destroyers, could England survive? In view of America's defense needs, were the ships expendable? What would happen to the vessels if Hitler managed to defeat Britain? Was there legal basis for a transfer? Would it provoke the anti-interventionists? A presidential election was only a few months away: what would be the political consequences? Would transfer of destroyers cause Germany to declare war against the United States?

One by one the questions received answers. By its effective resistance during June, England appeared able to survive the winter. U.S. military chiefs reported that the country could spare fifty destroyers, and the British pledged that in the "impossible contingency" of Germany overrunning the British Isles, the ships would not go to Hitler. Roosevelt's attorney general assured him that any transaction would be legal.

Supporters of Britain noted that the London and Washington governments had already discussed something even such anti-interventionists as the *Chicago Tribune* had long wanted: the possibility of American bases on British territory in the Western Hemisphere.

Why not exchange the destroyers for bases? For years, anti-interventionists had "demanded" hemispheric bases as a price for canceling the "war debts" of 1917–19. In June 1939 FDR himself had negotiated, though never implemented, a general agreement for such bases. In regard to the election, Roosevelt sought to offset the effect of a destroyer transfer by urging the Republican presidential candidate Wendell L. Willkie to announce his support. Willkie agreed to keep a destroyer-bases transaction out of the campaign but declined to support the move publicly. Roosevelt, confident that Hitler sought to avoid any clash, pressed on with the negotiations. In early August, a Gallup poll showed 60 percent favoring the destroyer transfer.

The president faced a final problem. Should he seek consent of Congress? Failure to do so would offend congressional sensibilities and bring charges of dictatorial action. Such a debate, however, would give anti-interventionists a forum, possibly leading to repudiation of the deal. In any event, the entire process would be long and drawn-out, and the British could ill afford to wait for the ships. The president decided to arrange for the transfer by executive order.

Negotiations ended on September 2, 1940, when Secretary Hull and the British ambassador signed papers for the transfer of fifty destroyers of World War I vintage. At the same time, the British leased locations for American bases scattered over 4,000 miles of ocean; they included the Bahamas, Jamaica, St. Lucia, Antigua, Trinidad, and British Guiana. Sites in Bermuda and Argentia, Newfoundland, were outright gifts. For political reasons, Roosevelt had needed a quid pro quo.

On the next day, Admiral Stark certified that possession of the bases rendered the destroyers unimportant to America's defense, whereupon the ships, described by Churchill as "more precious than rubies," steamed out of American ports. Viewing the trade of fifty old "four-stackers" for a string of bases as a sharp bargain, most Americans applauded. To calm Roosevelt's anxieties, the British government made a public statement, one pledging that if the British Isles fell, the Royal Navy would neither sink its own ships nor surrender to the Germans.

Roosevelt's foes harped on one issue: the president, they said, had acted high-handedly in failing to clear the transaction with Congress. Even the interventionist Willkie assailed the transfer by executive order as "the most dictatorial action ever taken by any President." FDR himself briefly feared impeachment over the matter.

The ships themselves were less than perfect. Any destroyer twenty-two years old, especially if mass produced and long out of commission, suffered from ailments similar to those of an auto of that age. Hull plating and piping systems leaked, boiler tubes gave out, and electrical systems and gunfire control circuits were defective. One British admiral later commented, "I thought they were the worst destroyers I had ever seen, poor seaboats with appalling armament and accommodation. The price paid for them was scandalous."

Yet if tactically the ships were of the lowest order and unsuited to the Atlantic weather, another admiral noted that "their mere presence threshing about in the water around the convoy afforded some sort of deterrent against the U-boat." They saw heavy action, and as the Director of Anti-Submarine Warfare in the Admiralty remarked, "Taken by and large, they gave invaluable service at a time of desperate need."

Two historians have borne the director out. Wrote diplomatic specialist Thomas A. Bailey and naval expert Paul B. Ryan, who himself served on a cruiser in the Atlantic in 1940, "The deteriorating four-stackers certainly did something to provide the difference between victory and defeat for Hitler on the high seas—and hence on the land." Kimball finds the arrangement "a good deal for America in every sense of the term." The nation's security was enhanced, Britain's ability to resist a common threat was strengthened, and by besting their long-standing rival and colonial progenitor, "Americans could grin a bit."

Offering a different focus, writer Robert Shogan claims no one can accurately measure the deal's contribution to Allied victory; the secrecy surrounding the negotiations, however, served as a destructive precedent for such surreptitious commitments as the Vietnam War and the Iran-Contra scandal. Kimball in turn responds that premature public debate would have almost certainly brought the wrong answer—as far as FDR, Britain, and history itself are all concerned. Not only does "sheer practicality place foreign policy primarily with the executive branch," but Congress itself felt no overwhelming pressure to restrain presidential actions or change American policy. Certainly no one in Congress introduced legislation to nullify the deal and no private citizen filed charges against the president or his cabinet for violating the law. To FDR's own surprise, public opinion—as created and expressed in polls, print, and radio—supported the arrangement, as did the bulk of White House mail.

Not until March 1941, after protracted and sometimes bitter bargaining, were the precise sites and terms for the base leases settled. The United States found Argentia a priceless base for naval and air patrols protecting transatlantic convoys from German subs, and American installations in Bermuda played a similar if less crucial role. Roosevelt might have exaggerated the importance of the ships and Churchill oversold the significance of the bases, but the diplomatic results were important. The deal marked the abandonment of any pretense of neutrality. It was an act of war, for this time the United States did not even defer subtly to international law by first selling the ships to private agents.

Despite Roosevelt's departure from neutrality, it seemed that foreign policy would not be a campaign issue in 1940. During their national conventions both Democrats and Republicans had adopted almost identical platform resolutions on the subject, and the candidates Willkie and Roosevelt differed little on the entire matter. When, late in October, opinion polls showed FDR leading, Republican leaders persuaded Willkie to accuse the president of taking the country to war. Especially in view of his own interventionist leanings, the charges were contemptible. Willkie later confessed that "in moments of oratory in campaigns we all expand a little bit." But it was clear that the GOP candidate had struck a responsive chord.

Roosevelt countered with equally deplorable tactics, identifying Willkie with such Republican anti-interventionists as Representatives Joseph W. Martin, Jr., of Massachusetts, Hamilton Fish of New York, and Bruce Barton of New York. Playful repetition of the catchy phrase "Martin, Barton and Fish" brought roars of laughter from Democratic audiences, but it did little to reassure anxious mothers and fathers. So Roosevelt declared in a speech at Boston, "I have said this before, but I shall say it again and again: Your boys are not going to be sent into any foreign wars." When advisors suggested adding the words "except in case of attack," the president replied that "if somebody attacks us, then it isn't a foreign war." The statement served the immediate purpose, and Roosevelt won the election. The war issue could well have made a difference, for polls showed that had it not been for the global conflict, voters claimed to have preferred Willkie.

Roosevelt scholar Warren F. Kimball writes, "Clearly Roosevelt did not take the public into his confidence during the election campaign of 1940. He avoided and evaded answering awkward questions about how the United States could be neutral and still provide naval war vessels and war supplies to one of the belligerents." At the same time, Americans did not want to make unpleasant choices and, in a sense, "wanted to be lied to."

IV

By the fall of 1940, more general lines in the great foreign policy debate were being drawn. In themes echoed by such groups as the Committee to Defend America by Aiding the Allies and the Fight for Freedom Committee, Roosevelt repeatedly gave his reasons for aiding the Allies. In his "fireside chat" of December 29, 1940, the president claimed that "the Nazi masters of Germany" had made it clear that they sought "to enslave the whole of Europe, and then to use the resources of Europe to dominate the rest of the world." If Britain were defeated, "the Axis powers will control the continents of Europe, Asia, Africa, Australasia, and the high seas—and they will be in a position to bring enormous military and naval resources against this hemisphere." The Americas, he went on, "would be living at the point of a gun." The distance from Dakar, Africa, to Brazil was "less than from Washington to Denver, Colorado." Furthermore, at the northernmost end of the Pacific Ocean, America and Asia "almost touch each other." In addition, the flying range of bombers was drastically increasing, and planes already existed that could fly round-trip between the British Isles and New England without refueling.

In the president's eyes, the Axis threat was not purely military. Speaking to the Pan-American Union on May 27, 1941, Roosevelt claimed that a victorious Germany would pose a major economic challenge. By exploiting "slave labor in the rest of the world," Hitler would be able to undersell American goods everywhere. In order to survive, Roosevelt said, the United States would have to restructure its economy radically. Pointing to economic autarchy, loss of markets, and the elimination of collective bargaining, the president warned, "The whole fabric of working life as we know it—business; manufacturing, mining, agriculture—all would be mangled and crippled under such a system."

Interventionist columnist Dorothy Thompson concurred. She predicted that a German victory would create "the largest free trade area and the largest planned economy in the world," while the United States would be relegated to the role of an economic colony. In 1941, Douglas Miller, former American economic attaché in Berlin, wrote an entire book on the matter. Its title: *You Can't Do Business with Hitler.*

Roosevelt did not neglect matters of ideology. In December 1940, he noted that Hitler himself had denied any possibility of ultimate peace between Germany's political philosophy and that of the West. The following September FDR called Germany "an enemy of all law, all liberty, all morality, all religion."

The anti-interventionists were quick to respond. Even were the Germans and Japanese able to dominate Europe and East Asia, they maintained, the United States still could survive. They opposed a mass army, claiming that a new American Expeditionary Force would simply prolong the struggle overseas, work against needed negotiation between England and Germany, and ensure Soviet domination of Europe. Genuine defense, they argued, involved the strengthening of hemispheric deterrents, not the "dissipating" of armaments by sending them overseas. Far better to rely upon small highly trained mechanized forces, fighter planes, and a two-ocean navy. Air power was crucial, for the skies must be made untenable for any nation that dared to cross the oceans. In the words of Major Al Williams, a popular syndicated columnist, "The nation that rules by air will rule the world."

Furthermore, so critics claimed, the U. S. economy could survive quite well. According to the research division of the America First Committee, the leading anti-interventionist organization, a ravaged Europe would need so much food that Germany would simply be unable to exclude American trade. In fact, without American raw materials, European industries would be crippled.

General Hugh Johnson found the United States's unmatched industrial plant, raw materials, and gold supply giving it the commanding commercial position.

While most anti-interventionists did not question the brutalities of Nazism, many doubted if the Allied cause was that of democracy. Aviator Charles A. Lindbergh went so far as to say that "this is simply one more of those age old quarrels within our own family of nations." They also pointed to a long, and in their eyes sordid, record of British and French imperialism. Furthermore, so the opposition argued, any American effort to protect democracy abroad could mean its loss at home. Former President Hoover warned that during World War I, the U.S. became an effective dictatorship, with the government not only suppressing "much freedom of speech and the press," but telling the people "what to eat and what to wear."

How does the historian evaluate such claims? Any appraisal of America's policy depends upon whether one agrees with Roosevelt's fundamental premise, namely that Hitlerism menaced the United States and the principles on which it was founded, and that therefore it was in the national interest to engage in all-out support of Nazism's opponents, even at the risk of war.

By the 1960s, most historians found that by 1940 Germany had indeed been "a clear and present danger." Writing in 1967, Alton Frye documented Hitler's hostility to the United States, his plans for enlarging German influence in South America, and Nazi subversion throughout the entire Western Hemisphere. Furthermore, said Frye, had Germany conquered Russia and captured the British fleet, the United States would have been in serious jeopardy.

In 1976 Holger H. Herwig found the German dictator building a "Super Germany," stretching from the Atlantic to the Urals and supplied with raw materials from colonies in Central Africa. In the next generation, says Herwig, Germany would fight the United States from its advanced Atlantic bases. In 1994 Gerhard L. Weinberg, claimed that Hitler long assumed he would have to fight the U.S. and had begun preparations toward that end in both naval and aircraft construction.

Yet at least one scholar downplays any German threat. Political scientist Bruce M. Russett denies that Germany, or Japan for that matter, ever threatened American security. By the end of 1941,

American lend-lease aid and naval convoys assured Britain's survival, and Germany was totally bogged down on the Russian steppes. Hitler might rave of ultimately fighting the United States, but he lacked the capacity to wage such a war successfully.

Moreover, claims Russett, moral issues were not clear-cut. In June 1941, the United States became allied to Stalin, who had starved millions of kulaks and who, like Hitler, ruled by terror. Stalin's communist ideology had far more worldwide appeal than National Socialism, making it in some ways far more dangerous. Russett writes, "German 'medical experiments' and extermination camps were unknown to the world in 1941. Though the Hitler regime had anything but a savory reputation then, the moral argument too is essentially made in hindsight, not a primary motivation at the time war was declared." During the war, he continues, opportunities to bargain with the Nazis over Jewish lives were ignored. To argue that the horrors of Nazism were great enough to warrant U.S. intervention is perfectly reasonable, says Russett, first provided that *"one states it clearly"* (emphasis his) and second that one does not confuse a moral basis with an objective threat to American national security.

Yet Russett speaks for a decided minority, for historians largely agree on the gravity of the Nazi threat. Even in late 1941, so Russett's critics argue, it was far from certain whether Britain and Russia could survive without full-scale American entry. Moreover, one could claim that Russett sought a "miniwar," as he thought that American aid to Britain could have continued without full-scale troop commitments.

V

Despite Hitler's inability to mount an invasion of Britain, the summer and early autumn of 1940 saw the Axis star continuing to rise. In July, awed by the conquest of France, Hungary joined forces with Hitler. Independent Rumania expired peaceably in October, carved up by the Soviets and the Nazis. In mid-September Mussolini had carried the war to North Africa, moving Italian divisions against the British in Egypt. Two weeks later the alliance added a new partner, Japan, whose representatives met in Berlin with leaders of Germany and Italy and signed the Tripartite Pact.

Then the alliance began to lose some of its luster. In October 1940, Mussolini ordered his armies into Greece. The Greeks successfully counterattacked, and within one month the Italian invasion of Egypt ran out of steam. In December 1940, a British counterstroke sent the Italians flying back into Libya.

Hitler too was having trouble. Spain, fearing Allied reprisal, continued to resist alliance with the Axis. Even more important, Britain refused to collapse under merciless air attack. At the end of 1940, when it became clear that his bombers were not winning the Battle of Britain, Hitler turned his attention to England's oceanic lifeline, hoping that his U-boats might starve the British into submission.

As 1941 drew near, German submarines were not the only threat to Britain's survival; equally serious, British dollar reserves were running low, a situation that threatened its capacity to purchase supplies in the United States. When this problem had arisen in the First World War, help had come from American bankers and, after April 1917, from the government itself. This time, however, there were legal barriers to such transactions—the neutrality law's ban on loans to belligerents and the Johnson Act's prohibition of loans to countries that had defaulted on World War I debts to the American government.

On December 7, 1940, while on a Caribbean cruise, Roosevelt received an urgent communication from Churchill warning that Britain was in desperate shape. Unless America came to its rescue, it could well go under. On returning to the capital, the president sought a way to meet the problem. In the end, in what Secretary of the Treasury Henry Morgenthau, Jr., described as one of his "brilliant flashes," FDR divined a solution. Recalling that the United States had arranged to lend cargo vessels to Britain with the stipulation that they be returned after the war, the president asked: why not extend "lend-lease" to guns, tanks, and planes?

To outline his plan, Roosevelt, tanned and jaunty after a post-election cruise, held one of his most memorable press conferences. On December 17, after furtively disclaiming "any particular news," he opened the session by announcing that Britain's survival was important to the defense of America. He ridiculed as "nonsense" the traditional methods of financing war, based on "the silly, foolish old dollar sign," and proposed that the United States lend armaments to Britain.

Then came the parable of the garden hose: "Suppose my neighbor's home catches fire, and I have a length of garden hose four or five hundred feet away. If he can take my garden hose and connect it up with his hydrant, I may help him to put out the fire. Now what do I do? I don't say to him before that operation, 'Neighbor, my garden hose cost me fifteen dollars; you have to pay me fifteen dollars for it.' No! What is the transaction that goes on? I don't want fifteen dollars—I want my garden hose after the fire is over." With that homey analogy, Roosevelt's speech writer Robert E. Sherwood later wrote, "Roosevelt won the fight for Lend Lease." When asked if his scheme "takes us any more into the war than we are," he snapped, "No, not a bit."

The president's victory was not immediately apparent. Speaking to a national radio audience on December 29, he denied that lend-lease would push the United States toward war. To the contrary, helping Britain was the best way to defend the Western Hemisphere. "We must," he said, "be the great arsenal of democracy."

The lend-lease bill was deliberately numbered H.R. 1776 and, at the suggestion of Justice Felix Frankfurter, was titled "An Act to Further Promote the Defense of the United States." Its scope was sweeping. It authorized the president to provide military articles and information to any country "whose defense the President deems vital to the defense of the United States." Terms for transfer were left completely to the president's discretion. If the president so desired, the terms "defense article" and "defense information" could permit virtually anything to fall under one of the two categories. As *Newsweek* noted, Roosevelt would be given permission to lend "anything from a trench shovel to a battle ship."

Some anti-interventionists responded sourly. Senator Robert A. Taft (Rep.-Ohio) observed that "lending war equipment is a good deal like lending chewing gum. You don't want it back." Senator Wheeler compared lend-lease with the Agricultural Adjustment Administration's cotton "plow-up" of 1933: it was, said the Montana senator, "the New Deal's triple-A foreign policy; it will plough under every fourth American boy." Wheeler's remark prompted the only presidential retort in the entire debate: Roosevelt called the attack "the rottenest thing that has been said in public life in my generation," adding "Quote me on that."

*Above: President Herbert Hoover,
1928. In dealing with the Great
Depression, his administration was
immersed in domestic affairs, not
the worsening situation in Asia.*
Library of Congress, #LC-USZ62-
24155 DLC

*Right: An earlier photo of Senator
William Borah. Clashing with FDR,
he said, "I do not believe there is
going to be any war in Europe,
between now and the first of
January or for some time
thereafter."* Library of Congress,
#LC-USZ62-111352 DLC

Right: General George C. Marshall, army chief of staff, was in favor of a draft in 1940. To him, there was no other conceivable way to secure "trained, seasoned men in adequate numbers." "You cannot get a sufficiently trained force . . . just by passing an Act of Congress when war breaks out. . . ." Anti-interventionists questioned Marshall's assumptions. Shown here in later years, he was to become Truman's secretary of state. Library of Congress, #Rh-1261

Cordell Hull shown with Sumner Welles arriving for a conference with FDR. Hull supported FDR's cash and carry scheme. Before war broke out in Europe FDR's foreign policy advisor Welles traveled there to assess the situation.
© CORBIS

Top: FDR gives a fireside chat in Washington, D.C. Courtesy of the FDR Library

Bottom: FDR with Winston Churchill at the Atlantic Conference, 1941. Courtesy of the
FDR Library

Neville Chamberlain, shown here on June 6, 1937. In 1938, as Britain's prime minister, he tried to avoid a war with Germany by agreeing to cede parts of Czechoslovaki and the Sudentenland to Hitler's need for lebensraum. AP/Wide World Photos.

The fascist partners Mussolini and Hitler on parade during Il Duce's visit to Germany in 1937. In the 1930s, the National Socialist leader, Adolf Hitler, had become Germany's chancellor. Hitler wanted to reassert German power in the world, recover "lost" territories, and expand his nation's borders to provide living space. The Italian Mussolini also had thoughts of expansion. Austrian National Library.

Top: General Tojo Hideki, a short man whose quick intelligence gave him the nickname of "Razor Brain." He became Japan's prime minister in October 1941. AP/Wide World Photos.

Bottom: Admiral Yamamoto Isoruku mused, "Under present conditions I think war is inevitable. If it comes, I believe there would be nothing for me to do but attack Pearl Harbor at the outset, thus tipping the balance of power in our favor." The architect of the attack on Pearl Harbor, Yamamoto first broached this scheme in the spring of 1940. Shown here on December 12, 1941, shortly after the attack on Pearl Harbor. AP/Wide World Photos.

In June 1940, Roosevelt sought to give his foreign policy a bipartisan flavor by bringing [a] prominent Republican . . . into his cabinet—Henry L. Stimson (center)—as secretary of war. Stimson had not only been Hoover's secretary of state but two decades earlier had served William Howard Taft as secretary of war. Stimson was a strong interventionist. Here Secretary Henry L. Stimson is shown at the Lend-Lease Hearings in 1943. Library of Congress, #LC-USE6-D009156

Below: In Asia, the Japanese undermined China's Jiang Jieshi's (Chiang Kai-shek's) authority. America desired to bolster Chinese resistance. Jiang Jieshi is shown here in 1943 with Roosevelt and Winston Churchill. Courtesy of the FDR Library

Two captured Japanese photos. Top: Aerial view taken during the attack on Pearl Harbor. National Archives, War and Conflict #1133. *Bottom: Aboard a Japanese carrier before the attack on Pearl, Dec. 7, 1941.* National Archives, War and Conflict #1132.

Images of Pearl Harbor. Top: The wrecked USS Downes *and* USS Cassin. National Achives, NWDNS-80-G-9943. *Below: A damaged airfield.* Courtesy of the FDR Library. *Opposite top: Damaged warships.* National Achives, NWL-128-PHEX-8. *Opposite bottom:* USS Arizona. Courtesy of the FDR Library.

Top: The Purple Decoding Machine. By the fall of 1940, American cryptographers had cracked the Purple Cipher, Japan's highest diplomatic code. The new intelligence informed leaders in Washington of Japanese designs to the south, but this knowledge did little to relieve the agony of deciding what America's response should be. National Archives, NWDNS-64-M-276.

Below: President Franklin Delano Roosevelt signs the declaration of war on Japan, December 1941. Library of Congress, #LC-USZ62-15185 DLC

Yet most anti-interventionists did not endorse cutting off all aid to Britain. Rather they preferred a straight loan, even an outright grant. General Robert E. Wood, national chairman of the America First Committee, suggested selling spare U.S. ships to Britain and providing long-term credits for food and war supplies. Herbert Hoover recommended an outright gift of whatever defense material the United States could spare as well as some $2 or $3 billion to buy other items.

Both the administration and the anti-interventionists, however, saw just what was always behind such alternatives. If the United States simply lent or gave money, its stake in the war would be relatively limited. If, on the other hand, the United States lent major military items, such as planes, its material interest in a British victory would be much greater. Ultimately it all came down to the single question: was the United States willing to see the matter through?

To some critics, the matter of presidential powers remained foremost. Anti-interventionist historian Charles A. Beard found the bill placing "all the wealth, and all the men and women of the United States, at the free disposal of the President." Others found it weakening American defenses. Even an obsolete plane, said Representative Fish, was "actually worth its weight in gold, to train man power for the air power we need so critically today." Other critics feared that the inevitable war boom would lead to the equally inevitable bust, that the bill was a flagrant act of war, and that the British had not yet spent billions of securities they held in the Western Hemisphere.

Yet, although congressional debate over H.R. 1776 was sharp, the measure clearly had the necessary support. The House vote was 317-71, the Senate tally 60-31, and the polls indicated popular approval. On March 11, 1941, the president signed the bill. From Britain, Churchill hailed the legislation as a "new Magna Carta," declaring that "the words and actions of the President and people of the United States come to us like a draught of life, and they tell us by an ocean-borne trumpet call that we are no longer alone."

Ironically, given the long debate surrounding the measure, for the rest of 1941 lend-lease was not as generous as has long been believed. For two years, Roosevelt had envisaged the European democracies as America's front line. Yet the supplies were no gift, as repayment was postponed, not waived. Later administration discussions revealed that a final settlement was not necessarily expected to be in money or even in kind. Instead it involved participation in a postwar world economy, one in which the British commercial system of Imperial Preference would be abolished, thereby giving American goods much easier access to many markets where England had been supreme. During the 1930s, the Imperial Preference system did not only encompass such Commonwealth nations as Canada and Australia but over twenty other countries in Europe and Latin America.

In 1941, lend-lease conferred little benefit upon Britain. Only as the war continued was the British Commonwealth given some $31 billion in supplies and the Soviet Union some $11 billion. Throughout 1941, lend-lease provided only 1 percent of Britain's munitions total. (Another 7 percent came from the United States under older contracts, for which the British paid in cash.)

The bill, however, did mark a significant turning point, Robert E. Sherwood was later reminded of the Webster's Dictionary definition of a common-law marriage: "An agreement between a man and a woman to enter into the marriage relation without ecclesiastical or civil ceremony, such agreement being provable by the writings, declarations, or conduct of the parties." By assuming responsibility for Britain's long-term purchases, Roosevelt relieved the British government of a costly and cumbersome burden while demonstrating his faith in its survival. With that irrevocable commitment, a genuine Anglo-American alliance was forged. The later extension of lend-lease to the Soviet Union was equally significant. Without lend-lease, claim historians Bailey and Ryan, "The Russians probably could not have beaten Hitler on their front, at least not as soon as they did."

One need not accept conspiratorial arguments to acknowledge that lend-lease took the country to the very edge of the European conflict. Having gambled on Britain's survival, the United States was not apt to stand by if an Axis victory appeared imminent. Historian Warren F. Kimball notes that today few can quarrel with the stated purpose of the bill. Yet, because it was obviously a step on the road to war, "one is still disturbed and even shocked by the lack of candor displayed by the Roosevelt administration during the evolution of its legislation."

In the very speech proposing lend-lease to Congress, delivered on January 6, Roosevelt looked toward a world founded upon "four essential freedoms," a series of aims that he found fundamental to any future peace. Presented in his State of the Union message also on January 6, the freedoms included "speech and expression"; the right of "every person to worship God in his own way"; "freedom from want," which he further defined as "economic understandings which will secure to every nation a healthy peacetime life for its inhabitants"; and "freedom from fear," based upon "a world-wide reduction of armaments." Such aims, he continued, could be realized "everywhere in the world . . . in our own time and generation." (In a press conference held in March he conceded "they may not be immediately attainable throughout the world.")

By early spring, Hitler had turned to the south and east. In April, Erwin Rommel (the "Desert Fox"), his new commander in North Africa, sent the British reeling toward the Egyptian border. That same month Hitler's armies crashed into the Balkans. Resistance was fierce, but in less than three weeks, the Nazi banner fluttered over Yugoslavia and Greece.

Then the dictator wheeled his forces around and, early in the morning of June 22, 1941, astonished the world by launching "Operation Barbarossa," the invasion of the Soviet Union. It was the greatest onslaught in the history of warfare. Hitler had decided upon the invasion twelve months before, having discovered that the Soviets still retained aspirations in Finland and Rumania and would not heed his suggestion that they invade India and the Persian Gulf. Stalin, his officer corps decimated by the purges of 1937–38 and weakened by the Finnish war, was totally unprepared. Hitler invaded with 3.2 million men and 148 divisions ranged over a one-thousand-mile frontier from the Arctic Circle to the Black Sea.

Stalin had forbidden the Red Army from taking serious precautions, doing so out of the fear that such activity, in itself, might prompt German aggression. When a German deserter swam the Pruth River to warn Russia on the very night of the attack, Stalin had the man shot. Once the attack had begun, he still refused to believe that this marked full scale war. He would not even grant General

Georgi Zhukov permission to engage in hot pursuit. Bridges across vital rivers were captured intact. Soviet air fields were undefended, enabling the Germans to destroy 2,000 aircraft within forty-eight hours.

Although it could not be known at the time, the attack marked a crucial turning point in the war. Seldom in the history of the world has a conflict resulted in such devastation. Hitler himself told his generals two and a half months before his attack, "The war against Russia will be such that it cannot be conducted in a knightly fashion; the struggle is one of ideologies and racial differences and will haveto be conducted with unprecedented, unmerciful and unrelenting harshness." Possibly not since the struggle between Christians and Muslims in the Ottoman wars of the sixteenth century, notes British military historian John Keegan, had war been waged with such ruthlessness.

Although the initial German onslaught on Moscow was repulsed in early December 1941, only at Stalingrad in January 1943 and at Kursk in July 1943 did the tide begin to turn. By the end of the conflict, the total cost for Russia reached 11 million casualties on the battlefield, 2 million dying in German captivity, and 7 million civilians dead, the last figure excluding fatalities created by the Holocaust. It is estimated that 10 percent of the Russian population perished. Also as a result of the Russian campaign, 1.8 million Germans died, 1.2 million were missing, and half a million civilians lost their lives as well. Without the losses on Germany's eastern front, the risks associated with an cross-channel invasion, such as the one that took place at D-Day, were infinitely greater. As it was, the landing at Normandy on June 6, 1944, was by no means a sure thing.

Germany's move into Russia touched off an angry debate in the United States. Should lend-lease assistance go to the Soviets—leaders of world communism, parties to Hitler's crime against Poland, the rapists of Finland? Agreeing with Senator Bennett Champ Clark that "Stalin is as bloody-handed as Hitler," many Americans wanted to stand apart from the Nazi-Soviet war. Others endorsed the idea of Missouri's junior senator, Harry S Truman: "If we see that Germany is winning we ought to help Russia and if Russia is winning we ought to help Germany."

Not everyone agreed. The *New York Times* saw a German victory in Russia as the key to Nazi domination of the world. When German divisions smashed forward on all fronts, such reasoning became even more persuasive. Were Germany to command the vast human and material resources of the European heartland from the Urals to the Atlantic, it could end up virtually invincible.

Most American and British military analysts believed that such assistance was futile. At the same time, presidential troubleshooter Harry Hopkins, returning from a personal visit to Moscow, reported to Roosevelt that Stalin could hold out. With high-octane fuel, aluminum, and antiaircraft guns, the Russian dictator claimed, "we can fight for three or four years." In November, after Congress overwhelmingly rejected an amendment to a lend-lease appropriation bill prohibiting aid to Russia, the president declared the Soviet Union eligible for lend-lease assistance. To show he meant business, Roosevelt sent Averell Harriman, one of his closest advisers, on a relief mission.

Then there was the matter of the draft. The Selective Service Act, passed in September 1940, had limited the time of service to twelve months and had prohibited stationing draftees outside the Western Hemisphere. In April 1941, Chief of Staff Marshall told a House committee that selectees were going home when their year ended. In his biennial report of July 3, however, Marshall noted with alarm that as many as 75 to 90 percent of the regular officers were reservists, men whose term was coming to an end. As far as enlisted men were concerned, he found the outlook equally grim: the proportion of selectees, whose terms would soon be ending, usually ran from 25 to 50 percent of the total U.S. forces. Hit particularly hard would be such crucial support units as engineering, heavy artillery, and antiaircraft. Historian Forrest C. Pogue reports Marshall's perspective: "The Chief of Staff faced the prospect of seeing National Guard members, reserve officers, and trained selectees melt away within a few months." A few days after Marshall made his report, the War Department requested that geographical limits be lifted and time of service be extended.

On July 14, Roosevelt's congressional advisers flatly told him the House would never tamper with the restrictive draft law. Roosevelt did manage to secure endorsement for lifting the one-year limit, but only at the price of retaining the ban on serving outside the hemisphere. Nor did the public strongly back the president, as shown by an opinion poll indicating that only 51 percent favored eliminating the one-year termination.

In a special message sent to Congress on July 21, Roosevelt warned, "Within two months, disintegration, which would follow failure to take Congressional action, will commence in the armies of the United States." He noted that the 1940 law allowed Congress to extend the one-year training period if danger persisted. Claiming that the peril was "infinitely greater" than it had been a year before, he asked Congress to "acknowledge" a national emergency. Of course, FDR realized that if Congress declared such an emergency, it could automatically bring into force the provisions of the 1940 act empowering the president to hold the soldiers "for the duration." Marshall wanted to extend the time of service indefinitely, and with the Senate Military Affairs Committee supporting him, Congress braced itself for another fight.

The bill's sponsors encountered difficulties. On August 7, by a comfortable margin, the Senate tampered with the administration request. It offered only an eighteen-month extension, provided for a pay raise after one year's service, and sought to expedite the release of men over age twenty-eight. On August 12, the House narrowly passed the same bill, 203-202. The sudden news that unoccupied France was on the verge of becoming a full-fledged ally of Germany may have provided the necessary support. Furthermore, the close vote has often been misunderstood. Even if the eighteen-month extension had been turned down, undoubtedly a compromise would have been reached, and draftees would still have had to serve from six to twelve more months.

In midsummer 1941, with Hitler distracted in Russia, Roosevelt decided the time opportune for a meeting with Churchill. An informal exchange of views might open the way for even closer cooperation. Churchill was agreeable, and secret arrangements went forward for a shipboard rendezvous off the coast of Newfoundland near Argentia, a base recently transferred to the United States as part of the destroyer-bases deal. On August 3, Roosevelt, supposedly on a fishing cruise, boarded the yacht *Potomac* at New London, but once at sea he transferred to the cruiser *Augusta*. Churchill crossed the choppy North Atlantic on the new battleship *Prince of Wales.* The two men were in each other's company less than twenty-four hours.

The Argentia discussions focused on the problems of beating Germany and heading off Japan, but their main value, claims British historian David Reynolds, lies in the personal ties established between Roosevelt and Churchill. Posterity, however, long focused on what is now seen as an almost incidental byproduct of the conference: the famous Atlantic Charter, a joint declaration of Anglo-American war aims. Similar to Wilson's Fourteen Points, the charter announced that the United States and Britain sought no territory. The document favored "the right of all peoples to choose the form of government under which they will live." It endorsed "the enjoyment by all states, great and small, victor or vanquished, of access, on equal terms, to the trade and the raw materials of the world which are needed for their economic prosperity." It spoke of "the final destruction of Nazi tyranny," after which it envisioned "the establishment of a wider and permanent system of general security" that would guarantee such blessings of peace as freedom of the seas. Pending the establishment of this system, aggressor nations would be disarmed.

Fearful of its implications for such colonies as Egypt and India and seeing its "imperial preference," or sterling bloc, system threatened, Churchill, upon returning to Britain, felt forced to say that the Charter primarily applied to the nations of Europe lying under Nazi yoke. This circumstance, he added, was quite different from what he called "the progressive evolution of self-governing institutions in the regions and peoples which now owe allegiance to the British crown." In September 1941, Ivan Maisky, Soviet ambassador to Britain, announced that Russia accepted the Charter, but qualified the Soviet endorsement. Out to protect the recent Soviet annexations of the Baltic states, much of Poland, and certain strategic areas of Finland, he remarked: "The practical application of these principles will necessarily adopt themselves to the circumstances, needs, and historic peculiarities of particular countries."

What was the object of the charter? For Churchill it was a vehicle to bring the Americans a step nearer the war. Roosevelt thought more abstractly. Despite the joking informality of the Atlantic Conference, he did not fully trust the British, and he saw the joint declaration as a device to head off the type of secret agreements that had so troubled the world after the armistice of 1918. Moreover, the manifesto might rally people in occupied countries to defy the Nazis, and by pledging an equitable peace, might even move Germans to oppose Hitler. It could clothe the war in the guise of a crusade, and the experience of 1917–18 notwithstanding, Americans loved crusades. Then too, there was the hope that an eloquent charter would obscure the main business at Argentia, the discussion of war plans, and hence spike anti-interventionist criticism.

Historian Akira Iriye finds the Atlantic Charter a sweeping enunciation of the principle of collective security. Indeed, it was "Wilsonianism pure and simple, in its stress on territorial integrity and on collective action to punish the violators." Historian Waldo Heinrichs argues, however, the Charter was unremarkable. Both Americans and Britons took most of it for granted: "No other vision of the world had any standing." Its strength long lay in the sharp contrast between the world vision of the democracies, which was multilateral, and that of the Axis, so obviously self-serving. Theodore A. Wilson, who has written the most thorough account of the conference, notes that the document needed neither FDR or Churchill to help draft it; it could just as well have been drafted in Washington by Secretary Hull and Lord Halifax, British ambassador to the U.S.

VI

Yet if, as Roosevelt assured the country, the conference at Argentia did not take the United States along the road to war, events elsewhere around the Atlantic were doing just that.

At the beginning of 1941, as mentioned, Hitler put increased emphasis on the war at sea. At the very time Americans were debating lend-lease, the Battle of the Atlantic was expanding, and British losses were heavy. Churchill later confessed, "The only thing that ever really frightened me during the war was the U-boat peril." By March, the Nazis were sinking British vessels at the rate of over half a million tons per month. On a single night early in April, the Germans sank ten of twenty-two ships of a British convoy. To Admiral Stark, the situation was "hopeless, except as we take strong measures to save it." The question was obvious: how could the United States and Britain make sure that merchant vessels carrying lend-lease cargoes escape German submarines and cruisers and find their way safely to British ports?

There seemed only one answer: convoys. But convoys required escort, and the Royal Navy could not spare the necessary destroyers and cruisers. American warships were required. Early in 1941, fearful that the matter might prevent Congress from passing lend-lease, American interventionists hedged. At a news conference on January 21, Roosevelt implied that convoys risked all-out war. Ultimately the administration accepted an amendment to H.R. 1776 that read that "nothing in this Act shall be construed to authorize or to permit the authorization of convoying by naval vessels of the United States."

Still, it seemed idiotic to stand by and watch U-boats destroy lend-lease cargoes; some individuals playfully suggested that it would be simpler to dump supplies from American piers into the Atlantic. In truth, convoy escort by American naval vessels was inevitable.

As early as January 17, shortly after the bill was introduced, Roosevelt was preparing for the escort of U.S. shipping in the Atlantic. A significant step was taken on April 9, when Roosevelt signed an agreement with the Danish government that permitted the United States to occupy Greenland. The Danish minister in Washington, Henrik de Kauffmann, lacked the authority to enter into such an agreement, which was immediately disavowed by the Nazi dominated government at home. For the United States, the action was unprecedented, running counter to conventional international procedure. But no matter. In enemy hands, warned Assistant Secretary of State Adolf A. Berle, Jr., planes from Greenland could strike at New York. Yet, in friendly hands, the island was invaluable; it expedited the delivery of short-range aircraft to Britain and its weather stations were essential to later bombing raids on Germany.

Roosevelt realized that the anti-interventionists as well as the broader public still opposed escorting. He therefore turned aside appeals that he order the Atlantic fleet to escort lend-lease convoys. On April 18, 1941, however, he announced a "Western Hemisphere Neutrality Patrol" in the western Atlantic, though he lacked the ships to make it effective. Its mission was clear: to "observe and report" belligerent movements and keep war from "our front doors." (The U.S. Navy had wanted full-scale escort.) He settled on a North-South line down the twenty-sixth meridian, which ran halfway between Brazil and West Africa and which encompassed the Azores and most of Greenland. By flashing locations of German U-boats, of course, the patrol would alert merchantmen to veer away while inviting British cruisers and destroyers to attack. The U.S. neutrality or security zone would reach twenty-six degrees longitude west and would include all of Greenland plus the Azores. This vast expanse overlapped a German combat zone proclaimed on March 25, thereby assuring an eventual clash.

As American ships and planes had no authority to attack, Roosevelt insisted that the operation was indeed a patrol, and thereby limited to scouting, and not an escort, with its heightened risk of combat. In a press conference held April 25, he explained that there was the same difference between a patrol and an escort as between a cow and a horse: "if one looks at a cow and calls it a horse that is all right with the President, but that does not make a cow a horse." He compared the patrols to the escorts of a wagon train, whose job it was to find Indians and prevent ambush. Obviously such comparisons were colorful, but they skirted the severe risks involved.

Next Roosevelt turned to Iceland, an area that historian Waldo Heinrichs calls "the turntable of the Atlantic." Iceland was a sovereign state in personal union with Denmark, although it became totally orphaned once Germany occupied its mother country. Britain and Canada had stationed troops there for a year, but the president still feared a German takeover.

FDR's anxiety increased on April 11. The American destroyer *Niblack*, engaged in a reconnaissance mission to Iceland, fired at what it thought was a threatening German U-boat, an event taking place 500 miles south of its destination. It was undoubtedly a false alarm, what Bailey and Ryan call "the incident that never was," and somewhat resembled the Tonkin Bay incident of August 1964.

Encouraged by the British, Iceland accepted American "protection," and on July 7, a brigade of nearly 4,000 Marines arrived. Were the Germans to occupy that strategic island, said Roosevelt, they would pose an intolerable threat to all "the independent nations of the New World." Hostile naval and air bases there would menace Greenland, threaten shipping in the North Atlantic, and interrupt the steady flow of munitions, the last item "a broad policy clearly approved by Congress." In friendly hands, however, Iceland possessed two critical advantages: it provided indispensable refueling bases for convoys, and it controlled the Denmark Strait, a passage between Greenland and Iceland where German ships had been active. Had Roosevelt not acted, the CDAAA claimed, the Battle of the Atlantic would be lost, Britain itself face defeat, and the U.S. position in Greenland would suddenly become untenable.

Sixty-one percent of Gallup poll respondents endorsed the president's message, though anti-interventionists were furious. According to journalist John T. Flynn, "If the President, without the consent of Congress, can occupy Iceland, he can occupy Syria or Ethiopia." In the middle of July, the U.S. Navy started escorting American and Icelandic ships to its new outpost, the very development feared by foes of lend-lease.

How did Hitler respond to America's interference in the war at sea? Concentrating on the eastern campaign, he rejected his navy's appeal for authority to attack American ships, and in May 1941, when a U-boat sank the merchantman *Robin Moor*, he reiterated his wish that Germany "avoid any incident with the U.S.A." The *Robin Moor* was the first American ship to go down, though no lives were lost. The incident, which was not made public until June 10, took place in the South Atlantic, several hundred miles from both the bulge of Brazil and the west coast of Africa.

In a broadcast made on June 20, Roosevelt invoked the doctrine of freedom of the seas. The United States, he said, would not yield to "piracy." Yet unlike Woodrow Wilson in the case of the *Sussex* in 1916, he did not do what the anti-interventionists most feared, exploit the *Robin Moor* incident to take drastic measures. His one move, the freezing of German and Italian assets, had been planned earlier.

Still in all, the Führer would not be diverted from dealing with his enemies one at a time. Until he finished with the Soviets, he sought to avoid the Americans. His object was to divert American attention to the Pacific by encouraging the Japanese, which undoubtedly was his main purpose in bringing Japan into the Axis.

The matter of convoys was raised at the Roosevelt-Churchill summit of early August. On August 19, in reporting to the British war cabinet, Churchill claimed that at the Argentia conference, Roosevelt had committed himself to warlike acts. According to minutes declassified in the early 1970s, "The President said he would wage war, but not declare it, and that he would become more and more provocative. If the Germans did not like it, they could attack American forces." Roosevelt also remarked that the United States would assume responsibility for escorting North Atlantic convoys within the defensive zone west of twenty-six degrees west. Churchill said, "The President's orders to these escorts were to attack any U-boat which showed itself, even if it were 200 or 300 miles away from the convoys. . . . Everything was to be done to force an 'incident.'"

Yet when FDR returned to Washington, he was painfully slow in fulfilling any such promise. Although he had promised Churchill that the U.S. Navy would escort all Allied convoys west of Iceland and the Azores, he did not implement this policy. In fact, Theodore A. Wilson claims the conference did not put "the requisite iron in the presidential backbone." David Reynolds asserts that Churchill likely found the Atlantic Charter a poor surrogate for a declaration of war. An undeclared war, however, was obviously in the offing, for incidents were still inevitable.

On September 4, the American destroyer *Greer* and the German submarine U-652 exchanged shots in waters 200 miles southwest of Iceland. En route to Reykjavik with mail and passengers, the *Greer*, an old "four-stacker" dating from 1918, received a message from a British patrol plane that a sub lay submerged ten miles ahead. Alarm gongs sounded "general quarters" and the *Greer* set out after the U-boat. Its sounding devices made contact, while a message giving the submarine's location brought a British plane that dropped four depth charges. The submarine fired a torpedo, the *Greer* dodged, and the torpedo crossed a hundred yards astern. The *Greer* answered with eight depth charges. A few minutes later, the submarine launched another torpedo that also missed. The *Greer* emitted a few more depth charges, then proceeded to Iceland.

Roosevelt determined to make the most of the *Greer* affair. Although he had already quietly authorized the Atlantic fleet to escort lend-lease convoys as far as Iceland, he fretted over how to break the news to the country. In the *Greer* episode, he saw his opportunity. He would represent the decision to escort as a response to a German outrage. Portrayed as Nazi aggression, the incident also opened the way for orders removing restrictions on the neutrality patrol. Roosevelt would direct the fleet to "shoot on sight" at Axis submarines and cruisers operating in America's "defensive waters," defined as the entire Atlantic west of Iceland.

Because of the death of his mother, the president delayed his response for several days. On the evening of September 11, a mourning band on his sleeve, he entered the diplomatic reception room of the White House. Underscoring the historical importance were portraits of past presidents, a bust of Lafayette, and the large clock from the San Francisco Exposition of 1915. Sitting around the room were Mrs. Roosevelt, members of the family, friends, aides, and photographers. The president moved to a cluttered desk and sat down before a small microphone. Not mentioning that the *Greer* had provoked the U-boat, he said in solemn tones that the destroyer "was carrying mail to Iceland. . . . She was then and there attacked by a submarine. . . . I tell you the blunt fact that the German submarine fired first upon this American destroyer without warning, and with deliberate design to sink her."

Roosevelt also mentioned previous sinkings. The U.S. freighter *Steel Seafarer*, flying the American flag, had been bombed on September 7 while en route to an Egyptian port. A day later, the State Department had announced the loss of the *Sessa*, reported to have been sunk near Greenland several weeks earlier while carrying supplies to Iceland. Twenty-four crew members were lost; the rest were rescued. The ship, however, was not legally entitled to United States protection, as it was sailing under Panamanian registry, a common subterfuge used to evade Neutrality Act restrictions.

Pointing to "the Nazi danger to our Western World," the president declared that "when you see a rattlesnake poised to strike, you do not wait until he has struck before you crush him." Calling German submarines "the rattlesnakes of the Atlantic," he announced that American ships and planes "will no longer wait until Axis submarines lurking under water, or Axis raiders on the surface of the sea, strike their deadly blow-first." They would shoot on sight.

Then the president discussed convoy escorting. Explaining that the fleet had the duty of "maintaining the American policy of freedom of the seas," he announced that patrolling vessels and planes "will protect all merchant ships—not only American ships but ships of any flag—engaged in commerce in our defensive waters." When the president finished, one of the broadcasting networks played "The Star-Spangled Banner." Roosevelt and the others in the room stood at attention. The president had made no false statements, but he omitted a crucial fact, namely that it was the destroyer that had prompted the German attack.

Even historians William L. Langer and S. Everett Gleason, usually sympathetic to Roosevelt's policies, found it hard to defend this speech. Suggesting that perhaps the president's remarks rested on the best information available at the time, they add: "This does not, however, exonerate the President of the charge of having exploited the incident without awaiting a detailed report." Robert Dallek sees a "need to mislead the country in its own interest," but claims Roosevelt's "deviousness" injured "the national well-being over the long run." The president had "created a precedent for manipulation of public opinion which would be repeated by later Presidents in less justifiable circumstances." Conversely FDR biographer George McJimsey stresses that FDR was not the first president "to take steps that invited war while declaring peaceful purposes." Nor was he the first to lead his nation into a conflict that a large proportion of Americans were reluctant to accept.

Once the *Greer* incident took place, the United States Navy began escorting its first British convoys. U.S. "defensive waters" now extended as far as ten degrees west longitude, some 400 miles off the Scottish coast. There, for roughly three-quarters of the Atlantic, U.S. vessels were to escort friendly convoys and destroy any Axis forces encountered on the way. The sinkings of U.S.-owned vessels continued. On September 16, the State Department announced that the *Montana*, a U.S. freighter under Panamanian registry, was sunk between Greenland and Iceland. No one was injured. Three days later, the *Pink Star*, another American-owned vessel flying the Panamanian flag, was torpedoed in the same general locale. Some of the crew were lost. In October, four more U.S.-owned merchant ships were sunk.

With American ships being attacked, the administration worked harder than ever to repeal the "crippling provisions" contained in the 1939 Neutrality Act. Roosevelt particularly opposed the articles forbidding the arming of American merchantmen and prohibiting American ships from entering "danger zones." The president, of course, realized that Britain would receive far more aid if U.S. ships could sail directly to its borders. He also mentioned that although U.S. destroyers were escorting the merchant ships, these freighters—particularly those flying the U.S. flag—should assist in their own defense by mounting a gun or two.

Fully aware that the 1941 draft law had passed by the narrowest of margins, Roosevelt did not seek immediate repeal of the whole act; instead he focused on the sections affecting the Atlantic war. Speaking on October 9, the president urged Congress to permit the arming of U.S. merchant ships. "Although the arming of merchant ships does not guarantee their safety, it most certainly adds to their safety," the president said. The ships could choose whether to shoot the enemy on sight or keep their distance until help arrived. Fearing that Congress might not lift the ban on entering combat zones and delivering lend-lease goods directly to the ports of friendly belligerents, Roosevelt did not push the proposal; he hoped, however, that it would receive "earnest and early attention." He was, he declared, asking Congress to carry out the intent of the lend-lease act: "In other words, I ask for Congressional action to implement Congressional policy. Let us be consistent." Their spirits unimpaired, anti-interventionists rallied together against the presidential request.

On October 17 came news that German torpedoes had ripped the *Kearny*, a crack destroyer scarcely a year in service. The ship was responding to an appeal from a Canadian convoy, one attacked by a wolf pack raid some 400 miles away. Although it was damaged, not sunk, eleven lives were lost, and Americans saw their first naval casualty list of World War II.

Next came Roosevelt's sensational Navy Day speech of October 27, in which he announced that the *Kearny* was not just a navy ship:

"She belongs to every man, woman and child in the nation." He also revived memories of the Zimmermann Telegram of 1917, announcing that he had received a secret Nazi map that divided South America into "five vassal states" and that he knew of a Nazi plan to "abolish all existing religions." This time, however, the documentation was spurious; it is now suspected to have been planted by British intelligence.

Then came a new disaster, one involving the loss of a hundred seamen. On October 31, the destroyer *Reuben James* fell victim to a German submarine while escorting a convoy 600 miles west of Iceland. Of 160 men on board, only 45 were able to be rescued. In the following week, debate in Congress over revision of the neutrality act reached a climax, and on November 7, in an atmosphere heavy with tension, the Senate voted 50-37 to repeal the remaining restrictions, including the ones on combat zones. Six days later, by a tally of 212-194, the House responded similarly.

After his victory, Roosevelt remained cautious. Since the crucial parts of the 1939 Neutrality Act had been repealed, the president was empowered to send armed convoys directly across the Atlantic. Yet only on November 25 did the administration decide to do so. At that time, it decided to send unarmed vessels to Lisbon and armed vessels to the Soviet port of Archangel; ships flying the U.S. flag would start sailing to Britain, but presumably as part of a British escort. The decision about Lisbon alone was made public. Hence, the initiative remained in the hands of Hitler, who sought more than ever to avoid incidents.

On December 3, the *Chicago Tribune,* a leading anti-interventionist newspaper, published the U.S. Army's Victory Program, a contingency plan drafted by Major Albert Wedemeycr of the War Plans Division. It found invasion of Europe by American ground forces technically feasible, though it would involve 215 divisions and 6 million troops. No formal authorization of the plan was ever given; indeed, throughout the fall of 1941, the army feared cutbacks in manpower.

Was Roosevelt still seeking to avoid formal war with Germany on the eve of the Pearl Harbor attack? Historian David Reynolds answers affirmatively, noting several reasons. First, if the United States entered the conflict as a full-scale belligerent, the American public would insist that the nation keep the most vital supplies for its own war effort. Yet if equipment slated for its allies was cut back, there might be disastrous consequences for all concerned. Second, suppose Japan decided to honor the Tripartite Pact and come into the war on the side of Hitler. The United States would be forced to fight on two fronts. Current Anglo-American plans, which included postponing a Pacific conflict until Germany had been defeated, would be scrapped. Third, as the United States was already fighting, Roosevelt might have seen a formal declaration of war as making little difference. America's main contribution would still be through arms, not men. Historians Bailey and Ryan note that FDR could not tangle with any more submarines on the North Atlantic route than he was doing already, even had war with Germany been declared. Fourth, according to Reynolds, FDR genuinely believed that massive bombing, with the deliberate aim of hitting German towns as well as industrial centers, would make a large-scale army superfluous.

But irrespective of Roosevelt's motives, by December 1941 one thing was certain: the United States was now transporting unlimited aid to the Allies and skirmishing with Germany on the Atlantic. Partly due to Roosevelt's cautious but skillful leadership, both public opinion and Congress had moved far toward the acceptance of war with Germany. But one final push was required for full belligerency, a push provided by the Japanese attack on Pearl Harbor.

CHAPTER FIVE

Toward War in the Pacific

After the *Panay* affair of December 1937, the Japanese extended control in North China and secured the principal Chinese coastal areas. Step by step the imperial armies were fulfilling the vision of a "new order" in East Asia, one resting on Japanese hegemony in China.

In the fall of 1938, Roosevelt commissioned his secretary of the treasury, Henry Morgenthau, Jr., to make a $25 million loan to Jiang's government, to be repaid with proceeds from the sale of tung oil. Though the sum was small, the loan indicated America's desire to bolster Chinese resistance. Stronger action was risky, particularly in view of growing tensions in Europe. That November, Japanese Foreign Minister Arita Hachiro formally rejected the Washington system established in 1922. Ignoring U.S. protests, Arita claimed that former treaties and principles were no longer valid. In the words of historian Akira Iriye, "Japan, after long hesitation, finally crossed the bridge of no return."

At first, it appeared as if the West were withdrawing from Asia. On July 24, 1939, the British, preoccupied with the Polish crisis, recognized Japan's special position in China, including responsibility for law and order in the occupied areas. Two days later, Roosevelt moved to satisfy the popular urge for action, nonviolent of course, while giving pause to the Japanese. He sent out the necessary six-month notice of possible abrogation of the Treaty of Commerce and Navigation of 1911, an agreement that had regulated trade between the two countries. In 1938 the U.S. had supplied Japan with 44 percent of its imports, including such items as automobiles, machinery, copper, oil, iron, and steel. Abrogation would not necessarily end this commerce; rather it would deprive the traffic of legal protection, thereby putting it on a day-to-day basis. Commerce with Japan would henceforth lie at Washington's mercy. Similarly the U.S. Treasury would now be free to curtail purchases of Japanese silver and gold, Japan's chief source of foreign exchange and essential to its economic life.

In six months, that is by January 1940, the United States would be free to limit or terminate exports to Japan, even free to impose sanctions if Japan joined the Axis and continued its aggression in East Asia. Roosevelt realized full well that Japanese imperialism relied on American oil and scrap metal. He hoped the Japanese government might relax pressure in China rather than risk an economic boycott. The events in Europe of August and September 1939 left no time for self-congratulation, yet the president had cause for satisfaction over his move in the Far East. As historian Robert Dallek notes, "It encouraged London to be firm with Tokyo, raised Chinese morale, and received widespread approval in the United States." In Tokyo the leaders of Japan betrayed alarm lest the United States discard verbal protest in favor of sanctions.

I

There was, however, no weakening of Japan's determination to put together a Greater East Asia Co-Prosperity Sphere. Japanese armies continued to advance in China, air squadrons droned on, and European and American business came under new restrictions. Once the conflict subsided, the Tokyo government planned a puppet regime, to be located in Jiang Jieshi's former capital of Nanjing, and it increased the pressure of a diplomatic drive begun earlier in the year to persuade the British and French to leave China altogether. The Japanese were anxious to smooth over any difficulties with the United States.

They repeatedly assured American diplomats that once they resolved the "China incident," the trade door would swing open, and everybody, including the Chinese, would enjoy the rewards of Japan's imperialism.

Soothing words from the Foreign Office in Tokyo drew little response in official Washington, which was under no illusions about Japan's "new order." The Greater East Asia Co-Prosperity Sphere would obviously be a closed system, geared to function to Japan's advantage. And China? It would become a giant vassal.

In the view of some Americans, the best step would be a boycott of Japan, a move that would cut off American shipments to Japanese armies and align national policy to moral principle. To that end, several bills came before Congress in January 1940, although Roosevelt still opposed sanctions. Senator Tom Connally (Dem.-Tex.), anxious to punish Japan, complained that "we fired a few blank cartridges and then fell back." At the same time, FDR abrogated the 1911 agreement, a move that put all trade on a twenty-four hour basis. American war supplies were not severed but Japan was now kept on a high level of uncertainty. According to a Gallup poll, the public approved Roosevelt's move by a four-to-one margin.

In February 1940, another Gallup poll indicated that three-fourths of the public sought a Chinese victory. Far from all Americans, however, wanted to confront Japan. In July 1940 only 12 percent of those polled desired to risk war over the matter. The America First Committee undoubtedly spoke for many anti-interventionists when it said that November, "We sympathize with China. But we must not plunge America into war . . . for sentimental reasons."

Economic pressure was particularly opposed. If, so certain anti-interventionists reasoned, the United States slapped such a "friendly nation" in the face, Japan was bound to retaliate. No Japanese regime had ever submitted to foreign pressure. At the very least, it would blockade Chinese ports, shut out all imports, apply martial law wherever Japanese armies were located, and exclude all foreigners from China. Herbert Hoover warned against "sticking a pin in a rattlesnake." Wall Street lawyer John Foster Dulles found that sanctions would simply consolidate the Japanese people behind their army. Furthermore, said the foes of intervention, such an effort would certainly be ineffective, for Japan possessed alternative sources of supply.

There were several reasons for general anti-interventionist aloofness. First, there was the feeling that Japan's policy in China was "an Asiatic question," one that did not affect the Western Hemisphere.

Second, anti-interventionists denied that the United States had any vital interest in Asia worth its risking war. A Hearst columnist claimed that the sum Americans spent yearly on athletic events totaled more than the entire U.S. financial stake in China. Moreover, why sacrifice $400 million of the annual Japanese trade to protect $100 million worth of fixed investment in China?

Third, some anti-interventionists possessed a low opinion of China, and here they pointed to communist influence, the dictatorial nature of the Jiang regime, and China's general reputation for "backwardness." Conversely, despite the brutality of its armies, they found Japan bearing the earmarks of modern progress. Dulles, for example, called the Japanese "a people of energy, industry and ambition."

Fourth, Japan appeared to offer no military threat. As one anti-interventionist senator caustically remarked, "I suppose she is going to fly her big tanks over the Canadian Rockies. Or if she cannot fly them over, she will outfit all the Japanese soldiers with snowshoes so they can climb over the mountains in the winter time and get at us in that way."

Fifth, and conversely, anti-interventionists denied that Japan could ever be invaded. Operating out of its own bases, and possessing submarines, airplanes, and armies in abundance, the island empire could readily destroy any army within 4,000 miles. If American troops started out from Hawaii, it would take from three to four bloody years just to occupy islands some eight hundred miles away from Japan.

Even possible Japanese seizure of the Philippines did not change some minds. In 1934, Congress had passed the Tydings-McDuffie Act, a bill that targeted Philippine independence in 1946, provided for the removal of U.S. military posts, and envisioned negotiation over naval bases. Yet anti-interventionists, pointing to Japanese industrial and political influence, claimed that Japan had long been the dominant power there. Furthermore, the islands were deemed unprof-

Western Pacific, 1941

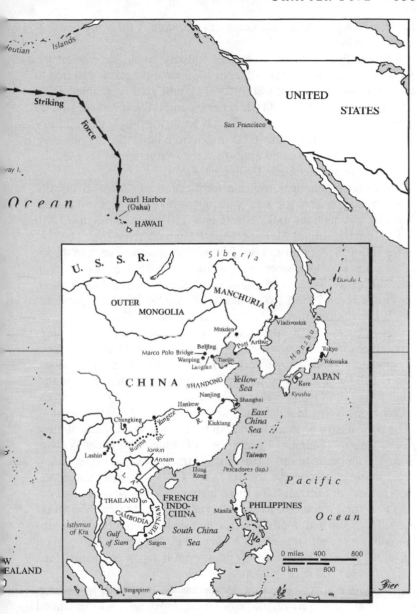

itable, costing the American taxpayer three dollars for every one dollar in benefits.

In addition, even the American military found defense of the Philippines well nigh impossible. In 1935 *Time* magazine referred to the islands as "a geographical Milky Way"; the chain contained 7,083 islands, of which only 2,441 had names and only 462 possessed an area of over one square mile. To rescue them, the American navy would have to operate some 6,000 miles from home. Japan, however, was so close that one could almost see the southernmost Japanese island from the northernmost Philippine one.

Anti-interventionists saw the fortification of Guam as equally risky. Acquired after the war with Spain and administered by the Navy Department, the rocky island, only 210 square miles, lay 3,850 miles from the natural Alaska-Hawaii-Panama defense line. The cost of major fortification would be $250 million, a sum more than the total investment of the American government and private investors in the Philippines, Japan, and China combined. When in March 1939, the House voted 205 to 168 against fortifying the island, Representative Bruce Barton quipped, "Guam, Guam with the Wind."

Asia itself, in anti-interventionist eyes, simply served as a playground for foreign imperialists, and the United States had no business becoming the bankruptcy receiver for Europe's colonial possessions. The Dutch had suppressed the native population of their East Indian colony, and the French had shot Annamese rebels by the hundreds. As for Hong Kong, Malaya, and India, the *New York Daily News* said, "The British have no more historic or racial right to be in any of these places than the Germans have to be in France." Journalist William Henry Chamberlin asked, "How many Americans, on a referendum vote, would choose to die for the Dutch East Indies, for Singapore, for Thailand or Senegal?" To those interventionists who stressed access to natural resources, Roosevelt critics claimed that sufficient oil existed in North and South America, that synthetic and Brazilian rubber could replace that made in Malaya, and that plastic was a good substitute for East Indian tin. Besides, even if Japan conquered East Asia, it would still need the American market.

As with Hoover close to a decade earlier, Roosevelt had reason for caution. Sanctions might provoke the Japanese, and the United States was not ready for a fight. Even if the threat of war passed, there was nothing to suggest that Japanese armies would stop dead in their tracks for want of American supplies. More likely, leaders in Tokyo would turn to Southeast Asia. There was, moreover, the war in Europe. Pacific involvements would be inimical to any American plans for helping fight Hitler. Roosevelt concluded that it was best to leave the Japan trade alone while searching for new ways to bolster China. As far as China went, problems were acute, for its finances were near collapse, and Japanese control of its ports required that most supplies find their way to Jiang Jieshi via the tortuous Burma Road.

All this time, the Japanese were continuing to offend the United States. From 1937 to 1940, the U.S. filed literally hundreds of protests concerning the bombings of civilian populations, damage to American property, and injury and insult to American citizens. By December 1939, even the Japanese admitted a total of 144 bombings and 73 other cases of destruction.

Equally serious were Japanese economic measures in China. U.S. diplomats repeatedly protested against exchange restrictions, currency manipulations, tariff revisions, and new Japanese monopolies. Americans saw these measures as part of a deliberate campaign —a campaign to drive all foreigners out of China.

Yet the U.S. still did not see its Far Eastern interests important enough to risk war, so it met the diplomatic and military incidents with diplomatic protests. It confronted economic discrimination by such countermeasures as abrogating the 1911 Commercial treaty. It answered such moral outrages as the bombing of civilian populations with moral embargoes on planes, bombs, and other war materials.

By early 1940, the Japanese had run into difficulty. War maps in Tokyo did not project China's vastness; the countryside seemed to swallow imperial armies. Nor could Japan convince Jiang Jieshi that its imperialism would benefit China; the Chinese leader continued to refuse Japan's hand of "friendship." In March 1940, frustrated Japanese civilian leaders reluctantly decided to go through with establishing a puppet regime. It was headed by Wang Ching-wei, formerly a Goumindang leader and man of the left. There was some concern lest the United States respond with a boycott, but establishment of the Nanjing government that month brought nothing more from Washington than a denunciation.

On March 29, American-British military conversations resulted in what American naval planners had already referred to as Plan Dog, the priority of a German defeat even if Japan entered the war. As an assumed corollary, it concluded that policy towards Japan must remain defensive. Roosevelt neither officially endorsed nor rejected what was called ABC-1, though Admiral Stark testified after the war that FDR unofficially approved the agreement.

That very spring, Hitler ended the "phony war" in Europe, one of his first victims being the Netherlands. In Tokyo, the Foreign Office asked who would dominate the Dutch East Indies, one of the world's richest sources of oil, rubber, tin, bauxite, nickel, and manganese. Would the Germans claim them? Or would the British attempt a "preventive" occupation?

Secretary Hull also wondered about the Dutch colony, but his main concern there was a Japanese takeover, He accurately surmised that Japan's plan for a "new order" in East Asia included the Netherlands Indies. To dissuade them from moving to the area, he reminded the Japanese that in 1922 they had agreed "to respect the rights of the Netherlands in relation to their insular possessions in the region of the Pacific Ocean." Any disturbance in the East Indies, he warned, would endanger peace in the entire Pacific. To reinforce the secretary's words Roosevelt ordered the Pacific fleet from San Diego to Pearl Harbor. It developed that the Japanese were in no hurry. Assured that neither the Germans nor the British would occupy the East Indies, they were content when, in June 1940, the Dutch pledged not to sever East Indian supplies to Japan.

Meanwhile, in Europe Hitler's *Blitzkrieg* had commanded the energies of France and Britain, who were forced to leave their Asian colonies almost defenseless. Would the poverty-ridden Japanese, seeing the Western world turning upside down, satisfy their national urge for treasure and grandeur by carrying the Rising Sun to Indochina, Malaya, and Burma? The answer seemed affirmative. Even before German troops had swept over France, the Tokyo government warned Great Britain that it could only avoid trouble in the Far East by closing the Burma Road and sealing the border between Hong Kong and the Chinese mainland. At the same time, the Japanese demanded that the French close the Indochina frontier and grant them the right to keep a control commission in the French colony. To show that they meant business, the Japanese sent warships to the Gulf of Tonkin and made military demonstrations along the Indochinese border. Both the British and French complied, though after three months the British reopened the Burma Road.

Some Japanese believed these policies too meek. In their view, the opportunity to cash in on Hitler's victories in Europe was too dazzling to let pass, especially when one measured a strike southward against the only alternative: carrying on a dreary, endless war in China. In the words of one prominent Japanese, "We should not miss the present opportunity or we shall be blamed by posterity." Charging that the government was moving too slowly, militants demanded a bolder policy. The Western democracies, they declared, had no choice but to yield to Japanese ambition. Japan should put aside its fear of America, join the Axis alliance, and stake out a claim to Southeast Asia by helping Hitler achieve his great purpose of overpowering Britain.

Early in July 1940, amid such calls to national greatness, Tokyo began to reverberate with rumors of the imminent downfall of the cabinet. Threats of assassination were frequent, and there were whispers that if Hirohito opposed a cabinet change, militant conspirators would not spare him. A fortnight later, the army handed the government an eviction notice. Leading the new regime would be Prince Konoye Fumimaro, who had been prime minister once before. Stemming from the prominent Fujiwara family, from which the empress was usually chosen, and possessing a wide popular following, Konoye was on good terms with the army and not apt to oppose its will. Matsuoka Yosuke became foreign minister. The very man who had defended Japan's occupation of Manchuria before the League in 1933, Matsuoka was a conceited and impulsive demagogue. Also powerful was the new war minister, General Tojo Hideki, a short man whose quick intelligence gave him the nickname of "Razor Brain." In a matter of days, the Konoye government set out its policy: firmness toward the United States, alliance with the Axis, an end to the war in China, better relations with the Soviet Union, and more vigorous diplomacy in Southeast Asia.

By now Washington was apprehensive, not so much because of Japan's change in government as because of the sudden increase in Japanese purchases of aviation gasoline and lubricants. Did the buildup signal a military expedition to Southeast Asia? Or were the Japanese storing oil for war against the United States? Whatever the reason, American leaders decided the time had come for a stronger stand.

On July 2, 1940, Roosevelt signed the National Defense Act, a bill that gave him authority to declare certain items vital to the national defense and thus eligible for export only under license. Just three weeks later, claiming that his nation's defense required new efforts to stockpile strategic materials, he imposed an embargo on the sale of high-octane fuels and top-grade scrap iron to Japan. True, Japanese planes could run just as well on medium-octane fuels, which were not blocked; hence Japan was able to buy 550 percent more aviation fuel in the five months following the embargo than in the five months preceding it. FDR's move did, however, serve notice that there were limits to U.S. patience.

Unimpressed by American policy, the Konoye government began to prod the Dutch. Seeking to increase in the flow of oil and other materials, leaders in Tokyo demanded the right to send a special mission to the Netherlands East Indies. Other plans were more sweeping. The Japanese had decided to try to cut the ties of the Indies to the Netherlands. Achieving that, they would coerce authorities in the Indies to recognize Japanese supremacy there. The Dutch saw through Japanese intentions and managed to keep concessions to a minimum.

The Japanese also turned up the pressure on Indochina. In August 1940, they demanded the right to send troops across Tonkin province and build airfields in the northern reaches of that colony. Their only purpose, they insisted, was to engineer Jiang's defeat and prevent hostile elements from taking over the country.

Obviously far more was at stake. The French hoped for American aid, but leaders in Washington, engrossed in the air battle going on over Britain, declined to make any promises. The French government at Vichy then toyed with the idea of resisting the Japanese. Perhaps in the steaming jungles of Southeast Asia, the armies of France could recover some of the luster lost in the recent humiliation by the Germans. Such thoughts were mere flights from reality, and after securing a pledge that Japan would respect French sovereignty, the doors of Indochina opened. Late in September 1940, 6,000 imperial

Japanese soldiers occupied three air fields in Tonkin, located in the northern part of the colony.

All this time, Japan was edging toward the Axis alliance. As was perfectly apparent, the target of any Rome-Berlin-Tokyo pact would be the United States. Both Hitler and Mussolini hoped that the United States would permit Britain's defeat rather than risk a two-theater war. For the same reason, some Japanese militants thought the Americans would submit to their nation's supremacy in East Asia.

Not all Japanese leaders were convinced, however. As negotiations went forward, an air of misgiving settled over Tokyo. The emperor privately took a gloomy view of Hitler, and the navy, fearful of war with America, saw the alliance as provocative. Undeterred, the army and other militants pressed on. They held the levers of power, it turned out, and their will prevailed.

Negotiations ended on September 27, 1940, when representatives of Germany, Italy, and Japan gathered in Berlin and signed the Tripartite Pact. Amid ceremonies climaxed by what historian Hans L. Trefousse describes as "the godlike entry of the Führer," the signatories recognized Japanese supremacy in East Asia and German-Italian supremacy in Europe. All pledged mutual support if any signers were attacked by "a Power at present not involved in the European war or in the Chinese-Japanese conflict." As the pact explicitly excluded the Soviets, there was only one clear target: the United States of America.

Japan had several motives for signing the agreement. It wanted to isolate the U.S. It sought German recognition of a Japanese sphere of influence for all East Asia. It desired to check the Soviets, who— Japan hoped—would be less likely to compete with Japan on the Asian continent.

Many anti-interventionists believed the United States had reaped the folly of its own policies. To Professor Borchard, the pact was "a perfectly natural response" to American "denunciation, chastisement, embargo, boycott, threat and an alleged moral superiority." To General Hugh Johnson, America's bluff was finally being called.

Until this time, the American public had not thought in terms of confrontation. Of course, it was strongly hostile to the Japanese cause, something bolstered by viewing the atrocities shown in

"March of Time" newsreels and the sympathetic picture of the Chinese people reflected in the film version of *The Good Earth* (1937). As *Time* noted as far back as October 1937, "To the U.S. public, China is symbolized by Confucius, Ming vases, heroic missionaries, clean shirts and Charlie Chan. Japan means hara-kiri, imperialism, post cards of Fujiyama, and the Yellow Peril." In 1938, Mr. Moto, the famous Japanese detective created by John P. Marquand, was dropped from the screen while Earl Derr Diggers's Charlie Chan became more popular then ever.

Until this point, the American national interest in the Far East was defined in terms of commercial access, something supposedly guaranteed by the Open Door; protection of the Philippines (really a matter of "national honor," for the U.S. had set them on the road to independence in 1934); traditional friendship for the Chinese people; and a growing dependence upon such raw materials as rubber, petroleum, and tin. Once, however, the Tripartite Pact was signed, the State Department linked the British battle against Germany and Italy to Japan's activities in the Far East, and thereby expanded what went under the rubric of national interest. For the Roosevelt administration and much of the American public as well, there was in reality one war, not two.

As America became increasingly entangled in Britain's cause, it saw itself needing to confront any Japanese moves that threatened British, Dutch, and French possessions in East Asia. In September 1940, a Gallup poll showed 60 percent of Americans finding the rise of Japanese power a serious threat to the U.S. When asked if they favored "steps" (unspecified) risking war to check Japan, 46 percent responded affirmatively.

On September 26, 1940, the United States was alarmed enough to embargo all scrap metal to Japan, not just the "top-grade" material. The embargo, announced the day before Japan joined the Axis, came as a blow to Tokyo's imperialists. Loss of American scrap meant that the Japanese would have to redouble efforts to build their own steel-producing facilities. They would also have to find new sources of iron ore and coking coal (three tons of ore and coking coal were required to turn out the equivalent of one ton of scrap metal). The resulting strain on the country's manpower, machinery, and shipping would be serious.

Would Japan retaliate against the embargo, denounced by the government in Tokyo as an "unfriendly act"? After holding their breath for several days, leaders in Washington began to debate new measures to contain Japanese imperialism. Some of the president's advisers counseled a hard line, including Ickes, Morgenthau, Stimson, and Knox; others, such as Hull, opposed intimidation, warning that the U.S. Navy was not prepared to fight Japan. Roosevelt weighed all arguments, then decided upon a "middle way." He would attempt to keep up pressure on the Japanese without inciting them to new violence. To that end, he set about coordinating Far Eastern policy with the British, and gave increased attention to Jiang Jieshi, whose forces in late 1940 were apparently close to exhaustion. Although FDR rejected Jiang's bid for outright alliance, he promised Jiang fifty modern fighter planes, pledged a $100 million credit, and took steps to provide passports to American military personnel who wanted to fly in Jiang's air force. He authorized Colonel Claire L. Chennault to lead the American-supported volunteer units, known as the Flying Tigers. On October 23, he ordered two squadrons of pursuit planes and two additional submarines sent to the Philippines. On December 19, he extended the ban on exports to Japan, ending traffic in iron ore, pig iron, steel, and many types of tools.

II

The advent of 1941 promised no moratorium on America's Far Eastern difficulties. In the first month of the new year, the Japanese set out to tighten their grip on Indochina and renew efforts to gain a foothold in the Netherlands Indies. They also were at work on other fronts, pushing their influence in Thailand, a strategic center in Southeast Asia, by sponsoring its claims to territory in Indochina, and sounding out the Soviets concerning an accord that would assure the northern frontier of the Japanese empire.

At this point, in January 1941, Roosevelt received Bishop James E. Walsh and Father James M. Drought, just back from Tokyo. Both belonged to the Roman Catholic Foreign Mission Society, based in Maryknoll, New York. For two hours, the president listened to a proposal that Foreign Minister Matsuoka had vaguely outlined to the two priests the previous month. As they understood it, the proposal had originated with Prime Minister Konoye. It suggested an agreement whereby Japan would support the United States in the event of a German attack; Japanese troops would leave China after termination of the "China incident" on "the basis of the secret truce terms offered last October by Chiang Kai-shek [Jiang Jieshi]"; the Open Door would reappear in China; and the United States would provide economic assistance to both Japan and China.

Had the offer been official and in good faith, it would have gone far to satisfy American aims in the Far East as well as to detach Japan from its Axis partners. Most historians, however, still question its legitimacy. Although seen as an expression of the views of Japanese moderates, it was not an official proposal of the Japanese government, and the State Department doubted that any government in Tokyo would be able to implement it. It did not, moreover, contain any pledge of restraint in Southeast Asia, leading Roosevelt and Hull to the conclusion that, in the unlikely event the Japanese did agree to leave China, they would merely increase the pressure in Indochina, Thailand, and the Netherlands Indies.

Roosevelt, his attention still centered on Europe, decided to continue the policy of firmness tinctured with caution. He urged the Dutch to maintain their stand against the Japanese. Then, as a warning to Tokyo, he sent warships on cruises to the western Pacific, where they called at the Philippines, Australia, and New Zealand. He bolstered American defenses in Guam and extended the embargo list, adding such items as copper, brass, bronze, zinc, nickel, potash, phosphate, and uranium.

In February 1941, a new Japanese ambassador, Admiral Nomura Kichisaburo, arrived in Washington. Nomura was an intense man of modest intellect who had been foreign minister late in 1939. He thought well of Americans, having been assigned to Washington during the First World War and having briefly become acquainted with Roosevelt. Tokyo hoped that he would head off trouble and at the same time make American leaders more sympathetic to Japanese policy in East Asia.

Unfortunately Nomura was not free to follow his own instincts, though he did try to move Tokyo in a more conciliatory direction. Still, in the absence of anything more constructive, it seemed wise to talk with him, and beginning in April 1941, the new ambassador and Hull had regular conversations, usually in the quiet atmosphere of the secretary's apartment at the Carlton Hotel. One may note that Germany strongly opposed these Hull-Nomura conversations, for were they to succeed, Japan's value to the Germans as a diverting influence on Washington would vanish.

The nine-month pattern of the Hull-Nomura talks became fixed at the first meeting. Nomura would arrive at 8:30 P.M., remaining for two hours. The secretary always felt frustrated, later recalling, "Nomura's command of English was so marginal that I frequently doubted whether he understood the points I was making. I took care to speak slowly and often to repeat and reemphasize some of my sentences." Only after Joseph Ballantine of the State Department was called in could communication be expedited.

In his memoirs Hull later noted that talks with Nomura always seemed "to come to a certain point and then start going around and around in the same circle." Hull kept reverting to his Four Principles: respect for the sovereignty and territorial integrity of every nation; noninterference in other countries' internal affairs; the principle of equality, including commercial equality; and changing the status quo by peaceful means alone. Over and over Nomura repeated arguments of his own: Americans did not understand Japanese intentions; by nature the Japanese were not warlike; only in the face of harassment and injustice by such "satisfied" powers as Britain and the United States had Japan decided that imperialism was the road to national salvation. As for an understanding, that was possible if the United States would restore trade with Japan, help the Japanese obtain materials (oil, bauxite, tin, etc.) in Southeast Asia, press Jiang to accept Japanese terms for peace, stop supporting Jiang if he rejected such pressure, and assist Japan in diplomatic maneuvers against the British in Southeast Asia. For their part, the Japanese would limit themselves to peaceful persuasion in Southeast Asia and keep to the letter of the Tripartite Pact, supporting Hitler only if Germany came under attack.

To American leaders, Japan's proposals amounted to exchanging pawns for rooks and knights, and they never for a moment considered them. Still, Hull avoided an unqualified rejection, keeping up the pretense that the United States might make concessions. He sought to avert a showdown in the Pacific, at least until the conflict over the North Atlantic subsided. Otherwise he made clear his belief that over the previous decade, Japan had been guilty of aggression, treaty-breaking, and violation of the principle of self-determination. Peace and stability, he stressed, could not come to East Asia until the Japanese withdrew to their home islands.

Although hoping that the Americans might cease their opposition to the "new order" in East Asia, Japanese diplomats also looked westward. Unaware that their Nazi partners had decided to ditch the Russo-German nonaggression pact of 1939, leaders in Tokyo were still seeking some kind of neutrality agreement with the Soviets. Japan's position in China and Southeast Asia, they believed, could be strengthened by eliminating its Russian flank.

In mid-March 1941, Foreign Minister Matsuoka left Tokyo, boarded a train at Vladivostok, and set out across the plains of Siberia on the long journey to Moscow. After a cordial hearing in the Soviet capital, Matsuoka went off to Berlin, there to inform his Axis allies of his aims. The Germans had hoped that Japan would join the war against the Soviet Union, scheduled only three months in the future; they therefore disliked Matsuoka's design for a Russo-Japanese neutrality pact. They decided, however, against telling the talkative foreign minister what they had in mind.

The Soviets meanwhile, having caught a scent of German intentions, decided that they too had a flank to secure, the eastern one opposite the Japanese empire. When in April 1941, Matsuoka returned to Moscow, the Russians agreed to a Russo-Japanese neutrality pact, pledging peaceful relations and respect for each other's territory. Not many weeks afterward, on June 22, 1941, German armies invaded the Soviet Union.

Although the Germans had not informed their Japanese ally, they expected Japan to join the fight. Matsuoka was anxious to oblige, but other Japanese leaders were opposed. Since the Tripartite Pact was only a defensive arrangement, the Japanese were under no commitment to support Hitler's attack. Furthermore, Japan was obligated to respect its neutrality agreement with Russia. Matsuoka's opponents also noted that a campaign against the Soviets would divert men and weapons from the Chinese front, postponing a conclusion of the

"China incident." In any event, the Germans probably would defeat the Russians in a few months without Japanese help, and after Russia's collapse, the British would be forced to make peace with Hitler. With Britain out of the war, the Americans would have to come to terms with the Axis, and in the grand division of spoils, Japan would become master of East Asia.

In the first days of July 1941, the Japanese charted their policy. On July 2, in a major strategic conference that included Emperor Hirohito, the government decided not to join Hitler's war against the Soviets unless the Germans were clearly winning. Japan would continue to concentrate on Southeast Asia, and in a few weeks complete the takeover of Indochina. Meanwhile the emperor's agents would step up the campaign to make Thailand a puppet state, then use the Indochina-Siam base to put fresh pressure on Malaya and the Netherlands Indies. If the British or Americans interfered, war would be risked. Such a policy, of course, involved a repudiation of the anti-Soviet Matsuoka, and a cabinet shuffle later in the month brought in a new foreign minister, Admiral Toyoda Teijiro, a more pliant man who was supposedly esteemed by the Americans.

By the fall of 1940, American cryptographers had cracked the Purple Cipher, Japan's highest diplomatic code. The code-breaking apparatus, known as Magic, informed leaders in Washington of Japanese designs to the south, but this knowledge did little to relieve the agony of deciding what America's response should be. Clearly the United States could ill afford merely to look on while Japan took Indochina and Thailand, but just as clearly, the country's first concern lay with the war in Europe. In the judgment of most officials, the United States did not have the means to stand up against the Nazis in the North Atlantic and fight the Japanese in the western Pacific. American leaders faced the problem of how to resist Japanese aggression without provoking active hostilities. As Roosevelt wrote Interior Secretary Ickes on July 1, "it is terribly important for control of the Atlantic for us to help keep peace in the Pacific. I simply have not got enough Navy to go round—and every little episode in the Pacific means fewer ships in the Atlantic."

On, July 24, 1941, news reached Washington that troop transports flying the Rising Sun were steaming toward Saigon, the major city in southern Indochina. By terms of an arrangement made between Japan and Vichy France, Japan would have the use of eight air-fields in southern Indochina and naval bases at Saigon and Camrahn. Fifty thousand Japanese troops were dispatched to the area. The island empire was well poised for further action. It secured land access to Thailand and Rangoon, Burma, where American materials bound for China were being stored. Singapore and Manila now lay only 600 miles away.

After extensive consultation, Roosevelt decided to "freeze" Japanese funds already in the United States. Such an order would place Japanese-American trade under even stricter presidential control, for only a license issued from Washington could release the "frozen" Japanese dollars needed to pay for transactions in the United States, such as the purchase of gasoline. Should the Japanese fail to back off from Indochina, the president could retaliate by refusing licenses. If he chose, he could terminate all commerce between the United States and Japan, a punishment the Japanese could ill afford. Despite restrictions of the previous year, trade with America remained essential to Japan's prosperity. And, as everybody knew, American oil was the lifeblood of the Japanese military mechanism.

But what if the Japanese refused to give way? What if a boycott provoked them to attack Malaya and the Netherlands Indies? Or even the United States? Roosevelt saw that a freezing order would be risky, for it might provoke the very war that he hoped to avert, or at least to delay. He believed, however, Japan's lunge in southern Indochina would so threaten American interests that a strong response was mandatory.

Before executing the freezing order, he decided to give diplomacy one more chance by hearing out Nomura. Roosevelt rejected the ambassador's argument that the move southward was intended to prevent "encirclement" of the Japanese empire by an Anglo-American-Dutch combine. Yet FDR promised that if Japan jettisoned the present maneuver, he would do everything possible to achieve neutralization of Indochina.

On the evening of July 25, when it became apparent that the diplomatic exchange had accomplished nothing, the executive office announced the freezing order. The next day the governments of Britain and the British Dominions imposed their own financial controls on commerce with Japan, and two days later the Dutch government-in-exile in London followed suit. Though FDR did not reveal his intentions, his order was soon processed through lower levels of the State Department bureaucracy into a full-scale trade embargo. Japan's all-important supply of American oil was halted.

Unless Japan backed off, war was now inevitable. On July 27, Roosevelt strengthened the American military presence in East Asia, for he placed the armed forces of the Philippines under U.S. command.

If much of the public was impervious, Roosevelt's economic move made anti-interventionists jittery. Mused legal scholar Edwin M. Borchard, "I wonder what difference it will make to an Indo-Chinese whether a French General or a Japanese General occupies the thatched hut in Cambodia." The New York chapter of the America First Committee attacked the "new and dangerous doctrine that if a foreign power (in this instance Japan) acquires bases of another foreign power (in this instance France), this may be construed as an attack on our country and treated accordingly."

Japan's economy was already in dire straits. The island nation was short of rice, tin, bauxite, nickel, and rubber. Now, with the freeze, Japan's naval oil stocks might last only eighteen months, the army's a year. One historian of Japanese policy, Michael A. Barnhart, suggests that the freeze backfired on the United States. Japan had not yet resolved its debate over advancing into Southeast Asia; indeed it lacked any real master plan. The U.S. embargo only served to unify Japan's ordinarily divided armed forces.

Roosevelt's intentions are still debated. Some historians, such as Irvine H. Anderson, Jr., and Jonathan G. Utley, deny that Roosevelt sought to sever all oil shipments. FDR, they claim, feared that total termination would result in war and therefore sought to keep some oil flowing. Inadvertently in Anderson's eyes and deliberately according to Utley, the State Department bureaucracy, led by Assistant Secretary of State Dean Acheson, levied a de facto total embargo. As Japan advanced, the United States thought that dismantling this embargo would be taken as appeasement, and in mid-September, Roosevelt and Hull approved the measure. In effect, writes Utley, "The Acheson embargo placed a time limit on peace in the Pacific."

Other historians, such as Waldo Heinrichs, see Roosevelt taking a more direct role and one that focused on the critical role of the Soviets. Suppose the Americans were to continue the oil shipments. Heinrichs writes that in FDR's eyes, Japan might "move with Germany against Russia, the survival of which now, at the end of July, was a matter of vital importance to the United States." Even if sanctions led to war, Japan was more likely to move to the oil-rich south than to strike at the critical Russian front. Moreover, in July 1941, the resources of Southeast Asia—as well as Britain's ties to Australia and New Zealand—already remained at Japan's mercy, and loosening the embargo might only threaten these areas further. There is still another factor: Heinrichs finds it difficult to believe that Acheson would pursue a course contrary to FDR's wishes.

One thing, however, was certain: over the next few weeks, the freezing order became the instrument for ending virtually all trade between America and Japan. Now, in a crucial step, Japanese imperialism was openly challenged. As Iriye notes, "From this time on it was assumed that there would be war in the Pacific when the Japanese made drastic changes in their policy. The only question was the timing."

A fortnight after the freezing orders, Roosevelt and Churchill had their Atlantic Conference off the coast of Newfoundland. In their meetings, they ranged over the whole problem of Japanese expansion. Churchill sought a militant American warning, and FDR's original draft message had been a strong one. Although Hull toned the message down before it was delivered, the president was now on record as admonishing Japan that further aggression would force him to take measures "toward safeguarding the legitimate rights and interests of the United States."

Such steps, however, were undefined. Churchill received no concrete commitment of American help. Once FDR returned to Washington, he disappointed the prime minister by omitting any reference to possible war. Furthermore, Washington refused to move parts of the American fleet to Singapore, Britain's major naval base in southeast Asia. Yet, if the British found the message reading like another one of Hull's general statements of principle, the logic was clear: either choose between the earlier framework of cooperation, epitomized by the Washington system of 1922, or isolate yourselves as part of the Axis.

In Japan there was confusion and dismay. The Japanese had expected some response to their incursion into southern Indochina, but the freezing order was more than they had bargained for. What should they do? Retreat before Anglo-Dutch-American pressure was unthinkable. That left one alternative: to avoid economic strangulation, Japan must bring the wealth of Malaya and the Netherlands Indies into its empire. Such a move, however, risked war with the United States. Only a few hotheads in the army felt enthusiasm for such a clash.

In their frustration, Japan's leaders first turned to diplomacy. Back on April 9, 1941, they simply offered to freeze troop levels in Indochina and to withdraw from the French colony once the "China incident" ended. In return they wanted the United States to restore normal trade with Japan, help bring Jiang Jieshi to terms, and recognize Japan's special position in Indochina. Now, on September 4, Japan said it would interpret the Tripartite Pact "independently" and withdraw from China once a treaty was signed.

Early in August, the Japanese proposed a meeting between Prince Konoye and President Roosevelt. At first Roosevelt expressed interest, but Hull talked him out of it. Believing that the Japanese prime minister could make no concessions, the secretary of state said that fundamental differences must be resolved before any summit could take place. Otherwise, it would be a waste of effort, if not an excuse for future Japanese skullduggery. Still, Roosevelt thought it a good idea to string the Japanese along, and through September 1941 he kept Konoye's hopes alive. Konoye meanwhile had a specially outfitted steamer, *Nitta Maru,* standing by at Yokohama, ready at a moment's notice to rendezvous with the American president.

Historians are divided concerning the merits of a summit. A Japanese historian, Tsunoda Jun, who is the editor of an eight-volume work on the Pacific war, claims that Konoye could have overridden military opposition. Although the army would have opposed compromise, the emperor, Tsunoda asserts, would have exercised sufficient pressure so as to force it to knuckle under. The army itself had regarded prospects for the negotiations' success at about 70 percent.

Akira Iriye denies that such a conference could have prevented war. Had the United States yielded to Japan's conditions, including its insistence on at least temporary military occupation of China, it would have alienated public opinion at home, embittered the Chinese, and undermined the Western alliance. Yet Iriye finds that rebuffing Konoye might well have been a tactical blunder. If some ambiguous agreement had resulted, war might have been deferred until the spring of 1942. In fact, it is possible that Konoye would have been able to stand up to Japan's military leaders. "In other words," says Iriye, "there might have been a way for the United States to keep encouraging Japanese hopes for some compromise," and doing so "without alienating the Chinese or actually giving in to Japanese demands at China's expense."

Iriye's view is not the only one. Robert J. C. Butow notes that War Minister Tojo told Konoye he could make no new concessions. Waldo Heinrichs accuses Konoye, "this melancholy nobleman," of having led Japan into such ventures as the war with China, the Axis alliance, and recent moves into Indochina. Always disdainful of Western liberalism, Konoye had endorsed the expansionist notions prevalent in the thirties. Could such a man, "ambivalent about power and flaccid in its use," be relied on to make a genuine peace?

III

By late August 1941, the nerves of the Japanese nation were becoming increasingly taut. One reason was the oil shortage. The United States had supplied 60 percent of Japan's oil; another 30 percent had come from the Dutch East Indies and the Caribbean. The Americans, British, and Dutch, first using one pretext and then another, had turned off the flow of petroleum products, compelling the Japanese to dip into precious reserves.

At the same time, the great British base at Singapore was receiving reinforcements. To its east the Americans had improved installations at Guam and, as noted, brought a squadron of B-17 bombers to the Philippines. As Japanese militants sized up the situation, Konoye's diplomats were living on borrowed time.

By September 1941, Japan's militants were determined to set plans for war with America in motion. When, on the 6th, an imperial conference of Japan's top leadership was convened, the conference decided on war with the ABD powers—the United States, Britain, and the Netherlands—if no diplomatic settlement was reached by October 15. At the meeting the military claimed that it could complete initial operations to the south within six months, thereby freeing its forces for a far more significant struggle. Hirohito recalled that in 1937 the army had made similar promises concerning a quick victory over China. "If," he said, "you call the Chinese hinterland vast, would you not describe the Pacific as even more immense? With what confidence do you say three months?" He then read a poem composed by his grandfather, the Emperor Meiji: "Throughout the world/Everywhere we are all brothers/Why then do the winds and waves rage so turbulently?" Hirohito gave in, however, when the navy chief compared Japan with a patient suffering a critical illness: drastic surgery might produce death, but it still offered the only chance of saving the patient's life.

In deference to the emperor's hope that diplomacy might yet achieve a peaceful solution, the militants agreed to give Konoye a few more weeks. If, in that time, his bloodless methods failed, they would unleash Japan's power in November or December, the last period for many months when weather would favor the kind of operations they had in mind. Historian Iriye goes so far as to call the results of the meeting, which had the innocent title of "Guidelines for Implementing National Polices," a "virtual declaration of war by Japan."

The militants sought Java, Sumatra, Borneo, and Malaya, a vast region rich in such resources as oil, rubber, tin, rice, bauxite, iron ore, and manganese. To bring them under control, the Japanese hoped to neutralize two obstacles, the American B-17 bombers in the Philippines and British ships and planes at Singapore. The big guns at Singapore pointed out to sea, for the British were only conscious of a frontal attack. Rather than face British cannon, the Japanese planned to land troops far up the Malay peninsula and send them southward through the jungle, striking Singapore from the rear. To destroy the B-17s stationed in the Philippines, the Japanese could launch a surprise attack from their nearest base, which was Taiwan, and thereby catch the Flying Fortresses on the ground.

Once secured, how would Japan protect its enlarged empire? The Japanese were counting on their Axis allies to support their drive to

Malaya and the Netherlands Indies by declaring war on the United States. But they knew that in the end protection would be up to themselves. To defend their empire they must first, they decided, destroy the American Pacific fleet based at Pearl Harbor. The fleet ought to be an easy target for a surprise attack from the air. U.S. attention would be riveted on Japanese moves in Southeast Asia, 7,000 miles west of Hawaii. Furthermore, the Americans lacked the aircraft necessary to patrol Hawaiian waters effectively, and American naval personnel naively thought the shallow channel at Pearl Harbor protected their ships from any torpedoes dropped from the air. Thus the Japanese had to keep the Americans focused on Southeast Asia, take care not to "telegraph" the strike at Hawaii, and put into operation new techniques for launching aerial torpedoes in shallow water.

While the American fleet was immobilized, Japanese soldiers would occupy a host of Pacific areas: the Gilberts, Bismarcks, Solomons, and Philippines as well as the Netherlands Indies, Malaya, Thailand, and Burma. By such moves, they would establish a defensive perimeter stretching southward from the Kuriles through the central Pacific and westward across Southeast Asia to the gates of India. From their maze of island bases, the Japanese could annihilate any task force. Americans would watch their sailors and airmen perish in futile attempts to breach Japan's defenses. Eventually they would find the struggle against Hitler too costly to permit any diversion. Growing weary of the fight, they would accept a settlement recognizing Japanese supremacy in East Asia.

Konoye continued his diplomatic efforts, but the piles of dispatches, memoranda, and statements yielded no hope that the United States and Japan might resolve their differences. The Japanese would consider nothing beyond an "independent" interpretation of the Tripartite Pact; i.e., only in the clear case of American aggression would they join their European partners in war against the United States. The United States wanted pledges of an early Japanese withdrawal from Southeast Asia and China, something Japan would consider only after "satisfactory" conclusion of the "China incident."

If Japanese moves in Southeast Asia had touched off the crisis in Japanese-American relations, by autumn 1941 it was clear that China remained a major obstacle to settlement in the Far East. One historian, Paul W. Schroeder, finds the China issue in itself leading to the

Pacific War. Down to July 1941, he writes, the United States had sought two limited objectives: splitting the Axis and stopping Japan's advance southward. With both these objectives suddenly within reach, the United States, argues Schroeder, concentrated upon a third: nothing less than the liberation of China. Washington, in a sense, was raising the ante, suddenly calling for Japanese withdrawal from all occupied territory in China.

According to Schroeder, "this last aim was not in accord with American strategic interests," which centered on avoiding armed conflict in Asia so as to focus upon defeating Hitler in Europe. Furthermore, so Schroeder argues, China was completely incapable of being liberated by peaceful means. Fulfillment of Hull's demands for total capitulation would involve the sudden dumping of a million occupation troops from China on the Japanese home islands and continued Russian and American buildups in the Pacific. Little wonder, argues Schroeder, Japan opted for war. He finds the Pearl Harbor attack an act of desperation.

One must make several observations about Schroeder's argument, for although first presented in 1958, it still finds adherents. First, Japanese leaders never intimated that they might consider a settlement without reference to China. Proposals emanating from the Foreign Office consistently listed resolution of the "China incident" as a condition of any agreement with the United States. When in November 1941, Kurusu Saburu, the special Japanese envoy to Washington, proposed a truce that would have left the China question in abeyance, he received a sharp rebuke from Tokyo.

Second, American leaders were less committed to the idea of liberating China than Schroeder suggests. Kurusu's overtures sparked interest in Washington, and late in November 1941, Secretary Hull drafted a proposal for a modus vivendi similar to that outlined by the Japanese envoy. Hull learned from Magic that the Tokyo government had rebuked Kurusu, and he concluded that such a proposal had no chance. In the face of rumors that he and Roosevelt were planning a "sellout" of China, he dropped the idea.

There is a third factor, perhaps the most important of all. As early as June 1940, diplomat Stanley K. Hornbeck wrote: "There is at present going on in the world one war, in two theaters; there are two countries today opposing force to force, China which has been fighting for three years, and Great Britain which has been fighting for nine months." Or as Roosevelt wrote Ambassador Grew in January 1941, "The hostilities in Europe, in Africa and in Asia are all parts of a single world conflict. Our strategy of self-defense must be a global strategy." Although Roosevelt always kept the Atlantic theater foremost in mind, he realized that if China opted out of the war, Britain's lifeline in Southeast Asia would be threatened. Were Britain to be deprived of that part of its empire that included Malaya, Burma, and Singapore, its situation would become still more perilous. Moreover, the threat to the "Eastern Dominions"—India, Australia, and New Zealand—was even more obvious. Deny Britain its Asian resources, and United States assistance across the Atlantic could never be adequate.

In short, the China question was never isolated. From the American point of view, Japanese evacuation was necessary, both as evidence of a wider change of heart and as insurance against the recurrence of general aggression. It was, however, believed that China at war served to pin down Japanese forces, thereby preventing Japan from assaulting the Russians via Siberia or the British via their Pacific outposts. At a time when Germany threatened to dominate all of Europe, the Atlantic theater remained foremost in the American mind. Hence, although Roosevelt was quite willing to practice Realpolitik by aiding the Soviets late in 1941, he never considered the option of compromise with Japan.

When, in mid-October 1941, it became clear that Konoye would achieve no diplomatic agreement with the United States, he and his cabinet resigned. The new prime minister was General Tojo, who had helped lead the China campaign. In asking Tojo to form a government, the emperor called upon the new cabinet to continue the search for peace. Tojo's biographer, Robert J. C. Butow, has noted that the general did not assume the prime ministership to lead Japan into war; rather it was to break "the deadlock of indecision which had threatened to prevail indefinitely under Konoe [Konoye]." Upon taking office, Tojo was given an imperial command to "wipe the slate clean," that is to review all past decisions, and to work for peace. The order was unprecedented, for no emperor had ever before rescinded a decision of an imperial conference. By his order, the emperor was saying that the September 6 conference was not binding.

When the passing days gave no promise of a peaceful solution, Tojo and his militant associates determined to act. The result: a five-hour imperial conference held on November 5, 1941, in which civil and military leaders set out Japan's course. To appease the emperor, Japan would play the diplomatic game a few weeks longer. If, however, by November 25 new overtures to the United States yielded no accord, the government would ask the emperor's sanction for an attack. Were the status quo to continue, Japan would have exhausted its oil supply, the conference reasoned, whereas the Western powers would have immeasurably extended their strength in the Pacific. Better to fight now, even if the long-range situation was uncertain.

In 1967, the records of such top policy conferences were published in English, revealing that Japan never considered invading the United States. The island nation risked war, and with it military defeat, in the hopes that it could stalemate America, and thereby preserve its dominance of East Asia. As Iriye notes, the lack of any extended vision was all too apparent. All the assumptions made by Japan were questionable: namely that Germany would be victorious, that the Soviet Union would be crushed, and that Britain would either surrender or sue for peace. Once these events took place, the American public would press its leaders to give up. The Japanese military totally ignored the recuperative capacity of the United States, and no less its general economic capabilities. Indeed, among the Japanese, it could be considered treason to warn of any alternative scenario.

Meanwhile Japan sought promises of armed support from Germany and Italy. At the same time, all elements of the Tokyo government agreed that Japan should not purchase German help by agreeing to fight the Soviets. On November 5, the day of the imperial conference, Japanese army and navy commanders learned that "war with Netherlands, America, England [was] inevitable; general operational preparations [were] to be completed by early December." Two days later, Japanese leaders fixed the date for attack at December 8, 1941, Tokyo time.

While American leaders listened in via Magic, the Tokyo government immediately warned Ambassador Nomura of the November 25 deadline. There was no mistaking the inference: after that date the Japanese would strike. The government also reported that an experienced diplomat would soon fly to Washington to expedite negotiation. The new man was Kurusu Saburo, a friend of Nomura and a former ambassador to Germany; in fact he had personally signed the Tripartite pact. As for instructions on continuing the diplomatic effort, leaders in Tokyo directed Nomura first to submit so-called Plan A, which focused on a general settlement. If, as expected, it was rejected, he was to present Plan B, which centered on a limited and temporary arrangement.

On November 10, Nomura handed Plan A to Roosevelt and Hull. Like the replay of a worn tape, the latest Japanese missive called upon the United States to restore normal trade with Japan and to persuade Jiang Jieshi to meet Japan's terms. If Jiang refused, the United States was to stop all aid to China. For their part, the Japanese would not automatically attack the United States if Germany and Italy went to war with the U.S.; rather they would decide any obligation "entirely independently." They appeared to be making other major concessions, but always with qualifications so severe as to make them meaningless. They would guarantee an "open door" to trade in their empire but only when all other parts of the world accepted that principle. They would evacuate troops from China—but only after establishment of peace and "the lapse of a suitable interval." (When pressed, Tojo said twenty-five years.) They would evacuate Indochina—but only after conclusion of the China incident. Within five days, the American government unceremoniously rejected Plan A.

On the same day, November 17, Kurusu first met with Roosevelt and Hull. He knew his mission was window dressing, and he carried no new instructions. He was certainly aware that his government was about to pull the switch that would signal war. Still, he was determined, in his words, to score a "touchdown" for peace. After conferring with Nomura, Kurusu concluded that the best prospect was a truce that would give the governments in Washington and Tokyo time to cool off. He sought a return to the status quo ante of July 1941—Japan would get out of southern Indochina, and the United States and its allies would lift trade restrictions. Such ideas aroused guarded interest among the Americans. The reaction in Tokyo, as mentioned, was different. A few days later, Magic revealed that Japan's leaders had rejected Kurusu's plan and rebuked the new envoy for exceeding instructions.

On November 20, Nomura placed Plan B before Hull. It embodied Japan's final gamble to detach the United States from China and the Dutch East Indies. If rejected, Japan would go to war. Plan A had concentrated on China; Plan B was more concerned with Southeast Asia. Although its language was occasionally cloudy, its meaning was always clear. Japan would advance no further in Southeast Asia and the western Pacific; it would withdraw from Indochina after a general settlement or the restoration of peace with China. The United States would unfreeze Japanese assets, supply Japan with "a required quantity of oil," press the Dutch to reopen the East Indies to trade with Japan, and discontinue support of Jiang Jieshi.

In short, Japan would refrain from further expansion in return for the relaxing of U.S. economic pressure. Power relations in the Pacific would revert to the situation as it existed before July 26. It was the final paragraph that assured rejection of Plan B, for under no circumstances was the United States prepared to terminate aid to China. According to Herbert Feis, historian and former State Department official, "whoever insisted on the last paragraph—Tojo and the Army certainly did—insisted on war."

Hull and his staff at the State Department refused to let the last chance for peace slide. Although they had grown weary in the search for terms, they worked long hours in the realization that November 25 marked Japan's deadline. They sought a truce, a three-month modus vivendi that would allow the United States and Japan more time. Knowing there could be no compromise concerning China, the State Department in turn decided to propose a return to the situation as it had been before July 1941. Japan would withdraw from southern Indochina and retain only 25,000 troops in northern Indochina. The United States would rescind the order freezing Japanese funds, although the resumed monthly oil shipments would be limited to a quantity sufficient for strictly civilian needs. The United States would put no pressure on Jiang but would not look with disfavor on Sino-Japanese negotiations. The experiment would last three months.

As Hull and his staff labored on, they learned from Magic that after November 29 "things are automatically going to happen." Since that date was only days away, it became increasingly clear that time was all too precious. Still, there seemed some advantage in going through the motions of proposing a last-minute armistice. In Hull's eyes, a modus vivendi did not center so much on stressing for the record that the U.S. had sought peace to the very end. Rather it was an effort to buy time until the B-17s could be transferred to the Philippines.

At any rate, the proposal of a modus vivendi died stillborn. The Chinese, catching the rumor of a deal, calculated that any agreement would be at their expense. Hence they pleaded with Washington to accept no terms that might compromise their interests. American newspapers friendly to Jiang Jieshi took up the cry, and corridors and cloakrooms of Congress buzzed with talk that the State Department was selling out China.

The British too objected, with Churchill cabling Roosevelt: "What about Chiang Kai-shek [Jiang Jieshi]? Is he not having a very thin diet? Our anxiety is about China. If they collapse, our joint dangers would enormously increase." As David Reynolds notes, "At this stage in the war, when the Red Army had been driven back to the gates of Moscow, a Chinese collapse would be disastrous."

On November 26, the president learned that five Japanese divisions, loaded on ships out of Shanghai, had been sighted south of Taiwan. He accused the Japanese of acting in bad faith and abandoned the modus vivendi proposal. It was a near certainty that the Japanese would reject the scheme anyhow. Japan's momentum was simply too great. Hull himself, like the rest of the Roosevelt administration, saw the need to maintain China's resistance. Furthermore, he was so weakened by tuberculosis and diabetes that he lacked the energy to campaign for a diplomatic settlement.

Jonathan G. Utley regrets that more imaginative proposals were never considered. In June 1941, for example, Harry Dexter White, special assistant to Treasury Department secretary Morgenthau, offered a scheme that Utley finds both exciting and innovative, a dramatic alternative to Roosevelt's lethargic diplomacy. White would resume normal trade with Japan, renounce extraterritorial rights, offer a major reconstruction loan, transfer the American fleet from the Pacific to the Atlantic, and ask Congress to remove the 1924 immigration exclusion. In return, Japan would withdraw all troops from China (though not Manchuria), give

China its own reconstruction loan, send up to 50 percent of its shipping to the U.S., and sign a nonaggression pact with the Asian powers.

Magic had revealed secret Japanese deadlines, deployments, and stiff bargaining terms. The crisis of the Russian front and discouraging news of Africa, where General Rommel remained supreme, called for Allied solidarity. Above all, says Heinrichs, the presence of Japanese troop convoys in the South Seas made any conciliation sheer appeasement.

On November 26, Hull secured Roosevelt's approval for a ten-point proposal, which he submitted to the Japanese envoys later in the day. Provisions included the withdrawal of all Japanese forces from China and Indochina, neutralization of French Indochina, and Japanese participation in a nonaggression pact with the Allies. In return, the United States would remove the freezing orders, lift the tariff on raw silk, and otherwise encourage increased trade.

A reiteration of principles that Japan had refused many times and submitted strictly for the record, the proposal was sure to elicit a rejection. As Iriye notes, the U.S. was inviting Japan to help reestablish a Western-oriented brand of order in the Pacific. "If Japan refused to do so, then no compromise could be achieved." Nevertheless, Hull had sought to keep the historical record clear.

Physically, emotionally, and mentally exhausted, he wrote Stimson on November 27: "I have washed my hands of it, and it [the situation] is now in the hands of you and Knox, the Army and Navy." That same day a "final alert" went out to commanders in the Pacific, the message to Admiral Husband E. Kimmel at Pearl Harbor reading: "This dispatch is to be considered a war warning. Negotiations with Japan looking toward stabilization of conditions in the Pacific have ceased and an aggressive move by Japan is expected within the next few days."

In Tokyo preparations were underway to play out the final ritual. Late in November, the Japanese government learned that Germany and Italy would declare war on the U.S. if new maneuvers brought on a clash. On December 1, Japan's leaders, relieved that it would not have to fight alone, met in the imperial presence to submit the decision for war. Tojo presided. The emperor uttered not a word, his face expressionless. Silence in such affairs amounted to assent.

Only one question remained: should Japan strike before breaking off diplomatic negotiations? To preserve the chance of surprise, the generals and admirals wanted to continue the diplomatic charade to the last moment. If the attack came without warning, civilian members of the government believed that Japanese honor would suffer irreparable harm. As a compromise, military and civil leaders agreed that Nomura and Kurusu should cut the cords of diplomacy twenty minutes before Japanese planes roared down on American targets—a warning, but too late to alert defenders. As it turned out, Nomura and Kurusu, because of confusion at the embassy in Washington, did not deliver the message ending negotiations until more than an hour after the first bombs had fallen on Hawaii.

In Washington, American leaders glumly awaited the Japanese blow. They knew from Magic that the Foreign Office in Tokyo had directed its embassies to burn diplomatic codes, a sure sign of war. Another intercept reported the Foreign Office's instructions to the Japanese ambassador in Berlin. He was to advise the Germans "that there is an extreme danger that war may suddenly break out between the Anglo-Saxon nations and Japan through some clash of arms and that the time of the start of this war may be quicker than anyone dreams." The Americans also knew that two large fleets of Japanese cruisers, destroyers, and transports were rounding the southern tip of Indochina, their destination apparently Malaya or Thailand.

On December 1, 1941, Roosevelt lunched with Lord Halifax. He told the British ambassador that if Japan attacked British or Dutch possessions in Southeast Asia, "we should obviously all be together." A Japanese strike at Thailand, by moving forces through the Isthmus of Kra, also met with a possible commitment. "We [British] could," Halifax reported home, "certainly count on their [the Americans'] support, though it might take a short time, he [FDR] spoke of a few days, to get things into political shape here." Roosevelt added that for constitutional reasons, he could make no guarantee concerning Thailand, but he indicated such joint action as the use of four-engined bombers stationed in the Philippines and a long-distance blockade, which, he added, "means shooting." Having felt themselves burned in the wake of the Newfoundland conference, when FDR appeared to make a hollow promise concerning the Atlantic, Churchill and his Defence Committee remained wary and cabled Halifax for clarification. After conferring with the president two evenings later, the ambassador responded that such backing definitely meant "armed support," though FDR did say he was unable to predict whether Congress would support him.

Historians read these conversations differently. Raymond A. Esthus sees them as evidence that the Roosevelt administration had finally succumbed to British entreaties for assurance. David Reynolds claims that at long last the British possessed the commitment that they had sought for so long. Warren F. Kimball differs, calling FDR "a master of indirection." "No British record," Kimball writes, "claims FDR uttered the simple key words: I will ask for a declaration of war on Japan if it invades British or Dutch colonies." Had the Japanese avoided any attack on American territory, Kimball notes, Roosevelt would have faced an awkward political decision, even though a Gallup poll taken in July 1941 registered 52 percent of Americans favoring war if Japan seized Singapore or the Dutch East Indies.

Roosevelt also told Halifax that the ABD powers should coordinate independent but parallel warnings to Japan concerning Thailand, Malaya, or the Dutch East Indies. He wanted the American admonition to come first, so as to convince American opinion that he was not simply following the British lead. Thinking along these lines, Roosevelt began to draft a message to Congress outlining American interest in Southeast Asia, doing so to warn the Japanese of a possible clash with America and to condition Americans to the prospect of hostilities. He planned to deliver the message on December 8.

On December 6, while the president worked on his message and on a last-minute appeal to the Japanese emperor, Magic began to decode a long communication to Nomura and Kurusu; it was the Tokyo government's reply to Hull's ten-point proposal of November 26. Thirteen parts of the fourteen-part message went to the White House that evening. Reading the intercept, Roosevelt said without emotion: "This means war." After breakfast the next morning—Sunday, December 7—Roosevelt received the fourteenth part. It announced that because of "the attitudes of the American government," negotiated agreement was impossible.

Later that morning Magic decoded another intercept, this one marked "Urgent—Very Important." It directed Nomura to submit Japan's reply to the ten-point proposal promptly at one o'clock that afternoon, and therefore indicated that something might break in the Pacific at that very hour. General Marshall was advised by his office that important information had come in, and after his usual Sunday morning horseback ride, he hurried to the War Department building. Once he consulted with Admiral Harold R. Stark by phone, he decided to send a new alert to San Francisco, the Canal Zone, Hawaii, and the Philippines. He dispatched the message via the army's message center, the channel least likely to tip off the Japanese that the United States had broken their diplomatic code. Encoded, the message went out by radio within thirty minutes. Operators quickly got through to San Francisco, the Canal Zone, and the Philippines.

Because of atmospheric interference, however, they could get no response from Hawaii. Unaware of the urgency of Marshall's communication, the signal officer in charge of the message center sent the warning by Western Union. Some two hours later in Oahu, a messenger, a Japanese-American youth wearing a green shirt and khaki pants, picked up a batch of cables. One was addressed to "Commanding General," Fort Shafter. As the young man steered his motorcycle toward the army base, his eye caught sight of antiaircraft bursts over Pearl Harbor.

V

Any evaluation of American diplomacy for the years before Pearl Harbor must center on Roosevelt's leadership, and here some historians are finding the president far more cautious than many supporters or critics have maintained. Diplomatic historian Waldo Heinrichs maintains the traditional view, claiming that FDR was "an active and purposeful maker of foreign policy, the only figure with all the threads in his hands." Roosevelt biographer James MacGregor Burns dissents, however, writing, "Roosevelt would lead but not by more than a step. He seemed beguiled by public opinion, by its strange combination of fickleness and rigidity, ignorance and comprehension, by rapidly shifting optimism and pessimism. . . . Not only did he evade strategic decisions, but he refused to let his military chiefs commit themselves on the most compelling matters." Such historians as Burns echo Secretary Stimson, who complained in April 1941 that the president "in effect surrendered the initiative to the Nazis" and "left it to them to choose their time to fight."

At the same time, such programs as the destroyer-bases deal and lend-lease were obviously steps toward war, Roosevelt's assurances to the country notwithstanding. Furthermore, the administration used guilt-by-association tactics, doing all it could to impugn the motives of its opponents. Indeed, it deliberately linked patriotic opposition to Nazism. It authorized wiretaps and G-men probes, and shortly before Pearl Harbor Roosevelt urged the attorney general to launch a grand jury investigation of the America First Committee. In the words of Wayne S. Cole, the leading scholar of anti-interventionism, "Freedom of expression and the right to dissent on foreign policy matters did not rank high in FDR's scale of priorities."

Although the president suspected that total war could well engulf the United States, American mobilization in those years was wheezing along on one cylinder. As late as the summer of 1941, factories were increasing the output of consumer goods. In autumn, as the country edged toward war in the Atlantic, popular magazines carried color advertisements of 1942 automobile models.

Defeat in the Pacific was not the only consequence. After Pearl Harbor, it took two years to mobilize American war industry, thereby initially forcing a strategy in Europe that was so cautious that it weakened the Anglo-American position vis-à-vis the Soviet Union and might have helped to open the way for the eventual communist takeover in Eastern Europe. Indeed many of America's frustrations in the Second World War were derived from the country's weakness at the time of entry.

Did the president ultimately see a need for full intervention? Warren F. Kimball expresses an increasing consensus in claiming that FDR "did not want to join the war against Hitler in the full, participatory sense—with American ground forces used to the fullest. Nor did he want to fight the Japanese. What he wanted was to gain victory and global political influence without paying the price." At most Roosevelt envisioned an air-sea role for the United States. If the president could keep Russia's vast armies from capitulating, he might—so he hoped—not have to send American troops to the European continent.

FDR biographer Patrick J. Maney offers supporting data. The president, Maney notes, rejected Stimson's advice to be brutally frank with the American public, that is to declare bluntly that entering the war as a full-scale belligerent was absolutely necessary. On July 3, 1941, Stimson drafted a message that, he claimed, FDR should deliver to Congress: It has become abundantly clear that, unless we add our every effort, physical and spiritual as well as material, to those free nations who are still fighting for freedom in the world, we shall ourselves be brought to a situation where we shall be fighting alone at an enormously greater danger than we should encounter today with their aid." In fact, Roosevelt did not even use the pretext of the *Greer* and subsequent incidents to ask for a declaration of war.

For Roosevelt to take the United States into the war as a full-fledged belligerent, and to do so in the absence of foreign attack, he needed to accomplish several things. First, he had to exert far more forceful leadership. Historian Jonathan Utley notes Roosevelt's disdain for detail and inability to translate general aims into concrete plans. One example follows another. His quarantine speech of October 1937 drew surprising popular support, but the president himself lacked any plan of implementation. That December, after the *Panay* incident, Roosevelt considered an Anglo-American naval blockade of Japan. Again, however, he advanced no concrete proposal, and the scheme died stillborn. In the fall of 1939, he told Ambassador Grew that the U.S. Navy would resist any Japanese move into Southeast Asia, but he offered no analysis on how one could intercept the Japanese fleet.

In 1941, the president completely turned over negotiations with the Japanese ambassador to his secretary of state; he preferred to stay out of such conversations, as they involved too much drudgery. During the final months of peace, the president only intervened once, to suggest a modus vivendi. But even here, he was opposed by his own advisors and foreign allies, and he let himself be talked out of the proposal.

Second, greater control over the government apparatus was needed. Historian J. Garry Clifford finds "the Byzantine atmosphere of feuding factions and palace intrigue" permeating the whole Roosevelt administration. As Heinrichs notes, FDR himself "liked to drive an ill-assorted team to see which horse pulled the hardest." Hence, the president often failed to function effectively in his crucial role as mediator of his own subordinates, much less to coordinate diplomacy with military and economic moves. Far too often, by not deciding major issues, he permitted bureaucrats, fate, or chance to make crucial decisions for him.

Bitter rivalries continually affected the foreign policy process. Within the State Department alone there were divided counsels. The departments of Navy, Treasury, and War long worked at cross-purposes, and by 1940 a host of lesser organizations gleefully entered into the chaos. Early that summer, for example, the army sought to stockpile weapons for hemispheric use, and the president agreed to make major aid to Britain contingent on its chances for survival. Unless he exercised tight control over the use of the B-17's sent to the Philippines in the fall of 1941, he might have surrendered a crucial initiative there to his military subordinates.

Third, there is the matter of Congress and the public. For several years, Roosevelt had received major setbacks at the hands of both. In 1937, he was unable to alter the composition of a hostile Supreme Court. In 1938, he could not purge the Democratic party of anti-New Dealers or undertake a major reorganization of the federal bureaucracy. Hence, once war broke out in Europe, the president was understandably cautious.

In the summer of 1941, he hoped that the Newfoundland meeting with Churchill would galvanize public opinion. Yet, as noted by historian Theodore A. Wilson, "In the United States the meeting was a propaganda bust." With Americans remaining torn between the desire to aid Britain and Russia while still avoiding war, the conference offered no solution for what Wilson calls Roosevelt's "crisis in leadership."

The closeness of the House vote on draft extension was not a good omen. Nor was the surprising strength of anti-interventionism in November 1941, when the major neutrality restrictions were lifted.

Obviously the argument that one stays out of conflict by approaching the brink of war was singularly ineffective.

There is more, however, to the matter of public sentiment and presidential leadership. When one turns to the wider factor of public opinion, recent research has shown that a president's power to persuade is greatest during international crises, when a frightened populace tends to rally behind strong leadership. As early as 1940, pollster George Gallup observed that "the best way to influence public opinion" on any issue was "get Mr. Roosevelt to talk about it and favor it."

True, never at any time before Pearl Harbor did more than 17 percent of Americans polled favor a declaration of war against the Axis. The public support for convoys, however, might have given the president the leverage he needed. In May 1941, a Gallup poll indicated that 76 percent indicated that the United States should continue to supply England, even at the risk of war. "With clear public pluralities for decisive action," writes historian Michael Leigh, "the obstacle was not insurmountable." As commander-in-chief of the armed forces, the president had the necessary authority to initiate convoys, but for several months, as Leigh notes, "he was restrained by his own disinclination." Roosevelt said to Henry Morgenthau in mid-May, "I am waiting to be pushed by the situation." He certainly never spoke directly to the issue of what the U.S. could accomplish by full belligerency.

Even then, not all historians think Roosevelt would have been successful. FDR scholar George McJimsey argues that had the president executed a more assertive policy, yielding to the urgings of Stimson and Morgenthau, he might have led a divided nation into the conflict. In fact, the United States might have been more rent than in 1917, when Wilson led his nation into the previous war. "As it was," writes McJimsey, "American opinion provided him just enough room for activity to bring into war under the best political circumstances—but not in the icy waters of the North Atlantic." Kimball denies Roosevelt either misread public opinion or abdicated his role as leader. Given the lack of a unifying emotional issue, such as Germany's declaration of unrestricted submarine warfare in 1917, and given the closeness of the recent vote concerning the terms of draftees, FDR was just exercising "plain political common sense."

Most historians today find war with Hitler inevitable, and undoubtedly the great majority deny that Roosevelt exaggerated the long-term threat of the Axis. Yet one must concede that it was only the Pearl Harbor attack that truly united the nation, and here the responsibility does not lie entirely at the feet of the anti-interventionists. Roosevelt's guilt-by-association attacks on patriotic foes of intervention and his blatant deception on crucial matters did little to maximize consensus, much less educate the American public.

Although any national leader is often forced to act on an ad hoc basis, Roosevelt appeared to make an absolute virtue out of government by improvisation. His aversion to clear-cut decisions was deep-rooted and lasted his entire life. The president moved by fits and starts; there was little cohesion. J. Garry Clifford posits that if FDR did steer a course toward war, he did not know "his own speed or the exact location and identity of the enemy."

Roosevelt obviously sought defeat of the Axis, but to the end he was vague about full-scale intervention. Even in November 1941, after Congress had permitted the arming of merchant ships and their entrance into war zones, Roosevelt appeared irresolute. He still postponed any decision concerning the actual sending to Europe of U.S. convoys under U.S. escort. As historian David Reynolds notes, "In the end it was Hitler who would decide what constituted provocation."

Once in 1943, Roosevelt commented to Justice Felix Frankfurter in connection with a Copernicus Quadricentennial: "Strictly between ourselves, I have little sympathy with Copernicus. He looked through the right end of the telescope, thus greatly magnifying his problems. I use the wrong end of the telescope and it makes things easier to bear."

In a sense, the diplomacy of 1931 to 1941 reveals how such evasion of reality became the foundation of American foreign policy. But one thing is clear: if Roosevelt bore some responsibility for this evasion, it was not his alone but rather was shared by the majority of his fellow citizens.

CHAPTER SIX

Day of Infamy

In commenting on that famous dawn of December 7, 1941, presidential speech writer Robert E. Sherwood said: "Millions of words have been recorded by at least eight official investigating bodies and one may read through all of them without arriving at an adequate explanation of why, with war so obviously ready to break out *somewhere* in the Pacific, our principal Pacific base was in a condition of peacetime Sunday morning somnolence instead of a Condition Red (emphasis his)." Many Americans ever since have shared Sherwood's amazement, and perhaps the appearance of a devil theory was inevitable, that is the belief that Pearl Harbor was rooted in a monstrous plot hatched in the dark recesses of Washington.

According to a conspiracy thesis that emerged soon after the United States entered the war, by 1940 Roosevelt was afire with one thought: to take the U.S. into war with Germany. His purpose? To save Britain and later Russia, and to increase his own prestige and power. The destroyer-bases deal and lend-lease were part of the presidential scheme to provoke Hitler. As, however, the German dictator would not accommodate the president by furnishing any pretext for conflict, the Machiavellian Roosevelt simply increased the pressure upon Japan instead. Because of the Tripartite Pact, war with one Axis power would likely mean war with the other.

In this scenario, Roosevelt and his fellow conspirators—secretaries Hull, Stimson, and Knox, and General Marshall—deliberately, secretly, indeed diabolically—incited the Japanese to bomb Pearl Harbor. First, they pushed the Japanese into a position where they had to retreat from the Asian mainland or fight to retain it. The Roosevelt administration knew that faced with such a choice, the Japanese would fight. Second, to unite the country, the presidential cabal determined that Japan should strike the first blow. As a lure for a sneak attack, the president exposed the Pacific fleet at Pearl Harbor. The price of Roosevelt's treachery? Destruction of two battleships, immobilization of six others, loss of several lesser vessels, elimination of 188 army and navy planes, and the death of 2,403 Americans.

Advocates of the conspiracy thesis are part of a movement since called "World War II Revisionism." In 1948, only three years after the war ended, Charles A. Beard's *President Roosevelt and the Coming of the War* was published. In this volume, one of the nation's leading historians and political scientists accused FDR of calculated duplicity. The cost went far beyond the lives of the military personnel stationed at Pearl. Rather, said Beard, Roosevelt secretly usurped powers belonging to Congress and the people and thereby placed the whole principle of an American Republic in jeopardy.

In 1952 a more extreme account appeared: Charles Callan Tansill's *Back Door to War: The Roosevelt Foreign Policy, 1933–1945*. Here a professional historian began his narrative with the sentence: "The main objective in American foreign policy since 1900 has been the preservation of the British Empire." The tone is conveyed by his indictment of General Marshall's leisurely horseback ride on the morning of December 7, before he learned of the attack on Pearl Harbor, which Tansill contrasted to Paul Revere's "famous ride to warn his countrymen of the enemy's approach and thus save American lives."

A year later, the most ambitious effort of all appeared. Harry Elmer Barnes, a noted World War I revisionist and sociologist, edited *Perpetual War for Perpetual Peace* (1953), an anthology of revisionist authors. "In order to promote Roosevelt's political ambitions and his mendacious foreign policy," wrote Barnes in the concluding chapter, "some three thousand American boys were quite needlessly butchered at Pearl Harbor."

Today, years after the conspiracy thesis has been discredited, it still finds an occasional echo. In 1982, the popular writer John Toland accused Roosevelt and his inner circle of foreknowledge of the attack *(Infamy: Pearl Harbor and Its Aftermath)*. In 1991, two intelligence specialists, Englishman James Rusbridger and Australian Eric Nave, argue that it was Churchill, not Roosevelt, who knew of the attack beforehand; in fact the prime minister deliberately failed to warn FDR so as to drag the president into a war that would defend Britain's Far Eastern interests *(Betrayal at Pearl Harbor: How Churchill Lured Roosevelt into World War II)*. In 2000, journalist and navy veteran Robert Stinnett saw the U.S. deliberately provoking war in accordance with a prearranged plan designed by a junior naval officer *(Day of Deceit: The Truth about FDR and Pearl Harbor)*.

I

Toward the end of October 1941, a large part of the imperial Japanese fleet returned to its home islands. Stevedores were loading ships with equipment needed to operate in a tropical climate, undoubtedly Southeast Asia. But curiously enough, thirty-three of the vessels— carriers, battleships, cruisers, destroyers, and tankers—were taking on winter gear. To one of the ships, the giant carrier *Akagi* stationed off southern Kyushu, workmen were delivering a large crate. Inside was a mockup of the American naval base at Pearl Harbor. Also receiving attention were twenty-seven of Japan's *I*-class submarines. More than three hundred feet long, these were the finest subs in the world. Five of the big underwater boats were specially rigged to carry two-man "midget" submarines.

The proposed operation: one of the greatest surprises in all military history, an attack on the United States Pacific fleet located 3,000 miles away in Hawaii. Furthermore, strikes were planned against Singapore, Malaya, the Dutch East Indies, and the Philippines.

Aboard the flagship *Akagi*, a handful of top officers pulled apart the crate containing the mockup. Studying the model with particular intensity were Commander Genda Minoru, a young, talented staff officer in charge of the projected attack, and Lieutenant Commander Fuchida Mitsuo, the veteran flier who would lead the Attack Air Groups. Meanwhile, at scattered locations throughout Japan, the cream of Japan's naval air arm completed a long period of simulated attacks on stationary targets. Then, summoned by Genda, they made their way to the *Akagi*. When they assembled, Genda rolled out maps of the Hawaiian island of Oahu, showed them the mockup of Pearl Harbor, and explained that they would attack American vessels resting at their moorings. Hence the practice in hitting nonmoving objectives.

On November 11, those *I*-class boats not carrying midget submarines began, in groups of three, to leave their berths at Kure and Yokosuka. Seven days later those with midgets slipped into the Pacific: destination Hawaii. That same day, November 18, the thirty-three surface vessels, one by one, weighed anchor, steamed far out to sea, then swung northward toward Hitokappu Bay in the Kurile Islands. To deceive American monitors, radio operators still in port tapped out a stream of fake messages indicating that no task force had departed. Adding to the deception, large parties of sailors from Yokosuka Naval Barracks went to Tokyo on sightseeing tours. Naval leaders hoped that foreign observers would take note.

Hitokappu Bay, located in Etorofu, the largest of the Kuriles, was a gloomy, forsaken place. Snow capped the peaks that surrounded the harbor, walrus and seals sprawled lazily on the beaches. On a small concrete pier were thousands of drums of oil; sailors shivered as they loaded these on ships and lashed them to decks. Meanwhile, in briefing rooms of the *Akagi*, the task force's leader, Vice Admiral Nagumo Chuichi, went over plans with subordinate commanders and airplane crews. If the aviators were enthusiastic, the commanders were subdued, for they knew that if the mission were to succeed, the task force would have to plow undetected across three thousand miles of open sea. Complicating the operation was a major problem—the process of maneuvering tankers alongside warships every three days, a hazardous business in the cold, choppy waters of the North Pacific.

At length everything was set, and on November 25, the architect of the Japanese attack, Admiral Yamamoto Isokoru, personally radioed the order to proceed. That night three submarines moved out.

They ranged 200 miles ahead of the task force, watching for merchantmen that might tip off the Americans. At dawn the following morning, from the bridge of the *Akagi*, Admiral Nagumo gave the sign. Signal lights blinked, and through a dense fog the task force slipped out of the harbor into the icy waters. The course was almost due east—outside the lanes normally used by commercial vessels. To avoid detection the flotilla maintained radio silence. Rigid orders forbade any garbage dumping. When emptied, oil drums went into storage. Firing the ships' boilers was the best quality fuel oil, used to keep down the smoke. At night the fleet observed a total blackout.

Pilots memorized the entire terrain of Oahu, studied silhouettes of American ships, and went through calisthenics. The thin, grim-set Admiral Nagumo paced the bridge of the *Akagi*, worried lest he receive orders to return. On the night of December 2, his anxiety ended, for an officer handed him a message from imperial headquarters: "Climb Mount Niitaka." A mountain in Taiwan, Mount Niitaka was the highest peak in the Japanese empire; the message signaled the green light for the attack. Next day, as the task force steamed 900 miles north of Midway, ship captains summoned men to top decks and announced the fleet's objective: Pearl Harbor. Cries of "Banzai!" pierced the Pacific air. Seamen wept. Many wrote letters home, one man scribbling: "An air attack on Hawaii! A dream come true!"

After holding the same easterly course a few hours longer, Nagumo's ships veered to the southeast. At this point, the sea became heavy, gale-force winds lashed the task force, huge waves swept several men overboard. The ships never paused. Even when fog settled over the flotilla, raising the danger of collision, speed was maintained. On the morning of December 6, as the sea continued to churn, the tankers refueled the warships for the last time, and amid sentimental farewells, fell away from the striking force.

As it pressed down on the island of Oahu, the fleet received a radio message from Yamamoto: "The moment has arrived. The rise or fall of our empire is at stake." Ship captains again ordered men to top decks. Their voices blaring excitedly over loudspeakers, the captains read Yamamoto's communication, then issued their own patriotic calls to greatness. Seamen cheered. Up the mast of the *Akagi* went the same flag that had flown over Admiral Togo Heihachiro's flagship *Mikasa* in 1905, when the Russian fleet was annihilated in the Tsushima Straits. As the flag whipped in the wind, the men of the great carrier spontaneously broke forth with the Japanese national anthem. From the bridge of the *Akagi*, Nagumo now ordered full speed ahead: twenty-four knots. Radio operators monitored broadcasts from Honolulu stations KGU and KGMB for any hint that the Americans had detected the task force. All they heard were Hawaiian ballads and routine programs. The only distressing note came from Tokyo, a coded message revealing that the aircraft carriers of the American Pacific fleet presently were absent from Pearl Harbor .

Several hundred miles to the south, the submarine fleet already had taken position around Oahu. In addition to launching the midget submarines for an underwater sortie inside Pearl Harbor, the *I*-class boats were ordered to sink any American ships that tried to escape after the assault from the air. When darkness settled over the Pacific, the submarines rose to the surface. Seamen could see neon lights flashing in Honolulu; some could hear the strains of music drifting out from Waikiki Beach. In five of the vessels there was grumbling. Crews of the midget submarines resented the order restraining their attack until the airplanes had made the first run at the American fleet.

Meanwhile, through the night of December 6–7 (Honolulu time), Nagumo's task force plowed through the swelling sea. Few men slept. Then at 5:00 A.M., Sunday, December 7, crews began final preparations. Darkness still enveloped the fleet. At 5:30 two seaplanes catapulted to the air to make a final reconnaissance of Pearl Harbor. Soon the six "flattops" were alive with the roar of engines as mechanics made last-minute adjustments. On lower decks, airmen nervously slipped into clean uniforms, checking goggles, helmets, and other personal gear. Some carefully wrapped about themselves hashimaki headbands, traditional symbols indicating that the wearers must be prepared to die. Others knelt before little Shinto shrines, sipped ceremonial draughts of sake, and prayed that heaven would bless their mission. Next a quick breakfast. Then a final briefing.

A few minutes before six o'clock the airmen moved up to flight decks. Air crews on the *Akagi* lined up facing the ship's bridge and, on receiving the formal command to carry out orders, dashed to their planes. The carriers now were swinging in a giant arc, turning their noses into the north wind. In the lead aircraft, Commander Fuchida was pulling on his helmet when a mechanic leaped to the wing, handed him a red and gold turban made of silk, and asked: "Sir, may I offer you this with respect, from the mechanics?" Fuchida accepted the gift, wrapped it around his head, and started his engine. Other planes followed.

Within seconds, the first wave of planes was poised—engines screaming, blue flame spitting from cowlings. The commander, his turban flapping in the wind made by his propeller, peered down the flight deck. The sky was black; pale blue lights marked out the runway. He closed the canopy of his aircraft. At the end of the deck, the control officer, holding a green lamp, moved his arm in a circle. As the carrier rocked and pitched, Fuchida's plane lurched forward, roared down the flight deck, and took to the air. One by one, from all six carriers, the fighter planes (the famous Zeroes), dive bombers, torpedo planes, and high-level bombers repeated the maneuver—183 aircraft in all. Sailors cheered them on their way with cries of "Banzai!" At 10,000 feet, the planes assembled for the attack. Pearl Harbor lay 230 miles to the south and slightly west.

As the air squadron droned toward Pearl Harbor at 146 miles per hour, Fuchida noted heavy cloud formations. He feared he might find the target blanketed. Then, about seven o'clock, the clouds parted and out of the eastern sky a shimmering morning sun beamed across the Japanese planes. Visibility would be perfect. Forty minutes later, the commander, peering into the distance, could see the surf breaking against a shoreline: Kahuku Point, Oahu.

On reaching the point, the attacking force divided, one group peeling off for an assault on the American army's air base, Wheeler Field, near the center of the island; the other, under Fuchida, proceeding toward Pearl Harbor, on the south coast of Oahu. As the lush Hawaiian countryside passed beneath his wings, Fuchida pondered another question: which group of attackers should he send first against the American ships, torpedo planes or dive bombers? It would be better, he first thought, to lead with the torpedo planes, letting them launch their missiles before dive bombers spoiled targets. Yet, as torpedo planes were slow, they could be shot down more easily. In the event his squadron had lost the element of surprise, therefore, he would dispatch the dive bombers first, doing so in the hope that the confusion created by their assault would afford some protection for the torpedo planes.

Minutes later Fuchida and his airmen could see Pearl Harbor. They expected antiaircraft fire. There was none. No interceptor planes rose to meet them. And spread out below in neat alignment were main elements of the U .S. Pacific fleet, including eight battleships. Amazed, Fuchida wondered if the Americans recalled Japan's surprise attack on the Russian naval base at Port Arthur in 1904, the first action of the Russo-Japanese War.

Fuchida pulled back the canopy of his plane and fired a single "black dragon " signal flare, indicating that the attack was a surprise. The honor of striking the first blow at the American fleet had fallen to the lumbering torpedo planes. Taking aim on "battleship row," the planes swooped to sea level. They headed straight for the giant dreadnoughts, released their torpedoes, and banked sharply away. But Fuchida, thinking some pilots had missed his signal, had fired a second "black dragon." This time the flares, two in number, were the signal for "surprise lost." Seeing the second flare, dive bomber pilots thought the commander wanted them to go in first, and they screamed to the attack. Amid the confusion, the High Command's carefully integrated plan was ruined.

Although the Japanese found both waves of air strikes successful beyond all expectation, they failed to follow through. Therefore, the base itself was not pulverized. Nor were Oahu's vast fuel stores destroyed. Nor were American carriers at sea sought out and sunk. Indeed, one might well find such failure Japan's single greatest strategic error of the entire Pacific conflict.

II

There remains much legend concerning the Pearl Harbor strike. Late in July 1941, Japanese Admiral Yamamoto Isoruku mused, "Under present conditions I think war is inevitable. If it comes, I believe there would be nothing for me to do but attack Pearl Harbor at the outset, thus tipping the balance of power in our favor." Yet even Yamamoto's role has been unclear.

For one thing, contrary to myth, Japan had not been planning the attack for years. Rather, Yamamoto first broached this scheme in the spring of 1940. He realized that Japan could never achieve ultimate victory over the United States, but he hoped that a devastating blow would break America's will to resist Japan's Pacific advances. Personally no one in Japan desired war less than Yamamoto, and the Harvard-trained admiral was highly critical of Matsuoka and Konoye.

Furthermore, it was not Yamamoto but Commander Genda Minoru, a Japanese Billy Mitchell, who supplied so much technical knowledge that the plan could accurately be called the "Genda plan." (Years later, when Genda was visiting London, the press asked him if he had any second thoughts about the attack. He replied that Japan should have immediately invaded Hawaii, at which point the public outrage was so great that the Japanese Embassy promptly hustled him home.)

More legends have been shattered. In reality, the attack was not a supersecret, known only to a handful of Japanese. About a hundred officers, plus a few civilian leaders and Emperor Hirohito, knew about Operation Hawaii. Indeed, the attack force could not have been gathered without that number being informed. And even had the Japanese learned that Pearl Harbor was fully mobilized, they would not have turned back. Yamamoto specifically warned the First Japanese Air Fleet that it might have to fight its way to the target, incurring heavy losses in the process.

More important issues, however, have long been debated, and here it is necessary to examine the claims of the World War II revisionists. In the revisionist view, the economic sanctions upon Japan, completed in the summer of 1941, and Roosevelt's refusal to meet with Prince Konoye Fumimaro demonstrate that American leaders were seeking a back door to war. The revisionist case, however, has always centered upon Pearl Harbor: the idea that Roosevelt lured the Japanese to Hawaii by exposing the fleet and letting the raid come without tipping off army and navy commanders. Their questions are admittedly embarrassing.

Take the whole matter of the Magic messages. Certain diplomatic intercepts revealed Japan's unmistakable interest in U.S. warships at Pearl Harbor. Tokyo had asked Japanese agents in Hawaii to make meticulous reports, including specific identification of battleships, aircraft carriers, and cruisers at anchor. One message, sent on September 24 and decoded on October 9, read, "If possible, we would like [you to inform us] when there are two or more vessels alongside the same wharf."

Why then did leaders in Washington fail to provide Hawaii with one of the Magic decoders, particularly as both Manila and London possessed one? Did they fear that Hawaii's army and navy commanders would learn of their conspiracy? And what about the "east wind rain" code? Magic had revealed that the words "east wind rain" in Japanese weather broadcasts would be Tokyo's signal to embassies that a break with America was imminent. Revisionists are sure that a monitor picked up the signal and that officials in Washington suppressed the information. As intercepted messages, decoded in the first days of December 1941, indicated that a Pacific war was about to break out, why did Washington fail to reiterate the warning to Pacific commanders using the most forceful language—unless, of course, Washington secretly wanted surprise?

Other administration moves appear, on the surface at least, to be downright bizarre. Why did Roosevelt ignore the warnings of Admiral James O. Richardson, commander of the Pacific fleet, who in October 1940 personally warned Roosevelt that exposing his squadron at Pearl Harbor was an unnecessary risk? Rather than heeding Richardson's caveat, FDR removed him from command three months later, replacing him with Husband E. Kimmel. Had Richardson been allowed to keep the fleet at San Diego, it would have had an additional 2,000 miles of protection.

What else except conspiracy could explain the famous "maneuver" remarks, made at a White House gathering less than two weeks before the Pearl Harbor attack? According to Stimson's diary entry for November 25, 1941, FDR "brought up the event that we were likely to be attacked perhaps next Monday [December 1], for the

Japanese are notorious for making an attack without warning, and the question was what we should do. The question was how we should maneuver them into the position of firing the first shot without allowing too much danger to ourselves."

Why, on December 2, did Roosevelt order three small vessels, flying the American flag and armed only with one small gun and a machine gun, to patrol the "West China Sea" and the Gulf of Siam? What other reason than to insure American involvement before Japan knocked out British forces in Southeast Asia?

Why did Roosevelt, knowing war to be at hand, fail to send the battleship fleet to sea—unless he wanted it to come under attack? Why were the Pacific fleet's aircraft carriers absent from Pearl Harbor on the fateful Sunday morning? Was it because the president was willing to sacrifice battleships but wanted to save the carriers?

And why did General Marshall, on learning from an intercept that a Japanese attack might come at 1:00 P.M., December 7 (Washington time), transmit an alert to Hawaii by commercial telegraph? He could have used the "scrambler" telephone on his desk, a device that made phone conversations unintelligible to unauthorized listeners. Did he deliberately want the message to arrive too late?

Regarding revisionist questions about Pearl Harbor, more mainline historians offer "nonconspiratorial" answers for each indictment. Roosevelt, they claim, genuinely believed that the presence of the fleet at Pearl Harbor served as a deterrent. On Japan's interest in ships at Pearl Harbor, intercepts reveal that Japanese agents were collecting information on ships at several points, including the Canal Zone and Singapore; American intelligence saw nothing that unusual about inquiries concerning Hawaii. On failing to provide Hawaii with a Magic decoding device: such machines were difficult to assemble, and of course the more machines about, the greater the chance that the Japanese would realize that the United States had broken the Purple Cipher. Nor did access to Magic invariably lead one to discern Japan's aims accurately. After all, the Philippines possessed a Magic machine, but commanders there did not conclude from intercepts that they too faced imminent attack.

When we turn to the "east wind rain" signal, antirevisionists find shaky the testimony of the naval officer who claims to have seen it. Even had its existence been proven beyond question, it would have added little to what an ordinary newspaper reader could have learned. As for giving war alerts, on November 27 Washington had issued commanders a "war warning." As Stimson said later, "we assumed that . . . it would not be necessary to repeat that warning over and over again during the ensuing days."

Magic itself, one could argue, was a mixed blessing. If it permitted the U.S. to read diplomatic moves accurately, it caused American leaders to feel smug. In the words of military writer Ladislas Farago, "Mr. Roosevelt and his associates . . . assumed that thanks to the 'Magics,' they could learn well in advance everything the Japanese were planning, enabling them to apply whatever preventive or counter measures they deemed advisable and necessary." Thus, writes Farago, Magic was "partly responsible for the complacency with which the American authorities approached the final crisis in November and December 1941."

The "maneuver" statement does not prove conspiracy. According to antirevisionists, the secretary of war was anticipating a Japanese strike somewhere in the Pacific. He was therefore seeking an announcement, perhaps a presidential declaration, that such a blow would threaten American interests. If it fell, the president could claim that Japan had fired the first shot and ask Congress for war. Certainly the decision makers in Tokyo had already formulated a policy of force on their own and did not need FDR's machinations. Roosevelt's defenders see the "defensive information patrol" of three ships as a genuine intelligence effort, established to meet Britain's request for cooperation in tracing Japanese moves.

As for the president's failure to send battleships to sea, his naval advisers did not think any power could launch aerial torpedoes in a channel as shallow as that at Pearl Harbor. Therefore, they believed Hawaii the safest place in the Pacific for the fleet. On the absence of the carriers: those "flattops" available for duty were delivering planes for defense of Wake and Midway islands, under the circumstances a most legitimate enterprise. In regard to Marshall's failure to use the scrambler telephone, biographer Forrest C. Pogue notes that no one suggested its use: "If anyone had, Marshall would have not risked revealing that the United States had broken the Japanese diplomatic code by relying on the dubious security of the scrambler then in use."

Though the Japanese sought information on all Pacific installations, they showed far greater interest in the Panama Canal and the Philippines than in Hawaii. Furthermore, not one Japanese intercept earmarked Hawaii, or any other U.S. possession, for attack. Far more American intelligence would have been needed to predict such a strike. Moreover, the United States lacked spies in Japanese government offices; it did not make regular air reconnaissance of the Japanese navy or recruit observers of ship movements; and it failed to put code intercept units aboard ships sailing close to Japan. In short, not enough intelligence was collected, something not surprising when, as Dwight D. Eisenhower later conceded, the army general staff had treated intelligence as a stepchild.

Of course, Pearl Harbor was only one phase of a massive Japanese offensive that included the Philippines, Guam, and Midway. Had the Philippines alone been attacked, the U.S. would still have been at war. Revisionists stress Pearl Harbor, as historian Robert J. C. Butow notes, because after many years it still has the power to capture our attention.

According to Gordon W. Prange, whose definitive history of the attack appeared in 1981, the American command in Hawaii bears a heavy responsibility. Lieutenant General Walter C. Short, commanding general of the Hawaiian district, was preoccupied with training at the expense of fulfilling his primary task, which was to guard the fleet. Because of his obsession concerning sabotage, ammunition was not available when the strike came. In addition, he failed to use radar and ignored Washington's order to undertake reconnaissance.

Next at fault, writes Prange, was Rear Admiral Claude C. Bloch, commander of the Fourteenth Naval District in Hawaii and Short's counterpart as far as defending the base was concerned. Although entrusted with long-range air patrols, he was singularly apathetic, to the degree of being ignorant of the regular watch of the Aircraft Warning System.

Then, so Prange notes, there is Admiral Husband E. Kimmel, commander-in-chief of the U.S. Pacific fleet. All through 1941 Kimmel was priming himself for the eventual day of war, when he would lead his force into such Japanese mandates as the Marshall and Caroline islands. By the same token, he failed to see his mobile, potentially dangerous force as a prime target. He did not vary fleet schedules, did not place antitorpedo nets around the battleships, and ignored the significance of a Japanese order to destroy codes.

Of course, extreme revisionism has obvious drawbacks, and few professional historians have ever been recruited to its ranks. Only by the most tortuous reasoning could revisionists establish that the administration had special foreknowledge of the Pearl Harbor attack, much less deliberately permitted the death of American troops. The more militant of the revisionists made little allowance for human frailties, usually preferring to trace an unfolding plot. They seldom commented on possible Axis threats to the balance of power, stressing instead that captured Axis archives contained no plans to invade the Americas. In their desire to "expose" the personal guilt of Roosevelt and his advisers, they focused upon the activities of the historical actors, thereby neglecting deeper political and ideological currents. It is these deeper currents, revealed in events and ideologies of the years leading up to Pearl Harbor, that enable us to develop a genuine understanding of the origins of the Pacific war.

In fairness, however, one should note that some of Roosevelt's more militant defenders can also be made to look foolish, for they have gone so far as to find Roosevelt engaged in a kind of "nation-saving duplicity." One foe of the revisionists, naval historian Samuel Eliot Morison, declared that in 1940 the climate of American opinion forced Roosevelt "to do good by stealth. "Another opponent, diplomatic historian Thomas A. Bailey, wrote that "because the masses are notoriously shortsighted, and generally cannot see the danger until it is at their throats, our statesmen are forced to deceive them into an awareness of their long-run interests." It is one thing to claim that had not America entered the conflict, Hitler could well have defeated the Soviet Union, established bridgeheads in South America, and slowly strangled the United States. It is quite another thing to argue that in the same way that the doctor must temporarily lie to his patient, so the president dare not inform his own people of either the extent or the implications of his commitments.

Furthermore, the early revisionists raised some significant matters that are often overlooked. First, revisionists correctly stressed the constitutional limits of presidential war-making power and, in this sense, served as forerunners of critics of the Vietnam War. They pointed to presidential deception concerning such matters as the

Greer incident. The precedent of executive duplicity could backfire on interventionist liberals when they least expected it.

Second, revisionists pointed to dangerous illusions concerning the Open Door and the viability of Nationalist China. No self-respecting state, revisionists argued, could accede to headstrong American demands, such as prompt Japanese withdrawal from the Asian mainland.

Third, irrespective of motive, Roosevelt's "defensive information patrol" appears to be brinkmanship at its worst, with another *Panay* incident in the offing. Was such a maneuver necessary, especially as U.S. patrols were already surveying Japanese ship movements? Moreover, it was highly unusual for the president himself to give such detailed orders. Certainly the commander of one of the ships, Admiral Kent Tolley of the *Lanikai*, believed he was used as "bait" in a effort to decoy the Japanese.

Fourth, one does not have to believe in conspiracy to see the Hawaiian commanders as shabbily treated. If anyone should have been informed as to Japan's interest in the anchorage of the Pacific fleet, it obviously was its commander, Admiral Husband E. Kimmel. Yet Kimmel received neither copies of the actual messages nor summaries of them. Furthermore, he was not told that several times the Japanese had set deadlines for the completion of negotiations, after which, in the words of one of the intercepted cables, "things are automatically going to happen."

Far too often the warnings from Washington were ambiguous and lacked follow through, something quite inexcusable. A war warning to Kimmel, dated November 27, mentioned probable Japanese action against the Philippines, Thailand, and the Isthmus of Kra along with the possibility of an attack on Borneo. Yet it was silent about Hawaii, surely an indication that Washington held no such suspicions there. On the same day, General Marshall warned army commander Short: "hostile action possible at any moment." Short was told to undertake reconnaissance and "other measures you deem necessary," but he should not "alarm civil population or disclose intent." The Hawaiian commander replied that his forces were "alerted to prevent sabotage" and interpreted Washington's silence as approval. His alert, however, caused his planes to be bunched closely together, thereby presenting the Japanese with a superb target.

There is one other matter concerning Kimmel. Although he was long accused of failing to institute air reconnaissance, there were simply too few planes at his disposal and too much territory to cover. An adequate patrol needed 250 planes; Kimmel and Short possessed 49. Logistically, if there was an area to protect, it was southwest of Hawaii, in the direction of Japanese bases in the Marshalls and the Carolines, not in the north, from whence the attack came.

If, however, one can discount the conspiracy thesis, one can still explain the roots of unpreparedness by other factors. President Roosevelt himself showed much naiveté. In the spring of 1940, he ordered the U.S. Pacific fleet to remain indefinitely in Hawaii, as he thought it would act as a deterrent to Japanese advances. To the contrary, the stronger the fleet, the more Yamamoto wanted to strike, for the admiral's major target was always the fleet itself, not Pearl Harbor's military installations.

There were additional reasons for Japan's success. First, the weather was perfect, for smooth seas and thick fog hid the attack force. Second, Japanese agents in Hawaii, without violating any American law, reported to Tokyo frequently on fleet schedules that never changed. Third, while Magic had cracked the Japanese diplomatic code, it did not break the all-important military code, so dispatches dealing with the impending attack remained silent. Fourth, once Magic messages were picked up, decoding and translation took time. Finally, when the messages reached Washington, officials there set no priorities for decoding.

Even after the Japanese attack, many American anti-interventionists did not recant. In fact, like the revisionist historians whom they later supported with such zest, several privately blamed the United States. America First chairman Robert E. Wood claimed that Roosevelt had finally gotten America into war through the back door. Charles A. Lindbergh commented, "We have been prodding them [the Japanese] for weeks." Professor Borchard wrote, "The United States was asking Japan to perform acts which only a defeated nation could undertake."

Yet even had Roosevelt been the Machiavellian the revisionists claim, any "back door" efforts could have backfired on him. The Axis alliance was defensive. One recalls that Japan had been under no obligation to declare war in June 1941, when Germany attacked the Soviet Union. Similarly Germany was under no compulsion if Japan should attack the United States. Suppose Hitler had stayed aloof. The American government, forced to fight a major war in the Pacific, would have had a most difficult time convincing its people that Germany was still the greater enemy. Would the public have tolerated continued shipments of arms and planes to Britain when the nation was involved in a full-scale war with a major power?

III

One gnawing question remains: why, within four days after the attack, did Hitler declare war on the U.S.? Germany gained no appreciable military or economic advantages. Japan's attack did not direct Roosevelt's attention away from Europe and toward the Pacific. Japan did not reciprocate by declaring war against the Soviet Union and thereby relieving Hitler's major front. Indeed, the Axis effort was incredibly uncoordinated. As historians Bailey and Ryan note, the Japanese "fought their own war and went down in their own way."

Throughout 1941, as Hans L. Trefousse once observed, Hitler sought to avoid war with the United States while hoping that Japan would divert American attention to the Pacific. The Germans, Trefousse writes, were uneasy about any "departure from the Nazi practice of taking on one enemy at a time," but were powerless to prevent the Japanese from attacking the United States. If, however, Hitler "wanted to keep the Island Empire as an ally, he had to agree to war with America."

Historians James V. Compton and Saul Friedländer both note that Hitler wished to keep the United States occupied in the Pacific, doing so by encouraging Japanese hostility. Writes Compton, "In the face of abundant evidence that a Japanese expansion to the south would, in all likelihood, provoke an American reaction, the Germans pressed their allies toward aggression." A German declaration of war on the United States at this time, both authors argue, was a formality, for American policy in the Atlantic already had created a state of war. In the words of Norman Rich, an expert on Hitler's war aims, "For some time already Hitler had been convinced, and in this he was certainly correct, that Roosevelt was only waiting for an opportunity to intervene in the European war." The president's "shoot on sight" order probably would have given FDR the pretext he needed to intervene. Why, in Hitler's eyes, postpone an inevitable clash? Better to strike at American shipping before its defenses were properly organized.

Conversely, failure to honor the pledge might irreparably damage German relations with Japan, thereby ending any future possibility of joint action against the Soviets. Was it better to have the United States as an open enemy or Japan as a lost friend? Moreover, failure to respond to American provocation would seriously lower Germany's image in the eyes of its satellites and uncommitted neutrals.

There might well be still another motive for Germany's behavior. Failure to give assurances—suggest Trefousse, Compton, and Friedländer might have persuaded the Japanese to call off the attack, open new discussions with the Americans, and reach a settlement that would enable the United States to turn away from the Pacific and concentrate exclusively on Europe.

Still, from the vantage of German interests, did the need to maintain the Axis alliance and prevent a Japanese-American détente balance risks inherent in war with the U.S.? According to Friedländer, in late 1941 Hitler believed that the entire war would turn on the outcome of the Russian front. It would be many months, perhaps a year or more, before the United States could bring much power to bear against its European enemies. Let Germany quickly smash the Red Army and then turn its full might of the *Wehrmacht* on the West while, at the same time, organizing the vast territory from the Urals to the Atlantic. Once that point was reached, so Hitler reasoned, his Reich could hold off the Anglo-Americans and force a negotiated settlement that would leave him master of Europe.

Admittedly, much about Pearl Harbor and its immediate aftermath remains cloudy. But for the United States, December 7 finally ended the state of neither war nor peace. Moreover, two things remain undisputed. First, whatever had been the confusion in the air, the attack was one of the most brilliant strikes in military history. Second, America's long affair with isolation was over.

BIBLIOGRAPHICAL ESSAY

Though dated, the best general bibliography remains the *Guide to American Foreign Relations since 1700* (Santa Barbara, CA, 1983), edited by Richard Dean Burns and the Society for Historians of American Foreign Relations. It is currently being updated under the direction of Robert L. Beisner. For discussion of interpretation, see essays by Ernest C. Bolt, Jr., "Isolation, Expansion, and Peace: American Foreign Policy Between the Wars," and Gerald K. Haines, "Roads to War: United States Foreign Policy, 1931–1941," both in G. K. Haines and J. Samuel Walker, eds., *American Foreign Relations: A Historiographical Survey* (Westport, CT, 1981); Jerald A. Combs, *American Diplomatic History: Two Centuries of Changing Interpretations* (Berkeley, CA, 1983); J. Garry Clifford, "Both Ends of the Telescope: New Perspectives on FDR and American Entry into World War II," *Diplomatic History* 13 (Spring 1989); and Justus D. Doenecke, "The United States and the European War, 1939–1941: A Historiographical Review" and Michael A. Barnhart, "The Origins of the Second World War in Asia and the Pacific: Synthesis Impossible?" both in Michael J. Hogan, ed., *Paths to Power: The Historiography of American Foreign Relations to 1941* (New York, 2000).

Able treatment of Hoover's presidency and the following decade includes Martin L. Fausold's *The Presidency of Herbert C. Hoover* (Lawrence, KS, 1985); Gary Dean Best's *Herbert Hoover: The Postpresidential Years, 1933–1941,* 2 vols. (Stanford, CA, 1983); and Richard Norton Smith's *An Uncommon Man: The Triumph of Herbert Hoover* (New York, 1984). Volume two of *The Memoirs of Herbert Hoover,* subtitled *The Cabinet and the Presidency, 1920–1933* (New York, 1952), has occasional factual errors and should be used with care. Hoover documents can be found in William Starr Myers, ed., *The State Papers and Other Writings of Herbert Hoover,* 2 vols. (Garden City, NY, 1934), and Myers, *The Foreign Policies of Herbert Hoover, 1929–1933* (New York, 1940).

FDR still manages to evoke first-rate research. For general surveys that are as readable as they are scholarly, consult William E. Leuchtenburg, *Franklin D. Roosevelt and the New Deal, 1932–1940* (New York, 1963); Arthur M. Schlesinger, Jr., *The Age of Roosevelt,* 3 vols. (Boston, 1957–60), the latter taking the narrative down through 1936; and James MacGregor Burns, *Roosevelt: The Lion and the Fox* (New York, 1956) and *Roosevelt: The Soldier of Freedom, 1940–1945* (New York, 1970). Fresher material is included in Patrick J. Maney, *The Roosevelt Presence: A Biography of Franklin Delano Roosevelt* (New York, 1992), and George McJimsey, *The Presidency of Franklin Delano Roosevelt* (Lawrence, KS, 2000). David M. Kennedy puts forth a superior narrative of the entire FDR era in *Freedom from Fear: The American People in Depression and War, 1929–1945* (New York, 1999).

Volume four of Frank Freidel's *Franklin D. Roosevelt,* subtitled *Launching the New Deal* (Boston, 1973), covers the first year of the president's diplomacy. For Freidel's general interpretation, see *Franklin D. Roosevelt: A Rendezvous with Destiny* (Boston, 1990). *Franklin D. Roosevelt, His Life and Times: An Encyclopedic View* (Boston, 1985), eds. Otis L. Graham, Jr., and Meghan Robinson Wander, offers some strong entries on foreign policy. Robert Dallek's *Franklin D. Roosevelt and American Foreign Policy, 1932–1945* (New York, 1979), based on prodigious research in manuscript sources, remains the leading general work on this subject. Frederick W. Marks III's *Wind over Sand: The Diplomacy of Franklin Roosevelt* (Athens, GA, 1988) presents a far more critical view of much of the material that Dallek covers. Warren I. Kimball's series of essays, *The Juggler: Franklin Roosevelt as Wartime Statesman* (Princeton, NJ, 1991) has strong material on Britain and Russia in 1941. Wayne S. Cole stresses historical inevitability in "Franklin D. Roosevelt: Great Man or Man for His Times?" in Cole, *Determinism and American Foreign Relations during the Franklin D. Roosevelt Era* (Lanham, MD, 1995). An excellent picture of FDR's worldview is found in John Lamberton Harper, *American Visions: Franklin D. Roosevelt, George F. Kennan, and Dean G. Acheson* (New York, 1994).

Invaluable primary sources include Samuel I. Rosenman, ed., *Public Papers and Addresses of Franklin Delano Roosevelt,* 13 vols. (New York, 1938–1950); Elliott Roosevelt and Joseph P. Lash, eds., *F.D.R.: His Personal Letters, 1928–1945,* 4 vols. (New York, 1947–1950); Edgar B. Nixon, ed., *Franklin D. Roosevelt and Foreign Affairs,* 3 vols. (Cambridge, MA, 1969), which covers international correspondence from 1933 to 1937; the sequel volumes edited by Donald B. Schewe and covering the years 1937 through August 1939, 11 vols. (New York, 1979–1980); *Complete Press Conferences of Franklin D. Roosevelt, 1933–1945,* 25 vols. (New York, 1972); and Russell D. Buhite and David W. Levy, *FDR's Fireside Chats* (Norman, OK, 1992).

Henry L. Stimson offers personal accounts in *The Far Eastern Crisis: Recollections and Observations* (New York, 1936) and in an autobiography, written with the collaboration of McGeorge Bundy, *On Active Service in Peace and War* (New York, 1948). If particularly valuable on the years 1931–33 and 1940–41, the reader should beware of Stimson's exaggeration of supposed differences with President Hoover. Other work on Stimson includes Richard N. Current, *Secretary Stimson: A Study in Statecraft* (New Brunswick, NJ, 1954); Elting E. Morison's *Turmoil and Tradition: A Study of the Life and Times of Henry L. Stimson* (Boston, 1960); Robert H. Ferrell's *Frank B. Kellogg and Henry L. Stimson* (New York, 1963); and Godfrey Hodgson, *The Colonel: The Life and Wars of Henry L. Stimson, 1867–1950* (New York, 1990). Margot Louria, organizing her work around secretaries of state, offers appreciative chapters in *Triumph and Downfall: America's Pursuit of Peace and Prosperity, 1921–1933* (Westport, CT, 2001). For Cordell Hull, note his two-volume *Memoirs* (New York, 1948). In this ghostwritten account, he betrayed a faulty memory and often exaggerated his own influence. Still, the Hull volumes offer many insights to the problems and rationale of American policy before Pearl Harbor. Despite Julius W. Pratt's *Cordell Hull, 1933–1944* (New York, 1964), a new life story is needed. In *Secret Affairs: Franklin Roosevelt, Cordell Hull, and Sumner Welles* (Baltimore, 1995), Irwin F. Gellman finds Hull far too ill to bear the responsibilities he held. In contrast, Michael A. Butler's *Cautious Visionary: Cordell Hull and Trade Reform, 1933–1937* (Kent, OH, 1998) gives a surprisingly appreciative treatment.

Sumner Welles, a diplomat far closer to Roosevelt than Hull, produced such firsthand accounts as *The Time for Decision* (New York, 1944), and *Seven Decisions that Shaped History* (New York, 1951). Welles's son Benjamin offers a positive treatment in *Sumner Welles: FDR's Global Strategist* (New York, 1997) as does Frank Warren Graff, *Strategy of Involvement: A Diplomatic Biography of Sumner Welles* (New York, 1988). Gellman's *Secret Affairs* (see above) is more critical.

Other State Department memoirs include William Phillips, *Ventures in Diplomacy* (Boston, 1942); Hugh R. Wilson, *Diplomat Between Wars* (New York, 1941), and *A Career Diplomat, The Third Chapter: The Third Reich* (Westport, CT, 1973); Charles E. Bohlen, *Witness to History, 1929–1969* (New York, 1973); Nancy Harvison Hooker, ed., *The Moffat Papers: Selections from the Diplomatic Journals of Jay Pierrepont Moffat, 1919–1943* (Cambridge, MA, 1956); Fred L. Israel, ed., *The War Diary of Breckinridge Long: Selections from the Years 1939–1944* (Lincoln, NE, 1966); Philip V. Cannistraro, Edward D. Wynot, Jr., and Theodore P. Kovaleff, eds., *Poland and the Coming of the Second World War: The Diplomatic Papers of A.J. Drexel Biddle, Jr., United States Ambassador to Poland, 1937–1939* (Columbus, OH, 1976); and George W. Baer, ed., *A Question of Trust—The Origins of U.S.–Soviet Diplomatic Relations: The Memoirs of Loy W. Henderson* (Stanford, CA, 1986). John

Morton Blum, ed., *From the Morgenthau Diaries,* 3 vols. (Boston, 1959–1967), and *The Secret Diaries of Harold Ickes,* 3 vols. (New York, 1953–54) present "insider" material.

Though George F. Kennan only came to prominence during the Cold War, his recollections offer an unmatched picture of the American diplomatic service in the 1930s. See *Memoirs: Volume I, 1925–1950* (Boston, 1967); *From Prague after Munich: Diplomatic Papers, 1938–1940* (Princeton, NJ, 1968); and *Sketches From a Life* (New York, 1989). Work on Kennan includes Harper (see above) and David Mayers, *George Kennan and the Dilemmas of U.S. Foreign Policy* (New York, 1988).

Howard Jablon, *Crossroads of Decision: The State Department and Foreign Policy, 1933–1937* (Lexington, KY, 1983) gives Foggy Bottom few high marks. For superior biographies, see Russell D. Buhite, *Nelson T. Johnson and American Policy toward China, 1925–1941* (East Lansing, MI, 1968); Jesse H. Stiller, *George S. Messersmith: Diplomat of Democracy* (Chapel Hill, NC, 1987); H. W. Brands, *Inside the Cold War: Loy Henderson and the Rise of the American Empire, 1918–1961* (New York, 1991); Bernard V. Burke, *Ambassador Frederic Sackett and the Collapse of the Weimar Republic, 1930–1933: The United States and Hitler's Rise to Power* (New York, 1994); Shizhang Hu, *Stanley K. Hornbeck and the Open Door Policy* (Westport, CT, 1995); and Alfred L. Castle, *Diplomatic Realism: William R. Castle, Jr. and American Foreign Policy, 1919–1953* (Honolulu, 1998). Of the varied biographies of Joseph P. Kennedy, Michael R. Beschloss's *Kennedy and Roosevelt: The Uneasy Alliance* (New York, 1980) is the most helpful on the ambassadorial period. Particularly valuable is *Hostage to Fortune: The Letters of Joseph P. Kennedy* (New York, 2001), edited by Amanda Smith. The views of an anti-British assistant secretary of state are described in Jordan A. Schwarz's *Liberal: Adolf A. Berle and the Vision of an American Era* (New York, 1987) and Beatrice Bishop Berle and Travis Beal Jacobs, eds., *Navigating the Rapids, 1918–1971: From the Papers of Adolf A. Berle* (New York, 1973). A host of other diplomats are covered in Richard Dean Burns and Edward M. Bennett, eds., *Diplomats in Crisis: United States–Chinese–Japanese Relations, 1919–1931* (Santa Barbara, CA, 1974) and Kenneth Paul

Jones, *U.S. Diplomats in Europe, 1919–1931* (Santa Barbara, CA, 1981).

Warren I. Cohen, *The American Revisionists: The Lessons of Intervention in World War I* (Chicago, 1967) is excellent on its subject. Typical works of American disillusion concerning World War I include Harry Elmer Barnes, *The Genesis of the World War: An Introduction to the Problem of War Guilt* (New York, 1926); Walter Millis, *Road to War: America, 1914–1917* (Boston, 1935); C. Hartley Grattan, *Why We Fought* (New York, 1937); and Charles Callan Tansill, *America Goes to War* (Boston, 1938).

The Manchurian affair of 1931–33 has been the object of considerable study. L. Ethan Ellis, *Republican Foreign Policy, 1921–1933* (New Brunswick, NJ, 1968) stresses the failure of collective security. Robert H. Ferrell, *American Diplomacy in the Great Depression: Hoover-Stimson Foreign Policy, 1929–1933* (New Haven, CT, 1957) reveals the author's gift for superb prose. Armin Rappaport's *Henry L. Stimson and Japan, 1931–33* (Chicago, 1963) has sought to balance sympathy for Stimson's purpose with criticism of the consequences of his policy. Christopher Thorne, *The Limits of Foreign Policy: The West, the League and the Far Eastern Crisis of 1931–1933* (New York, 1972) presents the best perspective on Western statecraft. Gary B. Ostrower, *Collective Insecurity: The United States and the League of Nations during the Early Thirties* (Lewisburg, PA, 1979) offers far more than the title suggests. Justus D. Doenecke, *When the Wicked Rise: American Opinion-Makers and the Manchurian Crisis of 1931–33* (Lewisburg, PA, 1984) notes that despite bitter debates over coercion, there was far more internationalism than one first suspects. Doenecke has also edited *The Diplomacy of Frustration: The Manchurian Crisis of 1931–1933 as Revealed in the Papers of Stanley K. Hornbeck* (Stanford, CA, 1981).

Several excellent books discuss the Manchurian crisis, some going into subsequent events as well. See Yale Candee Maxon, *Control of Japanese Foreign Policy: A Study of Civil-Military Rivalry, 1930–1945* (Berkeley, CA, 1957); Takehiko Yoshihashi, *Conspiracy at Mukden: The Rise of the Japanese Military* (New Haven, 1963); Sadako Ogata, *Defiance in Manchuria: The Making of Japanese Foreign Policy, 1931–1932* (Berkeley, CA, 1964); Mark R. Peattie,

Ishiwara Kanji and Japan's Confrontation with the West (Princeton, NJ, 1965); James B. Crowley, *Japan's Quest for Autonomy: National Security and Foreign Policy, 1930–1938* (Princeton, NJ, 1966); and Michael A. Barnhart, *Japan Prepares for Total War: The Search for Economic Security, 1919–1941* (Ithaca, NY, 1987). For events leading up to Manchuria, consult Akira Iriye, *After Imperialism: The Search for a New Order in the Far East, 1921–1931* (Cambridge, MA, 1965).

Roosevelt's effort to bring U.S. domestic recovery without cooperation with other industrial states is revealed in Elliot A. Rosen, "Intranationalism vs. Internationalism: The Interregnum Struggle for the Sanctity of the New Deal," *Political Science Quarterly* 81 (June 1966). For firsthand accounts of the London Economic Conference, see Raymond Moley (with the assistance of Elliot A. Rosen), *The First New Deal* (New York, 1966), and Herbert Feis, *1933: Characters in Crisis* (Boston, 1966).

Thorough studies of Senator Gerald P. Nye, the Nye Committee, and neutrality acts include Wayne S. Cole, *Senator Gerald P. Nye and American Foreign Relations* (Minneapolis, 1962); Robert A. Divine, *The Illusion of Neutrality* (Chicago, 1962); John E. Wil[t]z, *In Search of Peace: The Senate Munitions Inquiry, 1934–36* (Baton Rouge, 1963); and Matthew W. Coulter, *The Senate Munitions Inquiry of the 1930s: Beyond the Merchants of Death* (Westport, CT, 1997). One gets a feel for the antiwar mood of the 1930s by reading H. C. Engelbrecht and F. C. Hanighen, *Merchants of Death: A Study of the International Armament Industry* (New York, 1934); George Seldes, *Iron, Blood and Profits: An Exposure of the World-Wide Munitions Racket* (New York, 1934); Charles A. Beard, *The Devil Theory of War: An Inquiry into the Nature of History and the Possibility of Keeping Out of War* (New York, 1936); and Edwin M. Borchard and William Potter Lage, *Neutrality for the United States* (New Haven, CT, 1937, rev. 1940).

Warren F. Kuehl and Lynne K. Dunn, *Keeping the Covenant: American Internationalists and the League of Nations, 1920–1939* (Kent, OH, 1997) is definitive. Michael Dunne, *The United States and the World Court, 1920–1935* (New York, 1988), explains why the United States ultimately rejected court membership. Consult also

Robert Accinelli, "The Roosevelt Administration and the World Court Defeat, 1935," *The Historian* 40 (May 1978), and Gilbert N. Kahn, "Presidential Passivity on a Nonsalient Issue: President Franklin D. Roosevelt and the 1935 World Court Fight," *Diplomatic History* 4 (Spring 1980).

For work on the Ludlow amendment, see Ernest C. Bolt, *Ballots before Bullets: The War Referendum Approach to Peace in America 1914–1941* (Charlottesville, VA, 1977); Richard Dean Burns and W. A. Dixon, "Foreign Policy and the 'Democratic Myth': The Debate on the Ludlow Amendment," *Mid-America* 47 (November 1965); Walter R. Griffin, "Louis Ludlow and the War Referendum Crusade, 1935–1941," *Indiana Magazine of History* 44 (December 1968); and Arthur Scheer, "Louis Ludlow's War Referendum of 1938: A Reappraisal," *Mid-America* 76 (Spring-Summer 1994).

Brice Harris, Jr., *The United States and the Italo-Ethiopian Crisis* (Stanford, CA, 1964) remains the best work on American policy toward the conflict in East Africa, but see also Herbert Feis, *Seen from E.A.: Three International Episodes* (New York, 1947); James Dugan and Laurence Lafore, *Days of Emperor and Clown: The Italo-Ethiopian War, 1935–1936* (Garden City, NY, 1973); and George W. Baer, *Test Case: Italy, Ethiopia, and the League of Nations* (Stanford, CA, 1976). For general studies of U.S. attitudes toward Italy, consult John P. Diggins, *Mussolini and Fascism: The View from America* (Princeton, NJ, 1972) and David F. Schmitz, *The United States and Fascist Italy, 1922–1930* (Chapel Hill, NC: 1988).

As for the Spanish conflict, note F. Jay Taylor, *The United States and the Spanish Civil War* (New York, 1956); Dante A. Puzzo, *Spain and the Great Powers, 1936–1941* (New York, 1962); Richard P. Traina, *American Diplomacy and the Spanish Civil War, 1936–1939* (Bloomington, IN, 1968); and Douglas Little, *Malevolent Neutrality: The United States, Great Britain, and the Origins of the Spanish Civil War* (Ithaca, NY, 1985). All find FDR too weak. Allen Guttmann, *The Wound in the Heart: America and the Spanish Civil War* (New York, 1962) is a sensitive picture of public response to the conflict. The memoirs of FDR's ambassador Claude G. Bowers, *My Mission to Spain: Watching the Rehearsal for World War II* (New York, 1954), should be used with care, for Bowers misrepresents the views he held during the crisis. Several books challenge the claim that Communists dominated American volunteers either exaggerated or flawed: Cecil Eby, *Between the Bullet and the Life: American Volunteers in the Spanish Civil War* (New York, 1969); Robert A. Rosenstone, *Crusade of the Left: The Lincoln Battalion in the Spanish Civil War* (New York, 1969); and Peter N. Carroll, *The Odyssey of the Abraham Lincoln Brigade: Americans in the Spanish Civil War* (Stanford, CA, 1994).

Until the 1960s, major works on United States diplomacy from 1939 to 1941 centered on revisionism and its critics. By far the best of the pro-administration accounts was the encyclopedic William L. Langer and S. Everett Gleason, *The Challenge to Isolation, 1937–1940* (New York, 1952) and *The Undeclared War, 1940–1941* (New York, 1953). Both works remain indispensable. Unusual insight into Roosevelt's thinking on foreign policy is found in Robert E. Sherwood, *Roosevelt and Hopkins: An Intimate History* (New York, 1948), written by a top FDR aide, though for Hopkins see also Henry H. Adams, *Harry Hopkins: A Biography* (New York, 1977), and George McJimsey, *Harry Hopkins: Ally of the Poor and Defender of Democracy* (Cambridge, MA, 1987). For more recent and able defenses of FDR, consult Dallek above and Waldo Heinrichs, *Threshold of War: Franklin D. Roosevelt and American Entry into World War II* (New York, 1988), which stresses the Russian factor. For a critique of the president's administrative practices, note Mark M. Lowenthal, *Leadership and Indecision: American War Planning and Policy Process, 1937–1942* (New York, 1988). In David Reynolds, *From Munich to Pearl Harbor: Roosevelt's America and the Origins of the Second World War* (Chicago, 2001), the author explains how FDR's World War II leadership led to such Cold War phenomenon as a new globalism, a bipolar worldview, the foundations of the military-industrial complex, and the origins of the "imperial presidency."

Among the revisionist works contending that Roosevelt maneuvered the United States into war are Charles A. Beard, *American Foreign Policy in the Making, 1932–1940: A Study in Responsibilities* (New Haven, CT, 1946) and *President Roosevelt and the Coming of the War, 1941: A Study in Appearances and Realities* (New Haven, CT, 1948); Charles Callan Tansill, *Back Door to War: The Roosevelt Foreign Policy, 1933–1941* (Chicago, 1952);

and Harry Elmer Barnes, ed., *Perpetual War for Perpetual Peace: A Critical Examination of the Foreign Policy of Franklin D. Roosevelt and Its Aftermath* (Caldwell, ID, 1953). For a detailed discussion of the first generation of revisionists, see chapter 5 of Justus D. Doenecke, *Not to the Swift: The Old Isolationists in the Cold War Era* (Lewisburg, PA, 1979). Studies of Beard include Ellen Nore, *Charles A. Beard: An Intellectual Biography* (Carbondale, IL, 1983) and the more hostile Thomas C. Kennedy, *Charles A. Beard and American Foreign Policy* (Gainesville, FL, 1975). For Barnes, consult Justus D. Doenecke, "Harry Elmer Barnes," *Wisconsin Magazine of History* 56 (Summer 1973). The political and strategic premises of the early revisionists and their critics are ably discussed in Wayne S. Cole, "American Entry into World War II: A Historiographical Appraisal," *Mississippi Valley Historical Review* 43 (March 1957). Revisionism is both updated and modified in Bruce M. Russett, *No Clear and Present Danger: A Skeptical View of the United States Entry into World War II* (New York, 1972).

For the argument that Roosevelt imperiled national security by continually surrendering initiatives to Germany and Japan, note two works by Robert A. Divine: *Roosevelt and World War II* (Baltimore, 1969) and *The Reluctant Belligerent: American Entry into World War II,* 2nd ed. (New York, 1979). A similar stress can be seen in Arnold Offner, *American Appeasement: United States Foreign Policy and Germany, 1933–1938* (Cambridge, MA, 1969) and *The Origins of the Second World War: American Foreign Policy and World Politics, 1917–1941* (New York, 1975); and John McVickar Haight, Jr., "France, the United States and Munich Crisis," *Journal of Modern History* 32 (December 1960). Offner points to American support for German rearmament, approval of the Anglo-German naval agreement of 1935, limited action in the Ethiopian crisis, and backing of Munich. Barbara Rearden Farnham challenges any indictment in *Roosevelt and the Munich Crisis: A Study of Political Decision-Making* (Princeton, NJ, 1997). Important are articles in David F. Schmitz and Richard D. Challener, eds., *Appeasement in Europe: A Reassessment of U.S. Policies* (Westport, CT, 1990), and in Melvin Small and O. Feinstein, eds., *Appeasing Fascism: Articles from the Wayne State University Conference on Munich After Fifty Years* (Lanham, MD, 1991), the latter covering a wider span than the title indicates. A more controversial defense of FDR is found in Robert Edwin Herzstein, *Roosevelt & Hitler: Prelude to War* (New York, 1989).

For emphasis upon economic factors in American foreign policy, see Lloyd C. Gardner, *Economic Aspects of New Deal Diplomacy* (Madison, WI, 1964); P. C. Hoffer, "American Businessmen and the Japan Trade, 1931–1941: A Case Study of Attitude Formation," *Pacific Historical Review* 41 (May 1972); Frederick C. Adams, *Economic Diplomacy: The Export-Import Bank and American Foreign Policy, 1934–1939* (Columbia, MO, 1976); Patrick J. Hearden, *Roosevelt Confronts Hitler: America's Entry into World War II* (DeKalb, IL, 1987); J. R. Herzberg, *A Broken Bond: American Economic Policies Toward Japan, 1931–1941* (New York, 1988); and Wolfgang J. Mommsen and Lothar Kettenacher, eds., *The United Sates, Appeasement, and the Open Door* (London, 1983). Arnold A. Offner, "Appeasement Revisited: The United States, Great Britain, and Germany, 1933–1940," *Journal of American History* 64 (September 1977), denies that competing economic systems caused conflict.

Superior general histories of World War II include B. H. Liddell Hart, *History of the Second World War* (New York, 1971); John Keegan, *The Second World War* (New York, 1990); Gerhard L. Weinberg, *A World at Arms: A Global History of World War II* (New York, 1994); and Williamson Murray and Allan R. Millett, *A War to Be Won: Fighting the Second World War* (Cambridge, MA, 2000). Superb naval history is offered in Samuel Eliot Morison, *The Battle of the Atlantic, September 1939–May 1943* (Boston, 1947), and *The Rising Sun in the Pacific, 1931–April 1942* (Boston, 1948), volumes 1 and 3 of his *History of United States Naval Operations in World War II*. Morison's *The Two-Ocean War: A Short History of the United States Navy in the Second World War* (Boston, 1963) is a fresher account. Aviation is covered in Michael S. Sherry, *The Rise of American Air Power: The Creation of Armageddon* (New Haven, CT, 1987) and Daniel F. Harrington, "A Careless Hope: American Air Power and Japan, 1941," *Pacific Historical Review* 48 (May 1979). For intelligence, see Ernest R. May, *Knowing One's Enemies: Intelligence Assessments before the Two World Wars* (Princeton, NJ, 1987). The thesis of Benjamin D. Rhodes, *United States Foreign Policy in the In-*

terwar Period, 1918–1941: The Golden Age of American Diplomatic and Military Complacency (Westport, CT, 2001) is revealed in its subtitle, though the book is far from narrow in its scope. Steven T. Ross covers strategy in his *American War Plans, 1939–1945* (Malibar, FL, 2000) as does Edward S. Miller in *War Plan Orange: The U.S. Strategy to Defeat Japan, 1897–1945* (Annapolis, MD, 1991). Mark A. Stoler skillfully captures prewar debates among the American military in *Allies and Adversaries: The Joint Chiefs of Staff, the Grand Alliance, and U.S. Strategy in World War II* (Chapel Hill, NC, 2000). For administration anxieties concerning the Western Hemisphere, see Irwin F. Gellman, *Good Neighbor Diplomacy: United States Policies in Latin America, 1933–1945* (Baltimore, 1979), and David G. Haglund, *Latin America and the Transformation of U.S. Strategic Thought, 1936–1940* (Albuquerque, 1984).

Among the strong biographies that reveal much concerning U.S. army administration are D. Clayton James, *The Years of MacArthur,* volume one, 1880–1941, 3 vols. (1970–1985); Barbara W. Tuchman, *Stilwell and the American Experience in China, 1911–1945* (New York, 1971); Keith D. McFarland, *Harry H. Woodring: A Political Biography of FDR's Controversial Secretary of War* (Lawrence, KS, 1975); and E. B. Potter, *Nimitz* (Annapolis, MD, 1976). Special attention has been given to George C. Marshall. Note volumes one and two of Forrest C. Pogue's life, *Education of a General, 1939–1941* (New York, 1963), and *Ordeal and Hope, 1939–1941* (New York, 1966); David G. Haglund, "George C. Marshall and the Question of Military Aid to England, May–June 1940," *Journal of Contemporary History* 15 (October 1980); and Larry Bland, et al., volume two of *The Papers of George Catlett Marshall,* titled *"We Cannot Delay": July 1, 1939–December 6, 1941* (Baltimore, 1986).

For naval leadership, see Walter Muir Whitehill, *Fleet Admiral King: A Naval Record* (New York, 1952); *On the Treadmill to Pearl Harbor: The Memoirs of Admiral J. O. Richardson* (Washington, DC, 1973); James Leutze, *A Different Kind of Victory: A Biography of Admiral Thomas C. Hart* (Annapolis, MD, 1981); and B. Mitchell Simpson III, *Admiral Harold E. Stark: Architect of Victory, 1939–1945* (Columbia, SC, 1989).

Naval issues are treated in Gerald E. Wheeler, "Isolated Japan: Anglo-American Diplomatic Cooperation, 1927–1936," *Pa-*

cific Historical Review 20 (May 1961); James H. Herzog, *Closing the Open Door: American-Japanese Diplomatic Negotiations, 1936–1941* (Annapolis, MD, 1973); Thaddeus V. Tuleja, *Statesmen and Admirals: Quest for a Far Eastern Naval Policy* (New York, 1973); Stephen E. Pelz, *Race to Pearl Harbor: The Failure of the Second London Naval Conference and the Onset of World War II* (Cambridge, MA, 1974); Patrick Abbazia, *Mr. Roosevelt's Navy: The Private War of the Atlantic Fleet, 1939–1942* (Annapolis, MD, 1975); James R. Leutze, *Bargaining for Supremacy: Anglo-American Naval Collaboration, 1937–1941* (Chapel Hill, NC, 1978); and Malcolm H. Murfett, *Fool-Proof Relations: The Search for Anglo-American Naval Cooperation during the Chamberlain Years, 1937–1940* (Singapore, 1984).

The United States's relation to Britain remains under intense study. Note Ritchie Ovendale, *"Appeasement" and the English-Speaking World: Britain, the United States, the Dominions, and the Policy of "Appeasement," 1937–1939* (Cardiff, 1975); C. A. MacDonald, *The United States, Britain and Appeasement, 1936–1939* (London, 1980); Richard A. Harrison, "A Presidential Démarche: Roosevelt's Personal Diplomacy and Great Britain, 1936–1937," *Diplomatic History* 5 (Summer 1981); R. A. Harrison, "A Neutralization Plan for the Pacific: Roosevelt and Anglo-American Co-operation, 1934–1937," *Pacific Historical Review* 57 (February 1988); David Reynolds, *The Creation of the Anglo-American Alliance, 1937–1941: A Study of Competitive Co-operation* (Chapel Hill, NC, 1982); D. Reynolds, "Lord Lothian and Anglo-American Relations," *Transactions of the American Philosophical Society* 73 (1983); William R. Rock, *Chamberlain and Roosevelt: British Foreign Policy and the United States, 1937–1940* (Columbus, OH, 1988); and Donald Cameron Watt, *How War Came: The Immediate Origins of the Second World War, 1938–1939* (New York, 1989).

For British activities inside the United States, see Nicholas John Cull, *Selling War: The British Propaganda Campaign Against American "Neutrality" in World War II* (New York, 1995) and Anthony Cave Brown, *Wild Bill and Intrepid: Bill Donovan, Bill Stephenson, and the Origins of CIA* (New Haven, CT, 1996). Thomas

E. Mahl's *Desperate Deception: British Covert Operations in the United States, 1939–44* (Washington, DC, 1998) contains valuable information but fails to distinguish between British plots and indigenous interventionism. Popular anxieties are described in John E. Moser, *Twisting the Lion's Tail: American Anglophobia between the World Wars* (New York, 1999).

Definitive work on specialized topics includes Raymond H. Dawson, *The Decision to Aid Russia, 1941: Foreign Policy and Domestic Politics* (Chapel Hill, NC, 1959); Warren F. Kimball, *The Most Unsordid Act: Lend-Lease, 1939–1941* (Baltimore, 1969); John McVickar Haight, Jr., *American Aid to France, 1938–1940* (New York, 1970); David L. Porter, *The Seventy-sixth Congress and World War II, 1939–1940* (Columbia, MO, 1979); and J. Garry Clifford and Samuel R. Spencer, Jr., *The First Peacetime Draft* (Lawrence, KS, 1986). For an account full of contemporary warnings, see Robert Shogan, *Hard Bargain: How FDR Twisted Churchill's Arm, Evaded the Law, and Changed the Role of the American Presidency* (New York, 1995). Charlie Whitham, "On Dealing with Gangsters: The Limits of British 'Generosity' in the Leasing of Bases to the United States, 1940–41," *Diplomacy & Statecraft* 7 (November 1996), stresses British reluctance. Thomas A. Bailey and Paul B. Ryan, *Hitler vs. Roosevelt: The Undeclared Naval War* (New York, 1979), captures the excitement of early Atlantic engagements.

The Roosevelt-Churchill relationship has received much attention. Warren F. Kimball's *Forged in War: Roosevelt, Churchill, and the Second World War* (New York, 1997) shows an able scholar at his best. Joseph P. Lash's *Roosevelt and Churchill, 1939–1941: The Partnership That Saved the West* (New York, 1976) still contains much of value. In 1972 the Roosevelt-Churchill correspondence was opened; the 2,000 items possibly compose the most significant set of communications in modern history. We now have two editions: Francis L. Loewenheim, Harold D. Langley, and Manfred Jonas, eds., *Roosevelt and Churchill: Their Secret Wartime Correspondence* (New York, 1975) and Warren F. Kimball's more detailed *Churchill and Roosevelt: The Complete Correspondence*, 3 vols. (Princeton, NJ, 1984). All such volumes reveal that Winston Churchill's six-volume *Second World War* (Boston, 1948–53) glosses over sensitive issues between the two men. The product of their first encounter is covered in Theodore A. Wilson, *The First Summit: Roosevelt and Churchill at Placentia Bay, 1941* (rev. ed.; Lawrence, KA, 1991) and Douglas Brinkley and David R. Facey-Crowther, eds., *The Atlantic Charter* (New York, 1994), 1–32.

General U.S.-Germany relations are skillfully treated in Hans W. Gatzke, *Germany and the United States: "A Special Relationship?"* (Cambridge, MA, 1980) and Manfred Jonas, *The United States and Germany: A Diplomatic History* (Ithaca, NY, 1984). For discussion of American representatives to Hitler's Reich, see Martha Dodd, *Through Embassy Eyes* (New York, 1939); William E. Dodd, Jr. and Martha Dodd, eds., *Ambassador Dodd's Diary, 1933–1938* (New York, 1941); Robert Dallek, *Democrat and Diplomat: The Life of William E. Dodd* (New York, 1968); Robert Hessen, ed., *Berlin Alert: The Memoirs and Reports of Truman Smith* (Stanford, CA, 1984); and Stiller, *George H. Messersmith,* cited above.

Increasing tension is traced in Hans L. Trefousse, *Germany and American Neutrality, 1939–1941* (New York, 1951); James V. Compton, *The Swastika and the Eagle: Hitler, the United States, and the Origins of World War II* (Boston, 1967); Saul Friedländer, *Prelude to Downfall: Hitler and the United States, 1939–1941* (New York, 1967); and Alton Frye, *Nazi Germany and the American Hemisphere, 1933–1941* (New Haven, CT, 1967). Holger H. Herwig, *Politics of Frustration: The United States in German Naval Planning, 1889–1941* (Boston, 1976), stresses a final reckoning with the United States. For claims that Hitler sought eventual war with the U.S. and an analysis of his declaration of war on December 11, 1941, see Gerhard L. Weinberg, *The Foreign Policy of Hitler's Germany,* 2 vols. (Chicago: 1970, 1980); *World in the Balance: Behind the Scenes of World War II* (Hanover, NH, 1981); and *Germany, Hitler, and World War II: Essays in Modern German and World History* (New York, 1995). Additional coverage of such issues is found in Klaus Hildebrand, *The Foreign Policy of the Third Reich* (Berkeley, CA, 1974); Milan Hauner, "Did Hitler Want a World Dominion?" *Journal of Contemporary History* 13 (January 1978); Andreas Hillgruber, *Germany and the Two World Wars* (Cambridge, MA, 1981; Norman J. W. Goda, *Tomorrow the World: Hitler, Northwest*

Africa, and the Path toward America (College Station, TX, 1998); and Norman Rich, *Hitler's War Aims* (New York, 1973).

John Lewis Gaddis, *Russia, the Soviet Union, and the United States: An Interpretive History* (2nd ed., New York, 1990) offers a perfect starting place to survey a most uneasy encounter. Standard works on the recognition issue and its aftermath include Robert P. Browder, *The Origins of Soviet-American Diplomacy* (Princeton, NJ, 1953); Donald G. Bishop, *The Roosevelt-Litvinov Agreements: The American View* (Syracuse, 1965); Edward M. Bennett, *Recognition of Russia: An American Foreign Policy Dilemma* (Waltham, MA, 1970); Joan Hoff Wilson, *Ideology and Economics: U.S. Relations with the Soviet Union, 1918–1933* (Columbia, MO, 1974); Thomas R. Maddux, *Years of Estrangement: American Relations with the Soviet Union, 1933–1941* (Tallahassee, FL, 1980); Hugh De Santis, *The Diplomacy of Silence: The American Foreign Service, the Soviet Union, and the Cold War, 1933–1947* (Chicago, 1980); John Richman, *The United States & the Soviet Union: The Decision to Recognize* (Raleigh, 1980); and M. Wayne Morris, *Stalin's Famine and Roosevelt's Recognition of Russia* (Lanham, MD, 1994). Edward M. Bennett has contributed two works: *Franklin D. Roosevelt and Search for Security: American-Soviet Relations, 1933–1939* (Wilmington, DE, 1985) and *Franklin D. Roosevelt and the Search for Victory: American-Soviet Relations, 1939–1945* (Wilmington, DE, 1990).

American ambassadors to the Soviet Union are covered in David Mayers, *The Ambassadors and American Soviet Policy* (New York, 1995), and Dennis J. Dunn, *Caught Between Roosevelt and Stalin: America's Ambassadors to Moscow* (Lexington, KY, 1998). For FDR's first ambassador to the Soviet Union, see Will Brownell and Richard N. Billings, *So Close to Greatness: A Biography of William C. Bullitt* (New York, 1988), which reveals the ambiguities in the character of FDR's first ambassador to Moscow. Consult also Beatrice Farnsworth, *William C. Bullitt and the Soviet Union* (Bloomington, IN, 1967). For Bullitt's own views, note Orville H. Bullitt, *For the President, Personal and Secret: Correspondence Between Franklin D. Roosevelt and William C. Bullitt* (Boston, 1972). The pro-Soviet memoirs of another Roosevelt ambassador, *Joseph E.*

Davies's Mission to Moscow, 1936–1938 (New York, 1941) should be used with care. Keith David Eagles criticizes his subject in *Ambassador Joseph E. Davies and American-Soviet Relations, 1937–1941* (New York, 1985) while Elizabeth Kimball Maclean's *Joseph E. Davies: Envoy to the Soviets* (Westport, CT, 1992) finds him at times perceptive. For FDR's personal liaison to Stalin, note W. Averill Harriman and Elie Abel, *Special Envoy to Churchill and Stalin, 1941–1946* (New York, 1975). Diplomats George F. Kennan and Loy W. Henderson, are treated above. Ralph H. Levering, *American Opinion and the Russian Alliance, 1939–1945* (Chapel Hill, NC, 1976) is a superior treatment of its topic.

Work on United States policy and the Finnish war includes Andrew J. Schwartz, *America and the Russo-Finnish War* (Washington, DC, 1960); Robert Sobel, *The Origins of Intervention: The United States and the Russo-Finnish War* (New York, 1960); and Travis Beal Jacobs, *America and the Winter War, 1939–1940* (New York, 1981).

For an early debate about American policy toward the Vichy government in France, see William L. Langer, *Our Vichy Gamble* (New York, 1947), and Louis Gottschalk, "Our Vichy Fumble," *Journal of Modern History* 20 (March 1948). Julian G. Hurstfield, *America and the French Nation, 1939–1945* (Chapel Hill, NC, 1986) and Mario Rossi, *Roosevelt and the French* (Westport, CT, 1993) offer able accounts. Admiral William D. Leahy's *I Was There* (New York, 1950) is the memoir of Roosevelt's ambassador to Vichy.

For partisan accounts of American interventionist groups, note Walter Johnson's study of the Committee to Defend America by Aiding the Allies, *The Battle Against Isolation* (Chicago, 1944) and Mark Lincoln Chadwin's study of the Fight for Freedom Committee, *The Hawks of World War II* (Chapel Hill, NC, 1968). Michael Leigh, *Mobilizing Consent: Public Opinion and American Foreign Policy, 1937–1947* (Westport, CT, 1976) is the leading work on public opinion, but be sure to consult the early polls presented in Hadley Cantril and Mildred Strunk, eds., *Public Opinion, 1935–1946* (Princeton, NJ, 1951), and George H. Gallup, *The Gallup Poll: Public Opinion, 1935–1971*, 3 vols. (Westport, CT, 1972). For a succinct analysis, see Ralph Levering, *The Public and American Foreign Policy, 1918–1978* (New York, 1978).

Anti-interventionism, a far more accurate term than isolationism, is now the subject of intensive study. Justus D. Doenecke offers over 1,500 entries in his *Anti-Interventionism: A Bibliographical Introduction to Isolationism and Pacifism from World War I to the Early Cold War* (New York, 1987). Definitive on their topics is the work of Wayne S. Cole: *America First: The Battle Against Intervention, 1940–1941* (Madison, WI, 1953); *Charles A. Lindbergh and the Battle Against American Intervention in World War II* (New York, 1974); *Roosevelt and the Isolationists, 1932–45* (Lincoln, NE, 1983); and his study of Senator Nye (see above). Manfred Jonas's balanced *Isolationism in America, 1935–1941* (Ithaca, NY, 1966) has become a classic. Thomas N. Guinsburg, *The Pursuit of Isolationism in the United States Senate from Versailles to Pearl Harbor* (New York, 1982), warns against exaggerating isolationist sentiment in either Congress or the public.

There is much material on the Great Debate of 1939–1941. Justus D. Doenecke offers a succinct treatment of FDR's foes in *The Battle Against Intervention, 1939–1941* (Malabar, FL, 1997) and a far more extensive one in *Storm on the Horizon: The Challenge to American Intervention, 1939–1941* (Lanham, MD, 2000). For different focuses, see Robert A. Divine, *Foreign Policy and U.S. Presidential Elections* (2 vols.; New York, 1974); David H. Culbert, *News for Everyman: Radio and Foreign Affairs in Thirties America* (Westport, CT, 1976); John M. Muresianu, *War of Ideas: American Intellectuals and the World Crisis, 1938–1945* (New York, 1988); James C. Schneider, *Should America Go to War? The Debate over Foreign Policy in Chicago, 1939–1941* (Chapel Hill, NC, 1989); and John W. Roberts, *Putting Foreign Policy to Work: The Role of Organized Labor in American Foreign Relations, 1932–1941* (New York, 1995).

For bibliographies on the pacifist movement, note Charles F. Howlett and Glen Zeitzer, "The American Peace Movement: History and Historiography" (pamphlet; Washington, DC, 1985) and Howlett, *The American Peace Movement: References and Resources* (Boston, 1991), the latter containing over 1,600 entries. Charles Chatfield, *For Peace and Justice: Pacifism in America, 1914–1941* (Knoxville, Tenn., 1971) remains the most thorough treatment. Cecelia Lynch, *Beyond Appeasement: Interpreting Interwar Peace*

Movements in World Politics (Ithaca, NY, 1999) offers a revisionist picture. Harold O. Josephson has edited a *Biographical Dictionary of Modern Peace Leaders* (Westport, CT, 1985).

Significant primary sources have come to the fore. For the movement as FDR's critics themselves saw it, consult Justus D. Doenecke, ed., *In Danger Undaunted: The Anti-Interventionist Movement of 1940–1941 as Revealed in the Papers of the America First Committee* (Stanford, CA, 1990). Also valuable are *The Wartime Journals of Charles A. Lindbergh* (New York, 1970); Anne Morrow Lindbergh, *The Flower and the Nettle: Diaries and Letters, 1936–1939* (New York, 1976); *War Within and Without: Diaries and Letters, 1939–1944* (New York, 1980); and her small book *The Wave of the Future: A Confession of Faith* (New York, 1940).

Among the better studies of congressional figures are Fred L. Israel, *Nevada's Key Pittman* (Lincoln, NE, 1963); Robert James Maddox, *William E. Borah and American Foreign Policy* (Baton Rouge, LA, 1969); C. David Tomkins, *Senator Arthur H. Vandenberg: The Evolution of a Modern Republican, 1884–1945* (East Lansing, MI, 1970); and James T. Patterson, *Mr. Republican: A Biography of Robert A. Taft* (Boston, 1972). See also Betty Glad, *Key Pittman: The Tragedy of a Senate Insider* (New York, 1986); and Richard Coke Lower, *A Bloc of One: The Political Career of Hiram W. Johnson* (Stanford, CA, 1993).

Work on leading anti-interventionists includes Bernard K. Johnpoll, *Pacifist's Progress: Norman Thomas and the Decline of American Socialism* (Chicago, 1970); Jerome E. Edwards, *The Foreign Policy of Col. McCormick's Tribune, 1929–1941* (Reno, NV, 1971); Michele Flynn Stenehjem, *An American First: John T. Flynn and the America First Committee* (New Rochelle, NY, 1976); and Ian Mugridge, *The View from Xanadu: William Randolph Hearst and United States Foreign Policy* (Montreal, 1995).

Biographies of prominent interventionists include Donald B. Johnson, *The Republican Party and Wendell Willkie* (Urbana, IL, 1960); John Mason Brown, *The Ordeal of a Playwright: Robert E. Sherwood and the Challenge of War* (New York, 1970); Ronald Steel, *Walter Lippmann and the American Century* (Boston, 1980); Roy Hoopes, *Ralph Ingersoll: A Biography* (New York, 1985); and Robert

E. Herzstein, *Henry R. Luce: A Political Portrait of the Man Who Created the American Century* (1994). Limiting his listing to those who were involved in efforts advancing world order, Warren F. Kuehl has edited a *Biographical Dictionary of Internationalists* (Westport, CT, 1983). Rorin M. Platt offers an intriguing study of one interventionist state: *Virginia in Foreign Affairs, 1933–1941* (Lanham, MD, 1991).

Although much of the primary literature surrounding the debate over intervention is ephemeral, there are thoughtful works. For the isolationist position stated at its best, see Charles A. Beard, *The Idea of National Interest: An Analytical Study of American Foreign Policy* (New York, 1934); Beard, *The Open Door at Home: A Trial Philosophy of National Interest* (New York, 1934); John Foster Dulles, *War, Peace and Change* (New York, 1939); and Hanson W. Baldwin, *United We Stand!: Defense of the Western Hemisphere* (New York, 1941). The most able proponents of interventionism include Edward Mcad Earle, *Against This Torrent* (Princeton, NJ, 1941); Raymond Leslie Buell, *Isolated America* (New York, 1940); and Allen W. Dulles and Hamilton Fish Armstrong, *Can We Be Neutral?* (New York, 1936).

For the argument that the Roosevelt administration deliberately linked mainstream opponents to the lunatic fringe, note Geoffrey S. Smith, *To Save a Nation: American Countersubversives, the New Deal, and the Coming of the New Deal* (New York, 1973); G. S. Smith, "Isolationism, the Devil, and the Advent of World War II: Variations on the Theme," *International History Review* (February 1982); and chapter 5 of Leo P. Ribuffo, *The Old Christian Right: The Protestant Far Right from the Great Depression to the Cold War* (Philadelphia, 1983). Overt political intimidation is described in Richard W. Steele, "Franklin D. Roosevelt and His Foreign Policy Critics," *Political Science Quarterly* 94 (Spring 1979), and Charles E. Croog, "FBI Surveillance and the Isolationist-Interventionist Debate, 1931–1941," *Historian* 54 (Spring 1992). For the claim that paranoia was at work, see Francis MacDonnell, *Insidious Foes: The Axis Fifth Column and the American Home Front* (New York, 1995).

Administration policy towards Jews and other refugees from Nazism is revealed in David S. Wyman, *Paper Walls: America and the*

Refugee Crisis, 1938–1941 (Amherst, MA, 1968); Henry L. Feingold, *The Politics of Rescue: The Roosevelt Administration and the Holocaust, 1938–1945* (New Brunswick, NJ, 1970); Richard Breitman and Alan Kraut, *American Refugee Policy and European Jewry, 1933–1945* (Bloomington, IN, 1987); and Bat-Ami Zucker, *In Search of Refuge: Jews and U.S. Consuls in Nazi Germany, 1933–1941* (Portland, OR, 2001). Irwin F. Gellman describes one controversial incident in "The *St. Louis* Tragedy," *American Jewish Historical Quarterly* 61 (December 1971).

For general accounts of United States–Asian relations, see William L. Neumann, *America Encounters Japan: From Perry to MacArthur* (Baltimore, 1963); Edwin O. Reischauer, *The United States and Japan* (Cambridge, MA, 1957); Charles E. Neu, *The Troubled Encounter: The United States and Japan* (New York, 1975); John K. Fairbank, *The United States and China*, 4th ed. enlarged (Cambridge, MA, 1983); Warren I. Cohen, *America's Response to China: An Interpretative History of Sino-American Relations*, 3rd ed. (New York, 1990); Michael A. Schaller, *The United States and China in the Twentieth Century* (rev. ed.; New York, 1990); and Walter LaFeber, *The Clash: A History of U.S.-Japan Relations* (New York, 1997). Raymond A. Esthus offers much revisionism on an earlier period in his *Theodore Roosevelt and Japan* (Seattle, 1967).

For perceptive analyses of Japanese-American relations, consult the essays by Waldo H. Heinrichs, Jr., and Louis Morton in Ernest R. May and James C. Thomson, Jr., eds., *American East-Asian Relations: A Survey* (Cambridge, MA, 1972). Dorothy Borg's distinguished works include *American Policy and the Chinese Revolution, 1925–1928* (New York, 1947) and *The United States and the Far Eastern Conflict of 1933–1938: From the Manchurian Incident through the Initial Stage of the Undeclared Sino-Japanese War* (Cambridge, MA, 1964). Borg finds Roosevelt acquiescing in Japan's continental expansion with a docility that in retrospect appears astonishing.

Other highly respected studies include Manny T. Koginos, *The Panay Incident: Prelude to War* (Lafayette, IN, 1967); Hamilton D. Perry, *The Panay Incident: Prelude to Pearl Harbor* (New York, 1969); Frederick C. Adams, "The Road to Pearl Harbor: A Reexamination of American Far Eastern Policy, July 1937–December 1938," *Journal of American History* 58 (June 1971); Paul A. Varg, *The Closing of the Door: Sino-American Relations, 1936–1946* (New York, 1976); Michael Schaller, *The U.S. Crusade in China, 1938–1945* (New York, 1979); and Brian McAllister Linn, *Guardians of Empire: The U.S. Army and the Pacific* (Chapel Hill, NC, 1997). Arthur Waldron has edited the famous 1935 memorandum of John Van Antwerp MacMurray, praised in George F. Kennan, *American Diplomacy, 1900–1950* (Chicago, 1951), in which the senior diplomat called for moderation in confronting Japan and restraint in backing China. See *How the Peace Was Lost: The 1935 Memorandum—Developments Affecting American Policy in the Far East* (Stanford, CA, 1992).

In examining FDR's quarantine speech, see Dorothy Borg, "Notes on Roosevelt's 'Quarantine' Speech," *Political Science Quarterly* 72 (September 1957); John McVickar Haight, Jr., "Roosevelt and the Aftermath of the Quarantine Speech," *Review of Politics* 24 (April 1962); Travis Beale Jacobs, "Roosevelt's Quarantine Speech," *The Historian* 24 (August 1962); and J. M. Haight, "Franklin D. Roosevelt and a Naval Quarantine of Japan," *Pacific Historical Review* 40 (May 1971).

For works on the Tripartite Pact, note Frank W. Iklé, *German Japanese Relations, 1936–1940* (New York, 1956); Ernst L. Presseisen, *Germany and Japan: A Study in Totalitarian Diplomacy, 1933–1941* (The Hague, 1958); James W. Morley, ed., *Deterrent Diplomacy: Japan, Germany, and the USSR, 1935–1940* (New York, 1976); and Johanna Menzel Meskill, *Hitler and Japan: The Hollow Alliance* (New York, 1976).

Former State Department official Herbert Feis defends the administration in his still valuable *The Road to Pearl Harbor: The Coming of the War between the United States and Japan* (Princeton, NJ, 1950). Detailed analysis by Japanese and American scholars is found in Dorothy Borg and Shumpei Okamoto, eds., *Pearl Harbor as History: Japanese-American Relations, 1931–1941* (New York, 1973). Robert J. C. Butow, *The John Doe Associates: Backdoor Diplomacy for Peace, 1941* (Stanford, CA, 1974) covers the Walsh-Drought mission.

Paul W. Schroeder advances his once provocative thesis in *The Axis Alliance and Japanese-American Relations, 1941* (Ithaca, NY, 1958). Irvine H. Anderson, Jr., *The Standard-Vacuum Oil Company and United States East Asian Policy, 1933–1941* (Princeton, NJ, 1975), and Jonathan G. Utley, *Going to War with Japan, 1937–1941* (Knoxville, TN, 1985), claim that despite the intentions of Roosevelt and Hull, Washington hawks were eventually able to engage in the economic warfare that led to military hostilities.

For other aspects of United States-Japanese relations, consult Raymond A. Esthus, "President Roosevelt's Commitment to Britain to Intervene in a Pacific War," *Mississippi Valley Historical Review* 50 (June 1963); Lester H. Brune, "Considerations of Force in Cordell Hull's Diplomacy, July 26 to November 26, 1941," *Diplomatic History* 2 (Fall 1978); Richard J. Grace, "Whitehall and the Ghost of Appeasement," *Diplomatic History* 3 (Spring 1979); Jonathan G. Utley, "Rooseveltian Leadership and the Coming of the Pacific War" (paper presented at a meeting of the Society for Historians of American Foreign Relations, Stanford University, June 1985); and Abraham Ben-Zvi, *The Illusion of Deterrence: The Roosevelt Presidency and the Origins of the Pacific War* (Boulder, CO, 1987).

Concerning the U.S. ambassador to Japan, Joseph C. Grew, Walter Johnson, ed., *Turbulent Era: A Diplomatic Record of Forty Years, 1904–1945,* 2 vols. (Boston, 1952) is superior to Grew's own *Ten Years in Japan* (New York, 1944). Waldo H. Heinrichs, Jr.'s *American Ambassador: Joseph C. Grew and the Development of the United States Diplomatic Tradition* (Boston, 1966) is not only splendid biography but a painless way of mastering the intricacies of United States-Japanese relations.

Fortunately, some historians are drawing upon Japanese sources. Foremost is Akira Iriye, a Japanese-American scholar whose work combines multi-archival research with sophisticated discussion of long-range policies. See, for example, *After Imperialism* (cited above); *Across the Pacific: An Inner History of American–East Asian Relations* (New York, 1967); *The Origins of the Second World War in Asia and the Pacific* (New York, 1987); and *Pearl Harbor and the Coming of the Pacific War: A Brief History with Documents and Es-*

says (Boston, 1999). Along with Warren I. Cohen, Iriye has edited *American, Chinese, and Japanese Perspectives on Wartime Asia, 1931–1949* (Wilmington, DE, 1990). The rigidity of Japanese diplomacy is stressed in Robert J. C. Butow, *Tojo and the Coming of the War* (Princeton, NJ, 1961). Japan's internal debates are covered in Nobutaka Ike, *Japan's Decision for War: Records of the 1941 Policy Conferences* (Stanford, CA, 1967). Hilary Conroy and Harry Wray, eds., *Pearl Harbor Reexamined: Prologue to the Pacific War* (Honolulu, 1990), and Robert O. Love, Jr., ed., *Pearl Harbor Revisited* (New York, 1995) offer debates among historians. The former volume includes Japanese scholars, containing Tsunoda Jun's analysis of a possible FDR-Konoye summit.

Also multi-archival in approach is the perceptive work of the British scholar Christopher Thorne. Note his *The Limits of Foreign Policy* (cited above); part one of *Allies of a Kind: The United States, Britain, and the War Against Japan, 1941–1945* (New York, 1978); and part one of *The Issue of War: States, Societies, and the Far Eastern Conflict of 1941–1945* (New York, 1985).

Several works have focused on Southeast Asia, their authors stressing in varying degrees the prominent role played by the region in the coming of war. One must note Gary R. Hess, *The United States' Emergence as a Southeast Asian Power, 1940–1950* (New York, 1986); Richard J. Aldrich, *The Key to the South: Britain, the United States and Thailand during the Approach of the Pacific War, 1929–1941* (New York, 1993); and Jonathan Marshall, *To Have and Have Not: Southeast Asian Raw Materials and the Origins of the Pacific War* (Berkeley, CA, 1995).

The Pearl Harbor attack will probably always be subject to inquiry. Definitive is the work of Gordon W. Prange with Donald M. Goldstein and Katherine V. Dillon, *At Dawn We Slept: The Untold Story of Pearl Harbor* (New York, 1981); *Pearl Harbor—The Verdict of History* (New York, 1986); and *Dec. 7, 1941: The Day the Japanese Attacked Pearl Harbor* (New York, 1988). Hans L. Trefousse's *Pearl Harbor: The Continuing Controversy* (Malabar, FL, 1982) combines significant documents with a learned defense of the Roosevelt administration. A noted scholar of Japan, R. J. C. Butow, critiques the revisionists in "How Roosevelt Attacked Japan at Pearl Harbor: Myths Masquerading as History," *Prologue* 28 (Fall 1996): 209–21.

American code-breaking is covered in Ladislas Farago, *The Broken Seal: 'Operation Magic' and the Secret Road to Pearl Harbor* (New York, 1967); Ruth R. Harris, "The 'Magic' Leak of 1941 and Japanese-American Relations," *Pacific Historical Review* 50 (February 1981); Ronald Lewin, *The American Magic: Codes, Ciphers and the Defeat of Japan* (New York, 1982); Rear Admiral Edwin T. Layton with Captain Roger Pineau and John Costello, *"And I Was There": Pearl Harbor and Midway—Breaking the Secrets* (New York, 1985); and Keiichiro Komatsu, *Origins of the Pacific War and the Importance of Magic* (New York, 1999). Weaknesses in communications gathering and intelligence are discussed in Roberta Wohlstetter, *Pearl Harbor: Warning and Decision* (Stanford, CA, 1962). Magic dispatches are themselves now reproduced. See *The "Magic" Background of Pearl Harbor,* 8 parts (Washington, DC, 1978).

Several works present broad military background, including Samuel Eliot Morison, *Strategy and Compromise* (Boston, 1958); John Toland, *The Rising Sun: The Decline and Fall of the Japanese Empire, 1936–1945* (New York, 1970); and Ronald H. Spector, *Eagle Against the Sun: The American War with Japan* (New York, 1985). John Dean Potter offers an able life of the man who devised the Pearl Harbor attack: *Yamamoto: The Man Who Menaced America* (New York, 1965).

For defenses of the Hawaiian commanders, see Rear Admiral Robert A. Theobald, *The Final Secret of Pearl Harbor: The Washington Contribution to Japanese Attack* (New York, 1954); Rear Admiral Husband E. Kimmel, *Admiral Kimmel's Story* (Chicago, 1955); Edward L. Beach, *Scapegoats: A Defense of Kimmel and Short at Pearl Harbor* (Annapolis, 1995); and Michael V. Gannon, *Pearl Harbor Betrayed: The True Story of a Man and a Nation under Attack* (New York, 2001). Admiral Kemp Tolley, in *The Cruise of the Lanikai: Incitement to War* (Annapolis, MD, 1973), finds himself an administration decoy, a claim challenged in Stanley L. Falk's *Seven Days to Singapore* (New York, 1975). In Admiral James O. Richardson's *On the Treadmill to Pearl Harbor* (Washington, DC, 1973), the former commander of the Pacific fleet argues that it should never have been sent to Pearl Harbor. Early conspiratorial views are summarized in Frank Paul Mintz, *Revisionism and the Origins of Pearl Harbor* (New York, 1985). Conspiracy theses find newer life in John Toland, *Infamy: Pearl Harbor and Its Aftermath* (Garden City, NY, 1982); James Rusbridger and Eric Nave, *Betrayal at Pearl Harbor: How Churchill Lured Roosevelt into World War II* (New York, 1991); and Robert B. Stinnett, *Day of Deceit: The Truth about Pearl Harbor* (New York, 2000). In Henry C. Clausen and Bruce Lee, *Pearl Harbor: Final Judgement* (New York, 1992), a former Pearl Harbor prosecutor presents the conventional picture of the commanders' negligence.

Even the subsequent investigations are coming under investigation. Martin V. Melosi, *The Shadow of Pearl Harbor: Political Controversy over the Surprise Attack, 1941–1946* (College Station, TX, 1977), and Bruce R. Bartlett, *Cover-Up: The Politics of Pearl Harbor, 1941–1946* (New Rochelle, NY, 1978) both find government investigations too biased. The varied investigations are all presented in U .S. Congress, Joint Committee on the Investigation of the Pearl Harbor Attack, *Pearl Harbor Attack: Hearings and Report* (Washington, DC, 1946).

SUBJECT INDEX

AUTHOR INDEX

From Isolation to War, 1931–1941, Third Edition
Developmental editor: Andrew J. Davidson
Copyeditor and Production editor: Lucy Herz
Proofreader: Claudia Siler
Printer: Versa Press